AF559999

VALUE-ORIENTED EDUCATION

VALUE-ORIENTED EDUCATION

Edited by

Dr. V. Dayakara Reddy

M.A., M.A., M.Ed., Ph.D.

Principal, Institute of Advanced Study in Education

Head, Department of Education

Sri Venkateswara University

Tirupati–517 502

Dr. Digumarti Bhaskara Rao

M.Sc., M.A., M.A., M.Ed., Ph.D.

Reader & Research Director

R.V.R. College of Education

Guntur–522 006

&

Member, Board of Studies in Education

Acharya Nagarjuna University

Andhra Pradesh

(India)

DISCOVERY PUBLISHING HOUSE

NEW DELHI-110002

First Published-2006
Reprinted-2010
ISBN 81-8356-051-2

Published by

DISCOVERY PUBLISHING HOUSE
4831/24, Ansari Road, Prahlad Street,
Darya Ganj, New Delhi-110002 (India)
Phone: 23279245 • Fax: 91-11-23253475
E-mail:dphtemp@indiatimes.com

Printed at
Arora Offset Press
Laxmi Nagar, Delhi–92

Dedicated
to
Lord Sri Venkateswara Swamy

Preface

Values are the socially accepted norms to be practised by each one and they form the backbone of the human society. Values are realised to the core only through value education.

Value education is a planned educational programme aimed at the development of values in students. It encounters with the total personality of the individual student keeping in view all aspects of human personality development—the intellectual, emotional and social. It makes an individual a good child, parent, adult and citizen, and keeps the people and society intact.

Considering the very role of value education to be imparted in educational institutions, a UGC National Seminar on Value-Oriented Education is organised in the Department of Education, S.V. University, Tirupati, Andhra Pradesh on 22nd and 23rd November, 2004. Several enthusiastic teacher educators from all around India participated in the seminar and expressed their views and opinions to their best. All went well and the seminar became a grand success in realising its objectives. Thanks to its Organising Secretary, Dr. V. Dayakara Reddy, for so cheerfully and successfully doing his business by making his brilliant presence of every point and moment.

The papers presented in the seminar are presented in this book for the benefit of people and personnel that involved in value education.

Long Live Values and Long Live Human Society.

—Dr. D. Bhaskara Rao

Sai Soudha

D-43, S.V.N. Colony

Guntur, 522 006

Andhra Pradesh

Contents

1

Value-Oriented Education

Dr. Nimma Vankata Rao*

In modern society, where individuals have a larger way of life and greater variety of choices than any time in the past, the formation of appropriate character has always become an important aspect as far as the purpose of education is concerned. Schools, in modern society, cannot be concerned only with a mastery of three 3 Rs. Among other things, they are expected to bring about the development of the cultural, aesthetic and social values for the young generation.

Unfortunately, these important aspects seem to receive little attention in the present system of education. Schools seem to be considered as institutions of formal learning whose concern is to communicate a certain prescribed quantum of knowledge, by keeping aside the issue of values.

The Concept of Value

Before the discussions of value-oriented education, it seems important to explain what the term "value" connotes. Value has different meanings depending on the context. For instance, when we say a Saint gives a lecture about the importance of leading a good life, people may exclaim, how valuable the lecture was! Here value stands for high thinking. Similarly, when we say Mahatma Gandhi led a valuable life, the meaning of value stands for "dignified" or "principled".

---

* **Associate Professor, Department of Education, Andhra University, Visakhapatnam.**

Value, as noted by Taneja (1990: 92) connotes any thing that fulfils the needs, satisfies the urges and helps man in realising his aspirations. This means, value of a thing depends upon how they satisfy our desires, wants, and urges. This implies that a thing or a condition or an act is more valuable or more worthy or better than another because it satisfies wants more or cause less deprivation of wants.

In relation to the determination of a thing or act educationists had put forward the following ideas.

- The value of a thing is due to the fact that the thing has power to satisfy our wants (view of life).
- Anything has value if it related to the perfection of life for which a man endeavours in his life (perfection theory).
- Anything which has utility.
- Anything which is helpful in organising society is called value.
- Anything which helps for existence.
- Values are determined by the notions of individuals and also by the circumstances in which they live, etc.

Nevertheless, educational interpretation of "value" does not signify a thing, but a thought or a point of view (Taneja, 1990). For instance, anything which is useful to an individual, becomes valuable to him and the same thing may be quite useless to another individual because of his different viewpoint or thought and as such it is of no value to that individual. So, things, conditions and acts can be classified as good or bad, beneficial or harmful, satisfying or annoying or possessing value only when they are seen from a particular point of view.

Educational values are, therefore, related to those activities, which are thought good or useful and valuable from the viewpoint to education. These values at any moment play a significant role in the life of man in enabling to lead his personal and social life successfully. They occupy an important place in education. They lead to motivation, which in turn results in desirable behaviour.

The Relationship Between Education and Values

Education is part of life and nearly our question about values and education are inseparable from larger question of values in life. This means values are embodied in educational practice. Thus, education develops a sense of discrimination between good and bad. This discrimination is based on values and these values are tested in schools.

In short educational values contribute the following advantages for individual and social life.

- Development of healthy and balanced personality.
- Capacity to earn livelihood and acquired material prosperity.
- Development of vocational efficiency.
- Creation of good citizenship.
- Adjustment with the environment and its modification fulfillment of the needs of man.
- Development of character.
- National integration and national development.
- Promotion of social efficiency, etc.

When seen from this perspective, values influence all aspect of educational process, techniques, policy and procedures. In education of any society, the selection of curriculum, the type of discipline, administration and supervision, the questions of teaching methods, etc. are questions of values.

Thus, the task of educator is not so simple like declaring some values as educational values. Every teacher, every school and every system creates value situation from which students take attitudes. Teaching should aim continually on keeping the aggregate of values alive and growing and should include all that the teacher hopes for students to learn so as life for them becomes as rich and fine as possible.

In this regard what is happening in our system of education in general in our schools in particular. What real problems India has as far as value orientation to the young generation is concerned.

Are really our schools shaping the youth in the way it should be? These and similar questions are addressed in the following brief discussions.

Current Educational System and Value Orientation

It is a known fact that we are in the era of globalisation and in era of fast technological developments when changes are taking place at breath-taking speed. Our educational system to bring India as a competitor country in this situation undoubtedly played very crucial role. It makes provision of a variety of knowledge and skills that helps to create good living conditions.

However, as indicated by Chandra, (2002: 250-252) in recent years, there has been an increased sensitivity to the failure of our educational system to live up to the hopes we entertain for it. The gap between the behaviour of even educated and individuals in their every day activities and what they have learnt at school is becoming increasingly chocking. Specifically some very serious problems are becoming evident of everyday phenomena. To mention few:

- In the present generation, self-interest dominates public interest.
- No respect is shown to elders and teachers.
- Common people have lost trust in religious practice.
- The attitudes like love, goodness, compassion, hospitality, kindness to animals etc. are slowly disappearing from the individuals and the society.
- In profession and business, deceit and cheat are replacing honesty and service mindedness.
- Violence, dictatorship and criminals have destroyed peaceful living in the society etc.

It is because of these and many other similar problems that we are highlighting value-oriented education. So, where lies the problem? With the teacher, the curriculum, or with other components of school activities. What should be the nature of value education? Why and how much? Which method should be adopted for value-oriented education?

Some of these problems and possible solutions are discussed as follows.

First, good education system can instill two kind of values- the basic (spiritual) and the life (social). Basic values are the foundations on which life values are to be built. However, our education system, according to (Chandra, 2002) fail to give priority to basic values like truth, beauty, love, righteousness and courage. Rather the attempt was to give precedence to live values over the basic values.

Secondly, practical experience shows that the most common way of teaching value education adopted by our schools is to teach moral education for one hour or two a week. This practice cannot help the development of appropriate value. This should be discouraged because spiritual and moral education cannot be taught with textbooks, blackboard and chalk piece. Value education is not amenable to be taught in small doses like History or Geography. It should take place as an *integral part* of general instruction without making it boringly explicit or tauntingly oppressive to children. This means there is no curriculum, syllabus or examination for value education. It is based on hidden curriculum as part and extension of the formal curriculum and syllabus in other subjects.

Hence, it is the responsibility of the teacher to use every small occasion available during instruction to the inculcation of values by drawing the attention of the students to the value content of each topic. The following are examples to simply indicate how it is possible to integrate value education in the teaching of other subjects.

— In language teaching it is possible:
  - Point out specific values involved in each topic.
  - Relate these values to our social and cultural life by suggesting suitable examples.
  - Relate these values to students' cognitive, emotional and intellectual development, etc.

— The teaching of science can be used to awaken students to:

- The scientists' devotion to truth and perseverance and sacrifices.
- The significance of scientific theories and inventions in eradicating irrational practices.
- The insignificance of the ego and the significance of humility in everyday life.

The teaching of social sciences should be oriented towards highlighting the following aspects:

- The basic and life values implied in each social movement, incident, innovation and idea.
- Relating these values to our cultural traditions and history.
- Distinguishing social events, ideas, movements and laws from the point of view of their value implications.
- Pointing out the social disharmony caused by contra versus.

This does not mean that our textbooks be rewritten according to the whim of the value-educators. It is not that we need a different set of textbooks but we need a different kind of interpretation of the contents in the already existing textbooks.

The other problems our education system has is related with the teachers themselves. That is, value instruction become meaningful and effective only if the teacher himself assimilates and practices the values he teaches. The presence of few, if not all, teachers who by their living example confuse and distort the value formation of students menaces our educational system today. The ideal teacher is one who guides his students to the source of knowledge and learning that will substantiate or refute their own beliefs and values. So the task of teacher is providing value clarification and this task should be effectively performed by those who exercise their life style and daily activities to ideals they preach. At any time they should play an important role in shaping and moulding the habits and manner of their students.

Parents have also a role in preserving and enhancing the values students assimilate in schools. The values taught in classrooms must find their reflection in the attitudes and life style of parents. Unless parents play this complementary role, whatever value-oriented education students receive at schools would be wasted away and a paradoxical situation of "what the schools do, the parents undo" will arise.

Concluding Remarks

We Indians, like any other nation, are living in a technological age fraught with possibilities of evil. To benefit from the technology and to protect our young generation from the evils that may bring harm, it is not debatable that value-oriented education is relevant. In this process, our schools are expected to lead the way to the achievement of goals of value-oriented education. They should provide suitable opportunities for individuals to develop ethical, social, personal, spiritual, and aesthetic values. They should inspire students to develop the inherited capacities and mould them to be worthy citizen having honesty, truthfulness, respect to law, duty mindedness, and respect for the right and privileges of others. In the school system a lot expected from the teacher. There should not be any contradiction between what the teacher says and what he or she does. If the teachers and the set-up do not become models, value-oriented education cannot be effective.

In all cases focuses should be:

— Bringing in practical value education, which provide, change in syllabus and emphasise experience.

— Developing and nourishing basic values which can reach the public and bring awareness through value education.

— Safe-guarding values by giving enough time for people to understand the situation and take decisions through proper discussion, observation and non-violent methods.

— Bringing in the practice in the society to adopt valuable principle for safe-guarding values.

REFERENCES

Chandra, Soti S. and Sharma, Rajendra V. (2002) *Principles of Education*, New Delhi: Atlantic Publishers & Distributors.

Saxena, N.R. Swaroop (2000), *Foundation of Educational Thought and Practice*, Meerut: Usha Printers.

Taneja, V. R. (1990), *Educational Thought and Practice*, New Delhi: Sterling Publishers.

2

Value Education

Dr. T.M. Geetha*

Value education refers to a programme of planned educational action aimed at the development of value and character. Every action and thought of ours leaves an impression in our mind. These impressions determine in our behaviour at a given moment and our responses to a given situation. The sum total of all our impressions is what determines our character. The past has determined the present and even so the present our present thoughts and actions will shape our future. This is a key principle governing personality development. The human values are resolved having lasting impact necessary for bringing about change in thought and conduct, in the 21st century.

Values are socially accepted norms to evaluate object, person and situation that form part and parcel of society. Values system is the backbone of a unified society. Values may change from one society to another society and also from time to time. For example, every society abides by certain moral values and these values are accepted by all the societies as "Global Values".

"Value" as a more concrete noun, for example, when we speak of a value or of "values" is often used to refer to what is valued, judged to have value, thought to be good or desired. The expression his values, her values system and refer to what a man, a woman, or think to be good. Such phrases are also used to refer

* Dept. of Studies in Education, Karnataka State Women University, Bijapur.

to what people think is right or obligatory and even to whatever they believe to be true. Behind this widespread usage lies the covert assumption that nothing really has objective value, that: "values" means being valued and "good" means being thought good. But the term "Value" is also used to mean valuable or good. Value means "Things that have value" things that are good or goods, e.g., for some users, also things that are right, obligatory beautiful or even true.

Nature of Values

Nature of value depends upon the basis of criteria of satisfaction. Value is that which gives satisfaction. Here the question arises as to who gets the satisfaction and of what type? It depends upon the analysis of the situation, anything, property, sentence and activity etc., can be valuable or has value. Values are determined by the situations. Value decision shows the nature of value. We must know some characteristics before deciding the values.

Necessity: The child/individual must know the necessity of values before. Due to the necessity of the meaning of some elements in a sentence it becomes valuable. The maximum value is given to those things without which we cannot exist. (Food, water clothes). Next we have to consider the things which provides comforts for us (books, radio, T.V.) later intoxicants and decorative.

Obligation: Some of the, value decisions are obligatory, it is difficult to put them in practice. They are different from general decisions. Education is valuable.

Based on the liking of decision makers: The values decisions are according to the liking of the decision-maker. One who is fond of flowers considers them to be the most beautiful thing in the world, those who have more respects for women. For them women is the best creation of God in the world. In this way differences in the value decision arises, nothing is intrinsically, valuable, but it has value because it is liked, is appropriate or necessary. According to GotShalk, there are three elements, in the formation of value, objectives subjective and rational depending on the situation, and the three elements possess values in the decision-making.

According to spiritualists, philosophers, the values are spiritual because spirituality is only the criterion. Of auspiciousness. According to materialists values are inherent in happiness. The object itself is not valuable but it has value only that it gives happiness. From the comparative studies of values. It comes to be known that all the values are measurable; the moral values are permanent, unique and original. They are not commensurable with other values, their knowledge leads to the emergence of duties, intelligence and moral obligations. Moral values are truth, beauty, and goodness, when all these values are united together, the ultimate aim of self realisation becomes a reality. It is a permanent ultimate value.

No value is completely objective or subjective. Both the aspects are present in a value, so it is inappropriate to divide values in to axiological subject and axiological objects. For the all round development of the individuals personality and self-realisation. No value can be neglected. In order to achieve the highest value of self-realisation, the lower values must be transformed. Their realisation is also necessary because in the harmonious axiological development no aspect can be left out.

Dharma was the universal guiding force in attaining self-perfection and social harmony, ancient Indian education were mostly value based and aimed to cultivate such virtues like non-violence, sincerity, honesty etc., in the form of ulterior value—Truth Beauty and Goodness (Satyam, Shivam Sundaram). The ultimate aim and purpose of education is self-realisation and divine perfection.

Truth beauty and goodness were the supreme value of ancient India and they served as the guiding lights for men in their lives. With dharma as the base. Artha and Kama were held as instrumental values to attain Moksha. That is spiritual freedom.

When the speed of change around us is increasing it is not easy to concentrate. Biologists have given us techniques of filtering the galaxy of external impulses, and neurophysiologists have given us the golden threads to hold and rich the chariot of time. It is scientifically possible to store the selected impulses in the huge "ocean" of instincts. The journey beyond this milestone is more to be experienced than expressed. The truth is that a man can thus have his intellect to be ready to catch a miracle, which is sure to happen.

"Satyam Bruyat, Priyam Bruyat Na Bruyath Satyam, Apriyam Priyam Cha na Anuratam Bruyat", (Speak the truth, speak what is pleasing, it is not possible to do so, do not speak that truth even, although pleasing to hear, yet do not tell a lie). This has been the norm for "Satyam" stipulated by our elders. To bring about the beneficial results from our truthful utterance, our mind should first be cleansed of lust and anger and be made pure.

Decline in Values

There is hardly any issue on which one may find complete unanimity of views in the society. The situation is no different in the case of the value system. Many people feel that there is, at present, a state of chaos in the society so far as moral values are concerned, however, a number of people do not share deep concern over the so-called deterioration of moral values the great scientist Darwin had remarked that mankind is continuously progressing on a course of evolution. He may not have been alluding to the biological factors only. The great spiritual leader Aurobind Ghosh had said that the Homo-sapien would steadily attain super manhood and there is no returning for him to the lower form of life. Some people say that cultural march of human race has failed to match its technological progress. There is a group of people who feels that man's cultural advancement excels his achievement in many other fields.

The data collected for the study indicated a convergence of views. Bulk of respondents feel that there has been a decline in moral values. To the statement that over the past 5-10 years moral values among Indians have declined. The student responds expressed their opinion as follows.

Out of total 881 non-student general category respondents 85 per cent concurred with the above statement, 5 per cent disagree and 7 per cent undecided. The value crisis perhaps became so obvious that the level of education did not make any significant difference in their viewpoint on this statement. The educationist experienced the highest degree of agreement. And the least by advocates. Reasons for this are perhaps; obvious even in the case of latter there is a high degree of agreement about the decline in value.

People of every generation always feel that the values have declined in time as compared to what they were in the Golden past. What is happening to our young people, they disrespect their elders, they disobey their parents, they ignore the laws. They riot in the street inflamed with wild notions. Their morals are decaying.

There may be valid reasons to learn over the loss of values in a society, but sometimes it may be difficult to point whether a value system is undergoing a metamorphosis or whether it is declining.

Causes for the Decline of Values

There are various causes for the decline of values in a society, (Teachers status, parent's role).

Studies were conducted to know the causes for the fall of values. From the study it came to know that 54.5 per cent of the cause is due to absence of proper religious teaching, 63.5 per cent due to fall in moral values of our political leaders, 54.9 per cent due to mass media adopting no proper policy to build moral standards in the society. From this it came to know that the political leaders have contributed significantly to greater extent than to other two values, it confirms the view point held by many people that the value system emerges from the seat of power. It is not only the politicians the impact that teachers and parents is deeper on the children as many other things.

There are some factors responsible for lowering the status of teachers. This may be the other reason for decline of values.

Lack of scholarship for teachers

Teacher's lust for money

Absence of sacrifice among teachers for their students.

Teacher had a place of reverence in India, he was the respiratory of knowledge, and a person of exemplary high character, during the period of education of the students, the guru assumed the responsibility of acting as the parent, the parents gave the physical birth to the child, and the teacher gave the second, the intellectual birth to him. Teachers are charged with an important responsibility of guiding their students. In order to fulfill this obligation they must raise their own level of conduct in their own eyes and in the eyes of public.

By the study it comes to know that 54.4 per cent of the teachers are towards lack of scholarships, 72.1 per cent of the teachers are having lust for money, and 72 per cent of the teachers show absence of sacrifice. Their lust for money and absence of the element of sacrifice among teachers have been considered almost equally important factor for lowering the status of teachers. So the ethos of the teachers needs to change from those of the merchants to those of the gurus.

The role of parents was also important. Younger generation will show more respect to their parents, if,

Parents give greater freedom to their children's

Parents spend more time with their children

Parents themselves keep adjusting the changing social values.

When the statements are ranked by the students it shows that all students whether in school or colleges, also want their parents to spend more time with them, for this greatly contributes to establishing emotional rapport between the parents and their children. Such a rapport is necessary so as to ward off psychological problems among children. In some cases where the parents are educated, dialogues and meetings between parents and children also enrich some good values by sharing their views regarding, good and bad. These meetings can be fruitful only if parents with the changing times keep on adjusting to the changing social values. Present day parents are not what their parents were and their children cannot be what they are. This is a fast changing world where scientific discoveries, mass media and international influences are revolutionising the thought processes which were so far circumscribed when these factors were absent or had a limited impact. In case where the parents refuse to adjust to the transforming social values, the rift between parents and their children is bound to ensure sooner than later. Young people have not accorded high priority to have greater freedom.

Other causes were the gap between the material and the spiritual progress is an important cause of the present value crisis. Nuclear capability is a great achievement, but our failure to co-ordinate it with moral values poses serious dangers to the human race.

The fall in values in modern times is attributable to over emphasis on wealth power, and consumerism.

Our weak spiritual and education background, contributed to our undermining the higher values of life.

Some of the unhealthy literature brimmed with sex, crime and violence. This had an adverse impact on the social ethos. What is true of literature is true of films also. Which is literature on a silvery-screen.

Urbanisations has ushered in the apartment—culture and pushed off the rural life values, including socialisation, with the ever increasing speed in life values and both the parents racing from one appointment to another, there is limited socialisation even at homes. All this has brought about changes in our outlook to the existing value—system. The trend needs to be rectified.

Approaches to Value Education or Institution

At the boyhood stage, individual physical development is concerned, during manhood and old age intellectual and spiritual values start dominating the corporal values. Therefore while imparting moral education educators must keep in mind that the young must be educated.

The education commission (64-65) has suggested that social, moral and spiritual values should be imparted both through indirect and direct method. It is not only the teachers in charge of value education are responsible for building character. Every teacher, whatever is the subject matter he must teach values. The school assembly the curricular and co-curricular activities, the celebration of religious festivals, work experience team games, and sports, subject clubs, social service programme—all these can help in inculcating the values. Of co-operation and mutual regard, honesty, and integrity, discipline and social responsibility.

At the early stages moral instruction can be imparted through parables, or stores, which have been an appeal to the emotions of the child. At the secondary stage there can be discussion between the teacher and the taught on the values to be imparted. Ethics can be taught through stories, religion, and sayings of great peoples and their lives. Films should be shown to them depicting temples, mosques etc.

Prizes may be given to the deserving persons for showing honesty, bravery, truth etc. The award should be given during school gathering. Contests may be organised on values of life.

Extension lectures based on morality or value-oriented education may be arranged in the institution.

The head of the institution and the teaching personnel should be living examples for values. Books must be provided for them on value education.

Conclusion

Value crisis in India has to be checked by one and all concerned with it directly or indirectly. Then and then only we can hope to see the bright future of the countrymen and see India as prosperous nation. There is need of re-consideration, re-planning and re-orientation. Let us also follow the views of different commissions or education for values and act wisely and rightly.

REFERENCES

1. Sachdev and Sharma, *Philosophical and Sociological Bases of Education* Pub. By Bharat Book Centre, Ludhiana.
2. K.L. Gandhi, *Value Education*, Gyan Pub. House, New Delhi.
3. Patro, *Value Profiles of School Students*, Pub. By Discovery Publishing House, New Delhi.
4. Yadav and Yadav, *Education in the Emerging Indian Society*, Pub. By Tandon Pub., Ludiana.
5. M.G. Chittakara, *Education and Human Values,* Published by Kul Bushan Nangia, New Delhi.
6. Ram Chandra Sharma, *Moral and Value Education,* Published by Book Enclave, Jaipur.

3

The Psychological Edifice for Value Education

Dr. (Mrs.) Kalpana Vengopal*

Ms. Priya Kumari**

There is an increasing awareness both in India and the world that the contemporary crisis is fundamentally the crisis of disbalancement of an exaggerated development of the outer structures and organisations and means of physical and vital satisfactions, on the one hand, and the neglect of ethical and spiritual dimension of human life, on the other. One, therefore, hears of the crisis of character, crisis of values and crisis of spiritual evolution. Gripped as we are in this crisis, we are bound to look for knowledge of ethics and spirituality, of values and of the knowledge that can bridge the gulf between the life of matter and the life of spirit. In the West, increasing number of leaders are now speaking of return to basics, and in India we have begun to conceive of programmes of value education (Joshi Kireet, 2000).

The anguish, anxiety and stresses of modern life are impelling educationists in various parts of the world to look for the inmost soul by the alchemic power of which calm and peace, equanimity and harmony, self-knowledge and self-integration are attained.

* **Lecturer, Regional Institute of Education (National Council of Educational Research and Training) Mysore–570 006.**

** **Lecturer, Amrita Shikshana Mahavidyalaya, Mosore–570 006.**

True education has to be value-oriented, since the fundamental aim of education is to prepare students for life. The most crucial component of such an educational model will be an unequivocal orientation towards values and ethics.

What is Value Education?

Value education is education for "becoming". It is an encounter with the total personality of the individual keeping in view all aspects of personality development—the intellectual, social and emotional, will and character. It involves developing sensitivity to and awareness of what is right, what is good, what is beautiful, ability to choose the right values in accordance with one's conception of highest ideals of life and internalising and realising them in thought and action (Seshadri, 1998).

The process of value education calls into play the three domains—knowing, feeling and doing. Not only should the learner be enabled to know the right and the good, but also to feel the appropriate emotions, concern and commitment and exercise the will to do the right thing. It is a process of interacting with the total human being with a view to develop capacities of reflective thinking and independent judgement on issues that are of critical concern to oneself and to humanity. It is a process of helping individuals to think freely and critically, to act responsibly and with courage and conviction. Eventually, it should given place to independent appraisal of a situation after rational deliberation and principled judgement.

Value education is not merely the cultivation of cognitive faculties, but also affective and conative. One cannot merely give a lecture on values. Just as swimming cannot be taught merely by lecturing, but by leading the learner to jump into the water and help him in the practical art of swimming in the midst of water. Similarly, value education requires of the teacher, the ability to inspire the student to enter into the waters of life's situations and give him practical abilities and art of practicing values in concrete situations in life with an attitude:

- to seek honour and act with truth
- for independent thought and action

- towards a strong sense of responsibility
- towards friendship and cooperation
- towards willingness to assume responsibility (Joshi Kireet, 2000)

Integrated Value-based Education

Integration of human values along with scholastic and co-scholastic activities of students in integrated value-based education, which is significant for the all-round development of the personality of students.

Every subject has values inherent in it, which the teacher can discover with the class and highlight, emphasis and reinforce these values through a variety of teaching methods and activities. There is more opportunity to draw out the essence of the subject. Integrated value-based education provides scope for a better understanding of the usefulness and value of each lesson with respect to life. In fact, the integrated approach enables the teacher to go deeper rather than remain at the information level (Kumari Priya, 2003). Values no longer need to be isolated as 'moral science' on 'human values', evaluated and assessed like any other body of information. (Saraf Somnath, 1999).

Teacher Education Curriculum

The whole teacher education curriculum needs rethinking. It should compulsorily train teachers to practice integrated value-based education approach in transacting a lesson. This may require inclusion of a paper on value education and the techniques of value education in various disciplines/methods. It is also necessary to sensitise teacher educators about the issues and concerns regarding the same (Gokak, Rohidekar, 1982). The existing population of teacher and school administrators may be trained in the techniques and practices of integrated value-based education through inservice programmes.

Process of Integrated Value-based Learning

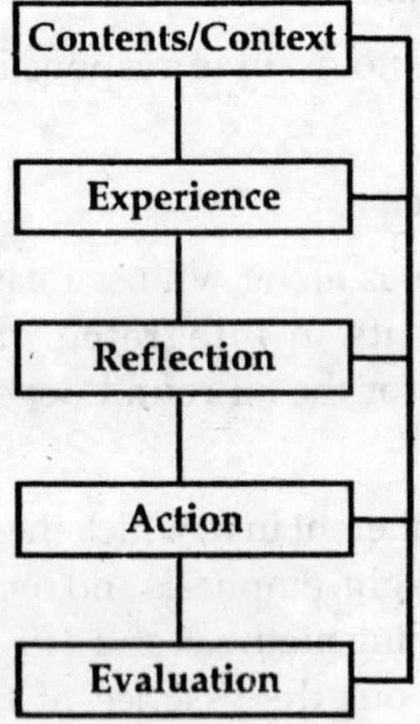

1. *Content/Context:* Subject content/school/classroom context for value orientation.
2. *Experience:* Direct/indirect experience.
3. *Reflection:* Thinking, feeling and appreciation leading to internalisation of values.
4. *Action:* External manifestation of internalised values.
5. *Evaluation:* By the teacher and the student (self-evaluation) of values internalised.

Psychology and Value Education

In the past, value education was a mechanical process of forcing the child's nature into arbitrary grooves of gaining knowledge—a process in which child's own attitudes and capabilities were of no consideration and the effort, both in schools and at home was to compulsorily shape his habits, thoughts and characters into a mode fixed for him by either conventional ideas or interests and ideals of teachers and parents. Value education, however, must be a process of bringing out the child's intellectual and moral capacity to the highest level possible and must be based on sound psychological principles of different age groups (Luther, 2001).

(i) Primary Stage: Age Group 5-8

(a) (For 4-5 Years Old)

- powers of expression do not always match their powers of comprehension;
- get easily frustrated when they are faced with difficult choices or have to decide on their own on what is right and what is wrong;
- not yet learnt to accept discipline and contend with disappointment;
- need considerable help from teachers so that the kind of egotism that is associated with infancy gives place to disciplined behaviour and recognition of themselves as individuals with specific capabilities.

(b) (Age Group 6-8 Years)

- very sensitive age;
- faced with the challenge of having to work cooperatively in a team;
- learn quickly what is fair and unfair;
- react strongly to being treated unfairly and react positively when they get a sense of fair play from their teachers and others;
- are promoted in their actions by the promise of reward or fear of punishment.

Programmes like groups songs, games, enacting, simple dramas, puppet shows, art, short stories and familiar folklore can be adopted to illustrate different values. Programmes developed for this group should be pleasurable and joyful, yet have a profound impact.

(ii) Middle Stage: Age Group (9-13) Pre-Adolescence

- sense of autonomy;
- increasingly social;
- capable of understanding and appreciating others' points of view;

- extremely eager to assume responsibilities;
- display an excitement for learning about the unknown;
- given a chance they want to script their own codes of moral and ethical values.

Values can be inculcated through issue-based classroom discussions, cultural activities which emphasis respect for all religions and cultures, encouraging to assume civic duties and responsibilities, introducing the study of biographies of famous personalities.

(iii) Secondary Stage: Age Group (13-17) Adolescence

- experience very rapid development—physical, intellectual, emotional, psychic and spiritual;
- very sensitive and are more amenable tc love and affection and family guidance rather than threats and punishment;
- evaluate authority and rules, rebels against blind adherence to rules;
- development of their own perspectives of reward and punishment;
- introduced to logic and reason.

Programmes to develop values include group discussions and debates about value-crisis, dilemmas and issues, culled from newspapers and magazines, role play of dramatics.

It must be noted that values and ethics cannot be promoted through a single course of instruction, but must form an integral part of all programmes and activities throughout the student's school life.

The Three Domains of Value Inculcation

Value inculcation like all learning needs to take place at three levels, cognitive, affective and conative. Value education must help in the cognition of the need and importance for human values in one's life. Proper understanding leads to appreciation which in turn helps students reflect and act upon values. Values need to be understood, experienced, felt and acted upon. True imbibing of values takes place only when they are cognised, appreciated, internalised and practiced.

Levels of value-development

Knowledge

Appreciation

Discrimination

Action with effort

Spontaneous manifestation

These levels represent the cognitive, affective and conative domains of learning. To be educated in the real sense of the term is to be able to think right, to feel the right kind of emotions and to act in the desirable manner. Objectives of value education should, therefore, be concerned with all the three domains (Rohidekar, 1998).

Conclusion

The National Curriculum Framework for School Education (2000) is emphatic about the importance of value-oriented education right from school level. Children, when young, are easy to mould and hence, 'integrated value-based education' right from elementary level would bring forth students with strong integrity with their roots firmly grounded in moral and ethical values.

Value development is a psycho-social process where children are guided by imitation, suggestion and identification. While designing models and programmes of value education, one has to take into account the psychology of the learner and the domains of learning in order to ensure fruitful internalisation of values (Luther, 2001).

We are not born with an internal set of values. We learn to measure the worth of things and ideas by observation and testing. Individual values are formed easily in life and are acquired from a variety of sources. Values are so deep-seated in our personality that they are never actually "seen". What we "see" is the way in which values manifest themselves through our attitudes, opinions and behaviour (Schmidt, Posner, 1982).

REFERENCES

Gokak, V.K. and Rohidekar (1982), *Teacher's Handbook for the Course in Human Values*, Sri Sathya Sai Bal Vikas Trust, Prashanti Nilayam.

Joshi Kireet (Ed), (2002). *Philosophy of Value-Oriented Education—Theory and Practice*, Indian Council of Philosophical Research, New Delhi.

Joshi Kireet (2000), *Education at Crossroads*, The Mother's Institute of Research, New Delhi.

Kumari Priya (2003), "The Study of Integrated Value-based Education of Sri Sathya Sai Primary School, Prashanti Nilayam, AP" Unpublished Dissertation Thesis. Regional Institute of Education (NCERT), Mysore, 2003.

Luther, M.M. (2001), *Values and Ethics in School Education*, Tata McGraw-Hill Publishing Company Limited, New Delhi.

National Curriculum Framework for School Education (2000), National Council of Educational Research and Training, New Delhi.

Rohidekar, S.R. (1998), "Inculcation of Values—How?" *In Value Education*, Edited by Venkataiah, N, APH Publishing Corp, New Delhi.

Saraf, S., (1995), *Education in Human Values: Programme Implementation*, Apeejay Education Foundation, New Delhi.

Seshadri, C., (1998), Education in Values—Why and How? *In Value Education*, Edited by Venkataiah, N, APH Publishing Corp., New Delhi.

Warren H. Schmidt and Barry Z. Posner, *Managerial Values and Expectations*, AMACOM, New York.

4

Fostering Values

A Challenge for the Society

Dr. N. Sobhana*

Introduction

Man is a unique creation in this universe who under certain parameters is free to make his own destiny. Now, if man has to make his destiny, the question of values in life comes up. He has to think naturally as to what should be the guiding norms of life process. It is therefore clear that the guiding factors for man, which provide the prime motivating force behind his thought, emotion and action, have to be moral and spiritual. The socio-cultural and spiritual life of man has to bring peace, progress and welfare for both the individual and the society. This is precisely the reason why the modern society is worried about the deterioration of values.

Having diagnosed the present problem, we have to find the remedy for this situation before there is further deterioration of values in the wider interest of the mankind.

Concept of Values

At this juncture, ask yourself a question. What are the pillars on which the citadel of 'life style' is built? The pillars are the 'values', which develop through an interaction of needs,

* Assistant Professor, Department of Education and HRD, Dravidian University, Kuppam–517 425.

perceptions, emotions, sentiments and attitudes. Values effect our lives every moment and will be the guiding force in all things we do and pursue. When our values are in congruence with our actions, we are in harmony.

Gupta, N.L. (1986), defined values as those standards or ethics for moral behaviour conditioned by one's cultural tenets and guarded by conscience, according to which human being is supposed to conduct himself and shape his life patterns by integrating his beliefs, ideas, attitudes to realise cherished ideals and aims of life.

In the present scenario of hope and despair, selfishness and competitions, the value', in its general sense, refers to what is good, desirable and worthwhile. In an objective sense, it refers to things, activities, persons or experiences, of individuals or groups that are deemed good. In a subjective sense, it refers to personal or group preferences among a number of possibilities. The concept of values differs from knowledge i.e., it has a normative element in addition to a cognitive element. 'Value' is a broader term which includes not only moral values but also aesthetic, cultural, intellectual, social, political and economic values.

Values

Values in education are classified in different ways. One such classification is:

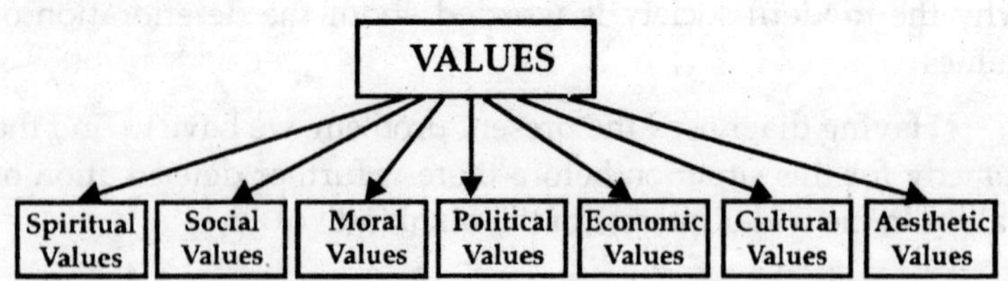

The Call for Values

In the history, our culture shows exemplary kings and common men who lives were shining examples of human values. Although our heritage is adored as the heart of spirituality by the outer world, we are still in darkness. It is indeed our misfortune that the might and the common men are afflicted with barbaric qualities of selfishness, favouritism and malpractice. Modernisation and other destructive forces give clear indication of the process of degeneration of human society.

Sharma (1986) rightly describes the current dismal social picture in Indian context where values are getting degenerated. He says "if values are missing, a nation loses ground". The vitality of human belief in values is dying everywhere i.e., in schools, colleges, universities, offices, assemblies, parliament and also at home. They blame each other for the deterioration of values in the society. Introspection is nobody's concern. As a result, the youth has started neglecting the religious epics giving room for erosion of values.

Whatever may be the reasons for the present value crisis, it is a fact, that decline of moral values in our life is creating social and cultural conflicts. The declining moral standards in personal and social life on one hand and the national ideological commitment to the values of democracy, socialism, secularism and modernisation on the other, constituted the driving force behind the recommendations stressing the importance of value education. Let us get back our (moorings) values before it is too late. Let the more enlightened ones take the lead. Let us select a handful of 'ideals' to guide us and strive hard to achieve those in the present society. In this perspective the present day society which includes parents, teachers, educators, administrators, educational system and mass media has a long way in making value education more meaningful and produce Indianised and sensitive youth who can work for the upliftment of the society.

Fostering Values: A Challenge for the Society

The effective tools to foster values in the youth are education, mass media and voluntary associations that involve the individuals.

The Kotari Commission report (Govt. of India, 1966) suggests that values should be taught to students/youth. Therefore, the National Policy on Education (NPE) 1986, (Govt. of India, 1986) has recommended various radical changes in present educational set-up and included in the policy, the parameters of the values themselves. They are as follows:

"The growing concern over the erosion of essential values and increasing cynicism in society has brought forces to, the need for re-adjustments in the curriculum in order to make education a forceful tool for the cultivation of social and moral values". In a pluralistic society like ours, education should foster universal and eternal values. Such value education should help to eliminate obscurantism, religious fanaticism and violence.

Education is expected to play a major role in promoting national development of all the faculties towards adequate preparation of life. Unfortunately, education is becoming day-by-day materialistic and traditions are being slowly given up. The modern Indian is being educated mainly with the aim of education to earn his bread and butter and as a result most of the youth are after money and comfort without concern for any values.

The present Indian educational system is reflecting more or less borrowed ideologies and philosophies and the national values are being relegated to the background. In our educational reconstruction the problem of an integrated perspective on values is pivoted, for its solution alone can provide organic unity for all the multifarious activities of a school or college curriculum and university courses/programmes. The curriculum should provide enough opportunities for the students to acquire considerable knowledge that is essential for morally responsible living in a democratic society. An integrated education can provide for integrated growth of personality and integrated education is not possible without integration of values. Language teaching and history teaching do reflect human values and value system. But our schools/colleges and universities have become examination centres and not value centres. Teachers at all levels do not have clear direction to the national values and ideals and ideologies that they have to foster in the youth. Hence they are not in a position to play their role as value educators.

Education should produce citizens with sound character and a healthy personality. Inspiring values, ideals, proper moral conduct and a life based on good principles is an essential requisite.

Role of Educational Institutions

How far the educational institutions are responsible and to what extent the teachers, administrators should make a deliberate effort to inculcate the values? Infact, onc of the responsibilities of the school is to expose young mind the diversity prevalent in the society.

There are three distinct steps that have to be taken care by educational institutions in value orientation/formation among the students.

(i) Making available appropriate reading material (biographies and views of great personalities who had certain values, ideals in life and who practiced against odds and sacrificed their very lives).

(ii) Creating institutional ethos in the institutions. The organisers and heads of the institutions should follow and practice values while running the institution.

(iii) Understanding the attitudes, emotions, feelings and motives of students is very important and plan activities accordingly.

Good institutions will impart students inspiring qualities like concentration, love, justice, wisdom, obedience, sincerity, honesty, faithfulness, mercy and respect for others to build equipment of life. This should be the central theme of value education.

Values can be taught through lectures, epics, textbooks and several co-curricular activities and the youth do catch them. But when they find elders and leaders to the society going the other way, they suffer from moral conflicts. Their conflicts may turn them into morally debased persons or hypocrites. On whom should this blame be laid? Obviously, the blame should be laid on elders and leaders of the society, for they do not provide good examples to the youth when they try to test the tenets of their moral values.

Role of Teachers

A true teacher never says "Do as I do" but shall say "Do whatever you deem right".

Teachers commanded high repute, respect and prestige in the past. The teacher-taught interaction used to play a very significant and effective role in the formation of character, personality development and cultivation of spiritual values in the minds of the pupils.

In our present set-up of society teacher-taught interaction is not found to be effective and as such the outcome is not the desired/expected one.

The teacher occupies a crucial role in imparting valued education to the students. The teacher should have commitment to the development of national autonomy in both thought and action.

Role of Parents

Moral education starts from the family i.e., from the parents before the children go to school. The most constructive factor of moral education is a happy, purposeful, stimulating home life which encourages the child to explore his/her powers while offering little guidance and setting appropriate limits to behaviour. Children acquire fundamental value education when the parents are educated and possess basic principles like self discipline, which is the basis of values and principle of existence and co-existence.

Role of Mass Media

Mass media like TV, newspapers should not highlight violence. Media should be able to create value awareness in the cross section of the society.

Television (TV)

Coverage of Kargil war has created nationalistic spirit among the younger generation. This has a positive effect on the youth. In a similar way sports and games also have a positive effect. But, the coverage in the same media on Mumbai blast, Godra episode in Gujarat etc., have brought in hatred against one other's religion which is a negative aspect.

Media, before highlighting an incident should imagine/ visualise the effects of projecting such information before the public. Proper judgement by the media in reporting or coverage will definitely inculcate high values in the younger generation.

Role of Religious Heads

Religious conventions or congregations are held in our country propagating the basic tenements of the respective religions. On many occasions sermons are delivered by the high priest/clergy/khazies on the importance of value-based ethics for understanding the importance of communal harmony. In some cased we also heard instigating speeches rousing the feelings of the youth which is highly objectionable. The religious leaders will have to understand the importance of the values of survival for the betterment of the community and the country.

Role of Administrators

An administrators should have exemplary conduct and ability to create congenial and conducive environment in the institutions. The teachers and other staff members in the institutions will naturally be influenced by the values practiced by the heads who by personal example would be able to do a lot in developing a right type of institutional ethos.

Role of Educators

The call for values in education is asking the educators to be the heroes. It implies educators to be leaders in realising the technology and materialism is not just enough, and that there is much beyond these things in life whose nomenclature is values. We know that real value based education is not something to be taught once in a week; it is at its best when integrated into the daily classroom experience. In any situation, a teacher can observe what is happening and reflect on the underlying values.

Teacher educators:

- Must tap the creative energy and universal values that each individual holds within.
- Should have the power to facilitate the development of universal values.
- Have to create open, flexible, creative and orderly value based environment. Obviously, the students will move

closer to understand their own values and develop their own way of thinking.

— Ought to generate learning experiences that create little time for students to reflect about their own values and practical implications.

— Must create an atmosphere that enables the students to recognise the importance of values and their own responsibility in making positive, personal and social decisions.

— Should be adult role models who exemplify those values.

Basically, as parents or teachers or educators or administrators, we need to possess some common skills to create a value-based atmosphere either at home or school/college/institution. They can be called something like parenting skills or facilitation skills or administration skills. They are skills of:

(i) Acknowledgement, encouragement and positive attitude building behaviour.

(ii) Balance of discipline.

(iii) Active listening.

(iv) Consistency in thinking/communication.

Let us first imbibe that so-called parenting skills, facilitation and administration skills to develop in our students so that they will be able to create a value based atmosphere around themselves and get ready to mould future generations with right values, attitudes and perspective of life.

Conclusion

We can say that there should be congenial conditioning in the society which includes parents, teachers, educators, and administrators for inculcating values in the students/youth. Preaching the values to the students and simply hearing those values is not enough on their part. They must experience and internalise them. If today's youth has to carry values into their personal lives as adults in future, they also need adult role models who exemplify those values. Promotion of human values in society depends on the promotion of good qualities among individuals. We must therefore, put necessary efforts to make our thoughts sacred by practicing those values and generate them among others. Value education should prepare individuals to participate in social life and accept social rules. Hence, schools, colleges and universities should provide a healthy atmosphere for sharing responsibilities, community life and relationships.

"Arise, awake and stop not till the goal is reached" must be our watchword. If we make our thoughts, words and deeds sacred there can be no better way of coming out of evil, ill will, and dependency. We must be prepared to put into practice the values that we proclaim to others. Therefore, the strategy of value education is a challenge for the members of the present day of society.

REFERENCES

Gupta, N.L. (1986), *Value Education: Theory and Practice*, Krishna Brothers, Ajmer.

Power, K.B. (2000), *Higher Education for Human Development*, Association of Indian Universities, AIU House, 16, Kotla Marg, New Delhi–110 002.

Prahallada, N.N. (1994), *Professional Competence in Higher Education*, Association of Indian Universities, A.I.U. House, 16, Kotla Marg, New Delhi–110 002.

Vanaja, M. (2001), *Need for Value Based Education: An Appraisal*, Paper Presented in Seminar on Value Education at Mysore.

5

Value Based Teaching

Need of the Hour

Dr. K.V. Raghupathi*

Aim of Education

The aim of education is to sharpen the intellectual abilities, sublimate the instincts, stabilise emotions, develop social traits and enable to cultivate morality and spirituality in the students and its ultimate goal is to achieve fullness and perfection in man. To realise this noble ideal of education teachers play a very constructive, positive and productive role. Indeed, they have a greater role to play than parents. If parents are regarded as the foundation, teachers are the pillars on which the whole edifice of student's life stands.

Status of a Teacher in the Vedic Times

In our Vedic times teaching was regarded as sacred and noblest of all noble professions. The teacher was upheld in high esteem, and regarded as a holy person. Even the kings used to bow before them in great reverence. They used to visit forests where they paid humble respects to their teachers. The teacher was almost treated as next to God. He is addressed as:

Guru Brahma, Guru Vishnu, Guruvai Sri Mahēswara/Guru Sakshāt Para Brahma Tasmai Sri Guruvai Namah.

* **7-55/Second Floor, Vasavi Nagar, Tirupati–517 502.**

The teacher is the creator, preserver and destroyer of knowledge, all blended into one in him. He is no other than the reflection of that *Para Brahma*. The function of a guru has been beautifully explained in the Sastras. In spiritual sense, the guru functions like a second thorn. He uses this second thorn to remove the first thorn of ignorance in the student. After this the student throws away the second thorn too. Which means the student once enlightened grows and lives all by himself without guru.

The word 'Guru' in Sanskrit stands for a *Jnāni* who dispels darkness in the student and lights the lamp. According to this tradition, a teacher should first be an enlightened soul before he could enlighten others. Only an enlightened soul could enlightened others. In this sense every teacher in the Vedic times as a *rishi*. The *rishis* were known as Brahmins. A teacher was identified in those times as Brahmin not by virtue of his observance of rituals but by virtue of having attained the knowledge of the ultimate reality, that is Brahman. Such was the status, position and nature of a teacher in those times. The teacher was also called as '*Vacha*'. A *Vacha* is one who possesses a sound learning.

Different kinds of teachers existed in the Vedic times. They are: *guru, āchārya, upadyāya, pradyāpaka, pravakta,* and *prachārya*. A *guru* is one who lights the lamp in others by burning himself. An *ācharya* does three things: he learns absorbs and trains up others in good behaviour *(ācharam grahagati itī āchārayah)*. A *guru* can be an *āchārya*. One who teaches is *upadyaya*. A seasoned teacher to teach advanced students or a retired teacher, or a teacher of teachers is called *pradhyāpaka*. A teacher who is an expert in *Siksa Sāstras* is called a *pravakta*. A retired teacher is called *prachārya*. Of these *Guru* was the highest term that was used for a teacher in those times.

Views of the Eastern and Western Thinkers

The position of teacher in the modern times as highlighted by great thinkers and philosophers is very much akin to the position glorified in the Vedic times In all their teachings greater emphasis has been laid on the moral and spiritual values of a teacher. Tagore compares the teacher with a living stream that flows ceaselessly. A stagnant pool gives only disease but not health. A stagnant teacher gives more information but not real knowledge and wisdom. The teacher according to him should be 'a living teacher'. From this we understand that a teacher should be a learner all through his/her life. Only a learner could impart more. A teacher should first and last remain as a student.

Gandhiji assigns a great place to the teacher. He is an important environmental factor, for he leads the student from untruth to truth, from darkness to light and finally guides him towards his perfection. To Gandhiji a teacher is born *firstly* when he has a zeal to go for an in-depth study of himself, *secondly*, only when he first practises whatever he realises, *thirdly*, when he dispels the ignorance in others and exhibits zeal to impart right knowledge and finally when he allows students to be nearer to him to receive what he gives.

Gandhiji preferred one good teacher to fifty indifferent teachers. A great teacher according to him is one who never entertains evil thoughts, evil words and evil deeds. It follows thus a good teacher should possess sterling character. Strong character is the foundation of life. Unless the teacher has this flawless character, it is hard for him/her to build up a character in others. As Swami Vivekananda says all education is ultimately aimed at man-making. This man-making is possible only when the teacher possesses an exemplary character. Gandhiji gives three cardinal principles for a teacher, namely, truth, non-violence and love. The teacher should be an embodiment of these three virtues, according to him. Addressing the teachers under basic education scheme, he said: "the cultivation of these cardinal virtues (truth and non-violence) is the foundation scheme. And if you do not show these in your daily contact with your pupils and a character in keeping with them, you will fail and so will your school". (Basic Education, p. 55-6).

Sri Aurobindo has advocated an integral education in which both teacher and student are partners in the process of learning. His concept of integral education encompasses an integral view of life which includes the training of the physical, intellectual, ethical, dynamic, practical, aesthetic and hedonistic faculties. For Aurobindo, "Education is a process of a harmonious and progressive awakening; education is a process of self-revelation of knowledge which is within. (*The International Centre of Education*, p. 2). It is the development of "psychic being". For this to happen the teacher must first be fit enough to mould himself/herself. Only a moulder can mould others. Unless the teacher is morally, upright, all moral education becomes merely conventional. Strong character is inseparable from the personality of a teacher. Not only to be morally upright but also to be spiritually strong. Spiritual training is the education of heart. Spirituality has to be lived, but never to be learnt, if learnt it can be learnt only as a creed, Sri Aurobindo says. A teacher according to him should contain this spiritual education. He says, "one must be a great yogi to be a good teacher". (*A True National Education*, p. 48). The Mother too observes, a true professor must be truly a yogi. His conception of teacher toes the line of Vedic tradition.

Sri Aurobindo has also given three fundamental principles of teaching: "The first principle of true teaching," according to him, "is that nothing can be taught. The teacher is not an instructor, or task master, he is a helper and a guide. His business is to suggest and not to impose". (*A True National Education*, p. 6). From this principles of teaching it follows that the entire responsibility of education lies with the student himself/herself. The teacher should act like a catalyst in this process of making the student learn by himself/herself. "The second principle is that the mind has to be consulted in its own growth. The idea of hammering the child into the shape desired by the parent or the teacher is a barbarous and ignorant superstition." (Ibid. p. 6). The second principle implies that a teacher is only a helper and not a dictator. "The third principle of education is to work from the near to the far, from that which is to that which shall be. The basis of man's nature is almost always, in addition to his soul's past, his heredity, his surroundings, his nationality, his country, the soil from which he draws sustenance, the air which he breathes, the sights, sounds, habits to which he is accustomed. They mould him not the less powerfully because insensibly, and from that then we must begin." (*Ibid*. pp. 6-7) In all these three principles of teachings, Sri Aurobindo has highlighted the role of a teacher.

For J. Krishnamurti right education means the awakening of intelligence, the fostering of an integrated life. He says, "Education is the change of the inner man". (*Krishnamurti on Education*, p. 39). Further he says, "The purpose of education is not to produce mere scholars, technicians and job hunters, but integrated men". (*The Education and the Significance of Life*, p. 51). This change of the inner man is done by a teacher in the initial stage. In the process of change the teacher plays the role of a helper, a pointer and a guide; and his/her role is purely democratic and spiritual in nature.

Among the Western thinkers, Maxwell Berston says that a teacher is "the child's third parent". This may be put in another manner, if the parents are the first teachers, the teachers are the second parents. The greatness of a teacher is very succinctly put by Robert Green, a distinguished poet, who says that "a teacher is greater than a thousand priests." For T.W. Emerson, the teacher is "the man who can make hard things easy". It means the whole life is made simple. Henry Louis Mencken observes that the mission of a teacher is "not to make his pupils think, but to make them think right". Such a teacher is a real teacher. "The object of teaching a child", Elbert Hubbard says, "is to enable him to get along without his teacher". The real value of a teacher was best put by Alexander the Great, who said, "I am indebted to my father for living, but to my teacher for living well". South also gives a similar view, he says, "he that governs well, leads the blind, but he that teaches him gives eyes".

In every tradition and in every country the place of a teacher not only in the institution but also in the society has been glorified. A teacher is not merely one who imparts information. Such a teacher is not a real teacher. According to a Japanese saying, a poor teacher tells, an average teacher teaches, a good teacher explains, an excellent teacher demonstrates and a great teacher inspires. A real teacher is one who should inspire the students, who should be able to take the text beyond the classroom, who should "enable the students to get along without teacher", (Elbert Hubbard), who should "not impart his opinions but to kindle minds". (F.W. Robertson) To inspire the students, a teacher should discharge twin roles—one to mould himself and the other to mould others. He should be "a burning candle", according to Tagore. A burning candle alone is capable of lighting other candles. Which means, every teacher has to learn in order to make others learn. Tagore says, "a lamp can never light another lamp unless it continues to burn its own flame". He should be everything to be a great inspirer. He should be a psychologist, moralist, spiritualist, environment-centred, a humanist, a naturalist, an eternal seeker of knowledge and wisdom, a pragmatist, compassionate, catholic, reformer, and a worthy, true honourable critic. Only teachers with the blended qualities can build a strong, dynamic, problem-free, hatred-free, violent-free society, and not teachers with mere certificates in hand. They should be spiritual beacons but not material or mechanistic giants. Only teachers endowed with such great moral and spiritual values alone can impart value-based teaching. All other teachers devoid of spiritual values can give only information. What we, therefore, need is not merely information but knowledge mixed with wisdom. What we need are not parrot like teachers and intellectual giants but teachers with Socrate's mind and Buddha's heart. This means that unless spiritual values are lived in no teacher can ever become an inspiring teacher. And his/her teaching will never be value based.

Current Position

Unfortunately, in today's Indian society the teacher stands for split personality. His/her position has been highly degraded, demoralised, and dehumanised because other external factors such as caste, political influence and money have crept into the temples of learning and vitiated the whole atmosphere. These factors are reigning supreme in colleges, especially in universities. The teacher has developed a dubious personality. He/she lacks moral fibre and spiritual elegance. His/her behaviour has become highly suspicious, corrupt, degrading and disgusting. Today's teacher looks more for monetary benefit and power than for the integrity and sanctity of the profession. He/she has grown more materialistic, egoistic, seeker of power and authority, insensible, indifferent to human suffering and misery and apathetic to students' needs. Values for which the ancient Indian teachers strived hard have taken a back seat.

Character is more important in a teacher than in any other person in society because the whole society depends on him/her for moulding and shaping. Character is the foundation of life. Swami Vivekananda says, knowledge without character will not stand, it crumbles. Knowledge stands as a super structure on the strong foundation of character. If character is lost everything is lost. Hence, knowledge and character are the twins, two sides of the same coin. As Swami Vivekananda states that even if one may not have knowledge but character, such a person is thousand times better than a mere knowledgeable person. But if a man of knowledge is devoid of character he/she is more harmful and dangerous to the society than a criminal. This character is nothing else than imbibing spiritual values such as adherence to truth, honesty, simplicity, contentment, sincerity, compassion, love, charity which are common and universal, present in every religion. If such values are cultivated and lived in every moment teachers will become great, inspiring, exemplary, emulative above all true gurus in the Vedic spirit. From their mouths, whatever comes is sacred, illuminating and their teaching will make an everlasting imprint on the minds and hearts of students.

Four Fundamental Duties

It is true value based teaching is the need of the hour. But this will become a reality if only the teachers are value-oriented. Unless the great spiritual values are learnt and lived, teachers can hardly create an impact on the students. A teacher has, therefore, to perform four fundamental duties: *One* is that he/she should be a learner all through life. He/she should have a perennial desire to learn. This learning should not be for the sake of learning, but for enlightening oneself, and this learning should be a comprehensive and all inclusive one. It is not merely procuring information from various sources but it should help improve and develop once own faculties, open ones own mind to a greater mind, from the ordinary mind to the higher mind to the illumined mind and the intuitive mind. His/her learning should be aimed at "growth of consciousness" to use Sri Aurobindo's words. It should literally help bring out the latent capacities in oneself. It should awaken the sleeping consciousness in oneself.

The *second* duty is that they should contemplate or reflect deeply upon the acquired knowledge. This contemplation is essential as it would change the ordinary mental consciousness which is externally determined by various factors. Contemplation has several advantages. It deepens ones own thinking, and widens consciousness—it moves from the local to regional, from regional to national, from national to global, from global to universal. It sharpens imaginative power and strengthens the spirit of inquiry.

The *third* duty is that the teacher should be able to absorb the worth and merit of learning in his/her life. The values he/she has learnt from his/her wide reading, observation and listening should be put to test in his/her life, and once they are proved as to be worthy to be lived, they should be completely absorbed in life. The cultivation of values should not be for the sake of obtaining any benefit from the external source or for seeking any due recognition but for deriving immense peace and happiness.

In the *fourth* and final duty, the teacher should become a beacon for others. He/she should shine like a star. He/she should train others in a tactful way but not simply rub it on them. Every teacher should ultimately in the end be useful for *lokakalyana*. But this fundamental duty becomes possible only when the teacher fulfills the first three duties. Such a teacher can be rightly called as *acharya* and *guru*. He is indeed the reflection of *Para Brahma*. Such a teacher indirectly helps for social reconstruction, works for peace, progress and prosperity of the whole world.

6

Value-Oriented Education

Need to the Day for Sustainable Development

Dr. G. Vijayasree*

"Good teachers radiate knowledge every where. They are unique, divine looking personalities. They inspire the young students and prepare them to face any challenges in life. They instill in them courage, hope, confidence and a sense of victory, values, so that they march on the path of brilliance to achieve their rightful destiny."

—***A.P.J. Abdul Kalam***
President of India

Introduction

Man is a social, rational and thinking being, living in the web of social relationships, interactions and processes. It is through socialisation the culture, traditions customs, mores, norms, values are being transformed to the younger generation. They are the important factors affecting the personality make up of individuals. A harmonious society needs individual with values, working towards developing the nations towards sustainable development. Values help to integrate a personality. They provide means by which conflicts tend to be solved and also help in maintaining order in the social structure. Present educational programmes

* **Graduate Assistant, Department of Home Science, S.V. University, Tirupati.**

should be designed in such a way to realise the aim of creating a society with sustainable development, as such our National goals of education are:

1. Increasing productivity
2. Social and emotional integration
3. Democratisation and modernisation
4. Development of social moral and spiritual values

Our Indian Constitution has certain important value based national goals such as secularism, democracy, equality, liberty, fraternity, sovereignty, justice, national integration, patriotism assuring the dignity of the individual and the unity of the nation. If all these are reflected in education it influences the total development and becomes the true education. So it is an unique investment in the present and excellent planning for the future.

Education

Education is a powerful instrument of change and progressive improvement of human behaviour. It has played an important role in shaping the destinies of societies. It tends to create a social order based on values of freedom, social justice and equal opportunity and fits a man perfectly for the time. Education in 21st century has to meet the emerging needs of mankind, as it progresses from the "local community to a world society", from social cohesion to democratic participation, from economic growth to human development, from unsustainable development to sustainable development.

Values in Ancient India

In ancient India, the Vedas, the Upanishads, the epics manifested and upheld the values of Indian society. More importance was given to morality, honesty, duty, truth, friendship, brotherhood (Vasudhaika Kutumbam). They were the themes of Indian culture, literacy and Indian society. The pupil could learn the first lessons of duty, devotion, dedication and discipline. The life of Guru used to be the role model for his disciples. Education was closely allied to practical life. Imparting value education and reformation of the society were the solemn aims and objectives for the teachers of the ancient age. Respecting womenhood is the most important cherished value. Value based education was emphasised to promote eternal values among students. This was the type of education we had, till few decades back.

Present Scenario

The population in India has been constantly rising, it has crossed one billion by 2001. Due to the explosion of population, advancement in science and technology, knowledge expansion, medical knowledge in curing diseases, industrialisation, urbanisation, mobilisation, IT revolution, globalisation, flow of western culture—the present society is rapidly changing and the life is centred round the wonders of science. Society is shaped by technical change, that is turn, is shaped by society. It is going through modernisation process thereby human life is full of problems, anxiety and struggle and became helpless victim and so he is at the cross roads of modernisation living in the midst of social, economic, political environmental and value crisis—which are all threatening the humanity in the society. Modernisation has led to the change of life styles, thinking processes, traditions and cultural norms. Inequalities persist between rich and poor, men and women, urban and rural. Over consumerism, selfishness, materialistic complex detaching man from real values of life. In a world based on science and technology, it is education that determines the levels of prosperity, welfare and security of the people.

Growing global poverty, pollution, hunger, diseases, unemployment untouchability, caste system, child labour, gender inequality, illtreatment of womenhood, violence, disability, exploitation of natural resources are causing crisis on the globe—all these are making man to loose honesty, sincerity, morality and humanity and as such there is a great transition in human society. To remove the problems of the present era, inculcation of values among individuals and promotion of values in education are essential. For real development we need integrated human personalities. The present educational system has to be reviewed in view of all the above and to meet the challenges in future.

Need for Value Oriented Education

People are suffering with problems like poverty, pollution, unemployment, depletion of natural resources on one side and on other side they are ignoring basic values like humanity, spirituality, Integration etc. On one side entire globe has become a village due to information technology revolution and another side people are leading a miserable life. Boosting economic development and disregarding the value of education are causing threat to the humanity on the globe. Overloaded curricula, home work, examination-oriented education, competition for ranks, seats, abnormal strength of children in the class, medium of instruction are hindering the values among students. Entire modern education is suffering from values in practice. Towards environmental destruction, over use or misuse of natural resources, environmental pollution, misuse of political power, ill-treatment of women and disabled, corruption, exploitation of children, youth-value oriented education is necessary. Here comes the role of education to play a vital role in overcoming all these and in harmonising the lives of the peoples' in India and also is establishing balance between the past and the present. There is a need to produce individuals with rationality, humanity and dynamism.

Sustainable Development

The true concept of development is the sustainability of man and environment on the entire globe by promoting harmony within humanity and between humanity and nature. Human welfare is the goal of development. Development without destruction of environment and human values is real development. Sustainable development seeks to meet the need and aspirations of the present without compromising the ability to meet those of the future. This can be done only with value-oriented human beings. For sustainable development there should be balance between science and humanity, ecology and economy, prosperity and peace. Sustainable development in-turn develop sastainability of man in particular, humanity in general. This stress the need for value-oriented education at all levels—family, community, local, national and global.

Strategies for Sustainable Development

For sustainable development, we have to give importance for the following areas of development:

1. Development of human resources
2. Maintaining biodiversity
3. Importance of biotechnology
4. Development of rural energy technology
5. Harnessing of solar and biomass energy
6. Gandhian concept of Gram Swaraj
7. Vocational education
8. Gardening and farming
9. Management of local resources by local people
10. Development of water harvesting and conservation of natural resources
11. Rural development
12. Cottage industries
13. Afforestation
14. Development of waste lands
15. Skilled manpower development for future

The philosophy underlying all these are work is worship, unity, co-operation, humanity, harmony, morality, character, self-confidence, self-reliance, democratic feeling, equality, creativity, self-sufficiency, dignity of labour etc.

Everybody must attempt to understand human society, its cultural foundation, its unity and diversity, aspirations and missions. We should also balance the spirituality and science to bring harmony in the human society.

Value-Oriented Education

Value-oriented education refers to a planned educational process aimed at the development of proper attitudes, emotions and character in the learner. It covers all the aspects of personality development. Values are standards according to which the behaviour of individuals is judged. Dimensions of value education are integrated in the entire curriculum. It is a comprehensive process, involves the awareness of what is right, or what is good and what is beautiful? All human faculties are involved in this process are knowing, feeling and doing. It is a process of education focusing on the development of critical thinking, rational choice and action. Realising the significance of value education, National Policy on Education 1986, gave priority to value education and stated that inculcation of values to new generation is a top most urgency to meet the challenges of the 3rd millennium.

Education of our population on this value oriented education is the prime requirement of the day. It should be taken up as a movement involving all the groups of the population. As the students are the most active group of the society they are to be oriented through curricular and co-curricular activities.

Among the several approaches for inculcation of value education, integration of value education with the curriculum is a better approach. The values are caught through activities under different approaches to value education. The content of value education can be viewed from individual point as well as social point, to make the human being a good person, and to make the society a good society. The national aspirations and goals to education must permeate through the curriculum, co-curriculum, hidden curriculum and the school atmosphere. The curricula, the textbooks, the teachers, the facilities available in the institution, and the environment of the institution from the point of values—would determine the status in respect of knowledge and values of those who come out of the system.

Role of the Parents

As parents are the first teachers, family plays an important role in imparting emotional, social, cultural, educational values to its members. The values institutionalised in the family are important to control any behaviour. It is a source of morality and decent conduct. The school, play groups, mass media, religion—play a significant role in promoting values and in determining the personality and character of child.

Schools should promote values like truthfulness, honesty, courage, tolerance, cultural heritage, equality, scientific outlook, democracy, dignity of labour etc., among children.

Mass media has a powerful role, in promoting some of the important values like respecting teachers, fellow beings are elders, brotherhood, Vasudaika Kutumbam (world is one family), unity in diversity, respecting womenhood, co-operation, empathy towards disabled and old age people, integration and inclusion of disabled in our society, conservation and preservation of natural resources and ecological development, girl child education, education for all, self-employment, vocational education, human rights etc. At the same time they should work for the removal of the evil thoughts like untouchability, caste system, child-labour, ill treatment of women, over competitive spirit, over-ambitious nature, destruction of environment, corruption, materialistic attitudes, malpractices etc., through well planned programmes.

Role of the Teacher

Todays children and tomorrows citizens and nation's strength. They are to be endowed with courage, competence and imagination. The teacher has a vital role to play in our effort to education to national development. It is the responsibility of the teacher to guide, inspire, and illumine his student, to enrich his discipline and to inculcate values which are in consonance with our cultural heritage and social objectives. Teachers should provide freedom and maintain discipline, he should be very realistic, natural and practical and inculcate values such as punctuality, honesty, truthfulness, self confidence, self reliance etc. required for healthy and happy life. Friendly relationship between the teacher and the taught is to be encouraged. They are the persons to develop a spiritual commitment towards democracy and public welfare, capacity to communicate, potential leadership with courage, decision-making, scientific temper and awareness of the world.

Values can be developed by the teacher at different levels i.e. pre-primary to higher education through general education and vocational education. At primary ages, values are learnt through consequences, at high school level, they develop through consensus. At university level, students develop values based on principles independently as such—the energy and idealism of the youth should be identified and channelised for the making of a socially, economically, politically militarily and spiritually glorious and dynamic India.

Through curricular subjects teacher could develop the important values in an integrated approach. The hidden curriculum, the school environment, personality of the teacher, functioning of the school transmits values. School subjects will inculcate scientific, social, economic, utilitarian, cultural, moral, education, intellectual, patriotic, aesthetic, literary values etc.

Through co-curricular activities values-citizenship, sympathy, empathy, courtesy, equality, tolerance, self-confidence, secularism, discipline, respecting others, dignity of labour, team spirit, accountability, forgiveness, positive attitudes towards environmental conservation obedience etc., can be developed. Values like helping aged, disabled, saving lives by donating blood, eyes, clean and green activities, gardening, healthy habits, service-mindedness, animal rearing, celebration of national festivals, awareness camps through mobile services, integration camps, helping people affected by natural calamities etc. are to be promoted by teachers at school level. Guidance programme can also be planned to develop the values, value-oriented curriculum textbooks, value-oriented training programmes for teachers at all levels, parents and administrators and policy makers. Such type of programmes are necessary to face new challenges in education. Professional code of ethics is needed by the teacher to do justice to their roles and responsibilities and to meet professional demands. Hence teacher plays a crucial role in providing value education message for which a teacher should be a set role model.

As value-oriented education is the need of the day for all the citizens, every institution or organisation should task the task of educating the public about the need for values and try to inculcate values. Mass media can be utilised as powerful weapon in this direction. But one has to evaluate whether the media is really functioning in this direction. Hence, there is a need to design the programme or issue meticulously to inculcate good human values, which helps people live with harmony and peace and to work towards developing society for a sustainable development.

Conclusion

For sustainable development, we need value-based education, spiritual education, ethical education, need-based education, global education for Vasudaiva Kutumbam, is what is necessary for making a man a human being with integrity. As all the famous, educationists visualised education is for the liberation of human mind, development of national consciousness and reconstruction of society. New education system is necessary to achieve all these and to meet new challenges. So, for sustainable development balance between science and human values is necessary, and hence value-oriented education is need of the day for all on the globe for development of integrated and balanced personalities.

REFERENCES

1. *Education in Emerging Indian Society* By Prof. B.P. Lulla.
2. *Education for Sustainable Development* By Prof. G. Guru.
3. *Self-Learning Material for Teacher Educators*—Vol. II, NCERT, New Delhi.
4. *Principles and Practice of Education* By D.S. Gordon.
5. *India 2020: A Vision for the New Millennium (1998)*. Dr. A.P.J. Abdul Kalam, President of India.
6. *Miracle of Teaching*, Quarterly Journal (2003).

7

A Need for Value Based Education in Modern and Complex Society

Sudha, H.R.[*]

India is the land of holy rivers, holy places and ancient cultural traditions. It is an auspicious land for many reasons. Every nation in the world holds a sacred view towards India; and tried to imitate and put feet on the rut of India's mark, due to the philosophical ideals to get banal, experience the soul's ecstasy and to realise the self. Whatever may be the length and breadth of scientific development, it is a void if there is no development of one's own self. Our ancient education catered for the fulfillment of the highest aim of life viz, self-realisation for which one should have truthfulness, beauty and goodness as the values in life. Human attitude, positive behaviour and progressive outlook can transform beasts into Homo- sapiens and, thereby, could help create a healthy-social order of harmony, peace and friendship healthy values are essential prerequisites for a progressive social order. The school curriculum and infrastructures play a complementary role. The teacher has to play the pivotal role in translating these objectives into reality. Thus, the teacher, the curriculum and all other agencies should help in cleansing society from all deviant and negative evils, draw people away undesirable practices and contribute to carving out highly evolved, shealthy and progressive civic order of peace, friendship and tranquility.

* **Department of Education, Bangalore University, Bangalore.**

What man is today is the result of the long evolutionary processes. There is a world of difference between ancient and the evolving human beings which is mainly an account of the scale of humane quality, rational behaviour, ethics, morality, conduce, attitude, aptitude, intelligence, accommodative, and co-operative culture, modesty, etc. These positive elements are by-products of knowledge acquired, enriched and supplemented by human values/the industrious, innovative, technological man is the offshoot of value-based education, implying the imperative importance and need for inculcating people with positive culture, values and knowledge. Thus, there is a need for effective value-based education, good curriculum, ideal teacher and desirable learning environment.

Concept of Value

Any human action is the reflection of an individual value whereas every human institution is an outgrowth of a social value and all reactions to human experiences are conditioned by the personal and group values. Therefore, it is however impossible to avoid the influence of values on human life. Since the inception of human society, the great philosophers of all the times have been greatly concerned with values which have their prior existence and human beings are continually valuing things and activities throughout whole of their lives. Values refer to a mode of conduct or end state of experience. A value is a conception of something that is personality or socially preferable. Values aim at perfection; self-realisation, satisfaction, development, integrity and cohesion etc. The different meaning of values are as follows.

Anything that is able to satisfy or desire is termed as values.

Educational values mean those activities, which are good, useful and valuable from the point of view of education.

Need for Values in Dynamic Society

Modern mass society presents a sharp contrast, as the young grow up. They are faced with confusions, delays and discontinuities. Adolescents in particular are uncertain about themselves. Some are in conflict with themselves, bewildered an insecure. In one-way or another, many children are out of step with the life. In short, society is less well coordinated today than at earlier time to advance children into adult.

It follows from what has been said that schools in many complexes industrially developing nation are faced with difficult tasks. They are asked to educate the young, not only in such skills as the three R's but also in many social aspects of culture; they are asked to acculturate young people.

Schools are expected to teach the moral values of society when the values themselves are in conflict. Moreover in the modern world, it is not enough to shape learners in the image of their elders. The aim is to transform young human beings, to teach them to be different—better, more successful and so on—than their parents. This effort to change, to improve, is the most striking feature of present schooling as compared to traditional, tribalistic education.

The problem of valued is a more general one, common to all fields of human activity, but often education is looked upon as the instrument for inculcating values.

Our present system of education lacks value education. Value education is the need of the hour. One should grow as a respectful citizens of the society and must learn to respect his own members of family. He should behave in a manner, which provides an impression of him having a good social background.

Values are usually influenced by the changing philosophical ideologies, cultural and religious perspectives, social, political and geographical conditions. In modern emerging Indian society, there has been a revolutionary change in the field of values due to many factors in addition to the influence of westernised culture, industrialisation, moderanisation, urbanisation, globalisation and multinationals. Therefore, it is necessary to make a synthesis of the traditional and modern social values. Now it is very essential to concentrate on holistic approach of education so that all types of values may inculcated in the learner group for their all round, harmonious development. It is very amazing that in the modern materialistic society, the individual has totally concentrated on the economic. Value and by all means, he bothers to earn money and it seems that this is the only prime aim of one's life now.

It is therefore essential to explore and identify concrete devices for the incorporation of values in education. Education should be a strong instrument to attain our national goals. Value education is at the root of this process, as values incorporate, digested in the system will enable people to achieve these goals.

Importance of Value-Based Education in Present Context

Educational values play a significant role in the individual, social and professional life of a person. Value-based education is very much beneficial in many ways such as:

- To develop the positive and healthy attitude towards life.
- To mould the balanced personality.
- To develop social, vocational and cultural competency and richness.
- To learn adjustment with the ever changing environmental conditions and modify the behaviour accordingly.
- To develop high degree of intellectual and moral maturity so that a person can lead his life independently with responsibility and caring others also.
- To develop some good habits supported by feeling and rational thinking.
- To inculcate moral values and reasoning for human caring and social motivation.

Through value education, we may promote a balanced development of physical, mental, social, cultural, emotional, moral and spiritual aspects of the learners so that we may produce balanced and adjusted citizens who strive to promote social progress and welfare.

In the context of social change, the main objective of education is not only to impart information. But to inculcate the values of humanism democracy, socialism, secularism, altruism and national integration.

Approaches in Valued Oriented Education

The development of values is not easy job. There is no magic formula, technique or strategy for the inculcation and development of values. The process of value education is very complicated task, influenced by a variety of hereditary and environmental factors.

The following activities are generally employed in value education:

- Teaching, instruction, explanation and discussion.
- Training of proper habits.
- Explore to work of arts, beauty in nature.
- Providing situations and opportunities to practice values.

Some models of teaching which can be utilised in the area of value education Juris Prudential Inquiry Model of teaching is one of such models which helps students to develop the capacity for analysing social issues to assume the role of others.

Inculcation of Values

The ways and means for inculcation of values are as follows:

- Morning assembly
- Redesigning the textbooks
- Extension lectures
- Compulsory subject
- Redesigning the curriculum
- Art and painting competition and exhibitions
- Celebration of birthdays
- Celebration of international days
- Use of mass media
- Book exhibitions
- Value-oriented projects
- Cooperative store
- Cooperative canteen

- Organising co-curricular activities
- Effective method of teaching
- Value oriented outlook

REFERENCES

Dr. Haseen Taj, *Current Challenges in Education*, Neelkamal Publication, Hyderabad.

Pani, B.K. and Singh, P., *Value Education*, National Psychological Corporation, Agra.

Veeraiah, B., *Education in Emerging India*, Hamalaya Publishing House.

8

Value Crisis in Contemporary Education

Dr. S. Indira*

Education is the main instrument for the development of any country. It plays a vital role in different walks of life like social, political, intellectual and cultural. Our country already made some progress in all these directions. But it is quite unbalancing and uneven. India has got the largest scientifically trained man power. Still we need to improve a lot on all the aspects. Education is one among them. The present education system is providing man with ample material comfort but has neglected his moral well being and spiritual advancement. This results in the weakness of moral fibre, great fall in the moral standards and emptiness in the spirit. The world today has become a hot bed of strifes of all kinds. Education means preparation for future life, it must be combined with some values. They are needed to establish and to maintain moral standards in life. In this context, I made an attempt to review the topic called "Value Crisis in the Contemporary Education".

Generally values are described as the desires and goals. They can be achieved through the process of conditioning, learning and socialisation. We give value to our desires and we want to achieve them through many ways. Values reflect different philosophical positions. They are closely associated with the concept of man. Their existence is very much needed in the field of education. But

* Reader, Department of Philosophy, Pondicherry University, Pondicherry.

in the present education system, there is value crisis. The Indian education system is struggling to resolve the paradoxes facing by the country. This is happening due to many reasons. The strength of the students is increasing day by day. But the facilities available are very less. The resources are also very limited. The nature of the student is also changing. Presently the students are coming from diverse social backgrounds. The strength of the women is also increasing. The progress in the education is determined by the factors like economic growth, agricultural development, social reconstruction and many other social and cultural factors. The regional differences within the country reflects mainly on the education system and also on other aspects of human development. Inequity in education development is one of the major crisis faced by the Contemporary Education System. It becomes a ritual without proper meaning and purpose. Large number of people are remaining illiterate and large section of children are not even privileged by primary education. This prevents from utilising the benefits. We need trained people with sharp abilities. The technological development is one of the factors that contributed to the today's value crisis. The other factors like personal greed, selfishness, indifference towards others are also the different means for value crisis in the contemporary education. The fall in the moral standards is also one of the reasons. The weakening of moral values in the contemporary education system and in social life creates serious social and ethical conflicts. Since the education system is becoming materialistic day by day, the moral standards are also falling. The modern Indian is being educated mainly with the idea of earning bread. As a result, most of the graduates run after money, power and material desires without caring for values. There is an urgent need to reform the values of human life and in the field of education. The Indian education system must be relevant to the changing contexts of life and also to our national needs.

Efforts must be made to impart the inspiring qualities among the students. Several moral virtues like infinite love, justice, honesty, purity, wisdom, humility, faithfulness, mercy, respect for others and sincerity in actions must be inculcated in the field of education. The contemporary Indian education system needs moral, religious and spiritual values. For majority of Indians, religion is the great motivating force. It is ultimately bound up with the formation of character and the inculcation of ethical values. The present Indian education system must fulfil the aspirations of the people. According to Einsteen "The most important human endeavour is the striving for morality in our actions. Our inner balance and even our every existence depends upon it. Only morality in our actions can give beauty and dignity to life". The present Indian education system is reflecting more on the borrowed ideologies. The natural values are neglected behind. The teachers are not having clear orientation. They must have clear ideas and natural values. The teacher must try to inculcate values in the students. The present curriculum also must reflect on human values. The schools an colleges should become the value centres. The individual's life will be judged on the touch stone of morality. Morality and virtues save man from worldly sorrows. In the present educational reconstruction, the integrated perspective on values must be pivotal. The practice of values can provide unity for all the activities of the educational institutions. An integrated education can provide growth of integration of values. Various commissions and committees recommended the value education at all levels. They must highlighten the point that the main function of education is to produce citizens with sound character and a healthy personality. Because good citizens are the hope for the progress and prosperity of the country. They should have inspiring values, ideals, proper moral conduct and also a life based on good principles. All these are the essential pre-requisites for a good citizen. The individual must put an effort in this direction. Such efforts may lead to the new beginning.

Good education results is harmony and peace in the society, when the members in the society have moral values. According to a French moralist by name E. Durkheim, "The first value that has to be inculcated in the student is discipline. Second is the attachment to social groups. The former is concerned with the development of the character of the individual and the latter is concerned with the relationship with others in the society. Both of these depend upon the education and training that the individual receives during adolescence". The moral values must be inculcated in the children before they come to the school. In the school they are subjected to systematic influence. Due to the complexity of modern society, the home is gradually loosing its importance. The school has taken over a number of functions from the home. So the school has to bear the great responsibility in moulding the children's character on sound scientific lines. They must give importance to secular morality, because our country has chosen the twin principles of democracy and secularism. For many children the school is the only source of regular moral influence, when compared to their homes. Many homes can offer little or direct help in promoting proper, moral growth among the children. Thus in the school there should be proper patterns of moral behaviour. The students must be encouraged to have proper value development. The teachers occupy pivotal role in imparting value education to the students. Counselling system is a must for the effective propagation of values, because it helps to understand the students properly. In the classroom it is not possible to make intimate interaction. The teachers cannot understand them within the scheduled time.

The curriculum must provide enough opportunity for students to acquire knowledge. The attitudes, emotions, feelings and motives of the pupils must be taken as important things to be considered. The teacher should be able to create the rational autonomy in both thought and action. The most important aspect of value development consists in the building and strengthening of positive sentiments for the people and also for ideals. Education should prepare individuals for participation and promoting values in social life. In addition to this the schools and colleges must provide healthy environment for sharing the responsibilities, relationships and community life. There should be universalisation of education at the elementary level, vocationalisation at the secondary level and specialisation at the higher education level. The teacher must emphasise that life is a precious gift. He must guide that the ambition is good. It can be achieved through the moral virtues. Above all the objective of education is the integration of the society. It must establish brotherhood on earth. In return it should impart human values. Our ancient Indians always called for peace through several shanti mantras namely:

"Sahanavavatu sahanaubhunaktu

Sahaviryam karavavahai

Tejaswinavadhitamastu

Mavidvishavahai

Om, santih santih santih".

It is chanted together by the teacher and the student and it is universal in its application.

While planning the curriculum, the values must be inculcated. It must promote the values of democracy, egalitarianism, social justice and secularism. It must emphasise high performance and excellence. As a mechanism of socialisation, it should prepare the generations with new design for living. It must promote the quality of life. In return the students will revive confidence. There must be commitment in inculcating values. Education must lead to continual growth of personality, steady development of character and qualitative improvement of life. A trained mind has the capacity to draw the spiritual nourishment from every experience. According to the American Journal by name *National Parent-Teacher Journal*, April 1955, the definition of current education is "the mysterious process whereby information pass from the notes of the professor to the note book of the student, through his pen without entering the mind of either of them". It is an apt description for the education in India today.

The educational stagnation can be removed only by treating education primarily as training of the mind. According to Swami Vivekananda education means "Life-building, man-making, character making assimilation of ideas". The entire educational method and programme should keep this an objective in the view. The education should help the common mass of people to equip themselves for the struggle for life. It must bring out strength of character, a spirit of philanthropy and the courage of a lion. It is the real education. The highest education is gained not from institutions, but from the illumined men and women. There is still higher education which yields the knowledge of the infinite self of man, the "Atman". Surplus human energy accumulated at the secular level of life, if it is not channelised properly into the spiritual direction, it will recoil on the personality. It creates disturbances and tensions. Today's children must develop the rich dimension of personality, physical, intellectual and spiritual growth. The British psychologist R.D. Laing refers in his book by name, *The Politics of Experiences* "The child born today in U.K. stands a ten times greater chance of being admitted to a mental hospital than to an university. It is our way of educating them that is driving them mad". We need education which brings transformation within man to be able to make him inclined and capable to use his enormous powers for peaceful constructive purposes. Education for both "learning to do" and "learning to be" is helped by the practice of meditation, because doing becomes an out flow of an enriched being within. Meditation given insight into one's own inner dimension and hidden possibilities. The student must combine meditation with work, that is inward penetration with outward action. With the help of this philosophy of yoga, we can transform modern civilization into a stable, rich and beautiful human achievement.

REFERENCES

1. *Moral Education: A Practical Approach* By K. Rama Rao, Published by Rama Krishna Institute of Moral and Spiritual Education, Mysore, 1994.
2. *Eternal Values of Changing Society* By Swami Ranganadhananda, Vol. 3, Bharatiya Vidya Bhavan, Bombay, 1995.
3. *Human Values for Universal Teaching and Application* Edited By V.R. Koraddi, Bangalore, 2001.
4. *Values and Personality, Dispositions of University Teachers* By Madhuri Sinha, Classical Publishing Company, New Delhi, 2000.
5. *College Teachers and Administrators—A Hand Book* By I.V. Chalapati Rao, 1992.
6. *Professional Competency in Higher Education,* Edited By S. Neelamegham and N.K. Oberoi, New Delhi, 2000.

9

Value Crisis in Contemporary Indian Education

Dr. V. Govinda Reddy*

Dr. D. Chenna Reddy**

"Values cannot be taught but caught" is the belief held by many people. Value education is coming into force to promote sense of morality, asesthetic and intellectual knowledge among the students. The existing knowledge can be upgraded through some of the curricular, co-curricular and extra curricular activities.

Value education has come to acquire increasing prominence educational discussions at all levels during recent times in our company. The issue has been projected as one of the national priorities in the National Policy on Education (NPE) 1986. This policy declares "the growing concern over the erosion of essential and an increasing cynicism in society has brought to focus the need for readjustments in the curriculum in order to make education a forceful tool for the cultivation of social and moral values".

Through value education we like to develop the social, moral, aesthetic and spiritual sides of a person, which are often undermined informal education. Value education teaches us to preserve whatever is good and worthwhile in what we have

* **Department of Education, Sri Krishnadevaraya University, Anantapur–515 003, Andhra Pradesh.**

** **Department of Education, Sri Krishnadevaraya University, Anantapur–515 003, Andhra Pradesh.**

inherited from our culture. It helps us to respect the attitudes and behaviour of those who differ from us. Value education does not mean value imposition or indoctrination.

Value education has the capacity to transform a diseased mind into a very young, fresh, innocent, healthy, natural and attentive mind. The transformed mind is capable of higher sensitivity and a heightened level of perception. This leads to fulfillment of the evolutionary role in man and in life.

The values are classified in the following manner. They are: (1) Utilitarian value; (2) Vocational value; (3) Intellectual value; (4) Cultural value; (5) Aesthetic value; (6) Moral value; (7) Creative value; (8) Interpretational value; (9) Experimental value; (10) Environmental value; (11) Psychological value (12) Disciplinary value; (13) Inspirational value; (14) Value of development of scientific aptitude; (15) Training in scientific method; and (16) Value for better living.

Factors Related to Value Education

(a) *Value Education Through Family:* The family is the first unit with which the child has continuous contact and it is also the most powerful medium through which value systems develop. The family plays one of the most important roles in the socialisation of the individual, which starts right from birth.

Parents, grandparents, elder siblings should become role models for the young children whom they can emulate and identify with. They should also expose children to the lives of contemporary great men so that they become role models to be followed. Parents and elders of the family are constantly under the scrutiny of children. Therefore, they should see that there is no incompatibility between their precepts and practice. Parents should not be overprotective and overanxious because this encourages the dominance of fear in the child. Parents should not be imposing or interfering in their zeal to infuse values in their children but they should encourage them in their growth by watching, helping and giving suggestions. Parents and other family members should sort out their differences in private or in a manner consistent with the dignity expected of them, so that children are not exposed to their bickering and quarreling. Parents should delegate some responsibilities on their children according to their capability in such a way that children feel responsible and not burdened. Parents should stop worrying excessively about their children's grades/marks in examination. Instead, they should focus equal attention of their children to other areas like sports and games, music, art, story reading and other hobbies. Parents and elder siblings should respect the right and dignity of the child in expressing his/her opinion. Family members should take sometime out of their busy schedule for outings, sight seeing, visiting places of interest like gardens, zoo, museum, historical monuments, science parks and the like. This is more advocated for urban child who is confined to the four walls of small flats. Parents should collaborate with school teachers of their wards to determine and decide what ideals should be imparted in value based education and how to do so.

(b) *Value Education Through Teachers:* The role of teachers is quite significant in the development of society. Teachers are real nation builders. It is the teacher community who moulds the future society. Teachers are the section of society who can influence the future generation towards a positive attitude with a healthy value base. The extent of influence, which a teacher casts up on the children, is well known and understood. The teacher is the role model for the child and what they imbibe gets multiplied subsequently in the society.

It was sounded in the Report of Education Commission as the Education Commission (1964-66) begins the report with the sentence, "The destiny of India is now being shaped in her classrooms". Educational institutions can impart values to influence human life along with imparting general instructions.

It would be possible for our teacher trainees to practice the value of love, brotherhood and fellow feeling, if something would be kept in his mind about these values. Our teacher education programmes should be placed to practice these values both by teacher educators and teacher trainees.

We expect much from our teachers for our development in terms of material and human aspects. Our expectation would be fulfilled, if we prepare real teachers through our teacher education programmes.

A teacher easily inculcates values if he has professionalism and love towards his profession and students. There is no need of prescribing any method to teach values for a devoted teacher who loves his pupils.

(c) *Value Education Through Textbooks:* The textbooks, supplementary reading materials and other materials for general reading in different subject areas will have to build in universal human values. These have to be written carefully and reviewed frequently so that they are not counter productive.

Hawq (1973) in his analysis of Hindi, History, Civics and English textbooks found neither a systematic pattern nor any consistency in the presentation of values. The mental maturity of pupils was not paid attention to. The languages texts of IX, X and XI classes were written entirely from literary point of view.

Chaudhari (1974) and Chaudhari (1976) analysed Hindi textbooks and found that scientific outlook, justice, simple living, and dutifulness were given the least importance in the text books prepared by the NCERT while patriotism was significantly presented in state corporation books.

Pillai (1976) analysed English and Tamil textbooks of the IX standard in Tamil Nadu State Board and found that the presentation of religious values was inadequate. Susheela (1977) found that secularism was prominently reflected in the social studies (Part–I) textbooks in the secondary level.

Usha Sri (1995) conducted an evaluation of value education is secondary schools. Teachers were asked to indicate the extent to which the listed characteristics were found in the textbooks of teacher's subject of specialisation. From the weighted scores, it was found that, in the textbooks of VIII, IX, X standards, the greatest attention is paid to examples given from life situations. Other characteristics that follow an order of descending weightage areas follows: 'Special mention is made regarding the qualities of discoveries, reformers, leaders etc., desirable values are emphasised wherever possible, a logical approach to problem solving is emphasised, questions given call for value judgement', and the good and glory of all religions is highlighted'.

According to science teachers, 'a logical approach to problem solving is emphasised as the most prevalent characteristic. The least perceived characteristic is the 'special mention made regarding qualities of discoveries, leaders reformers etc.

The social science teachers replied that the most emphasised characteristic in social science textbook is damage to humanity resulting from wars, followed by the characteristic examples that are given from life situation and 'desirable values are emphasised wherever possible'.

In Mathematics textbooks, a few characteristics only are perceived to be present by the math's teachers—'examples are given from life situation and a logical approach to problem solving is emphasised'.

(d) *Value Education Through Management:* Certain educational institutions in India are renowned for their commitment and exemplary programmes in value education. They illustrated us how in the context of value crisis, principled living is possible. The core group on value orientation of education (1992) reports some favours on deemed universities and the Rishi Valley school formulation.

Dayalbagh Educational institute has core courses emphasising on Indian culture. Rural service, co-curricular activities. Work experience is compulsory for students of various age groups. Ethical and moral values, National Integration tolerance and scientific temper are highlighted in its educational programmes.

Ramakrishna Institute of Moral and Spiritual Education (RIMSE), Mysore is founded on the twin principles of self-realisation and service to mankind, after Sri Ramakrishna Paramahamsa. Teachers and students of school and college levels are offered moral and spiritual education. The retreats organised by RIMSE are well known for their value related programmes. The B.Ed. course provides value education in theory and practice of National unity, sensitivity towards environment, spirit of service to the community and a healthy attitude towards life.

National Seminars, extension activities and national integration camps cover a wide range of lectures discussions, screening of films and programming highlighting moral, spiritual and scientific values.

The philosophy of J. Krishnamurthy is reflected in Rishivalley School. It advocates for absolute freedom, helping the child to flower in goodness, responsibility, a spirit of inquiry without bias and a concern for man and environment that are integral to the scheme of education.

Sri Aurobindo International Centre for Education (SAICE), Pondicherry is an institution to provide integral education as envisioned by Sri Aurobindo and the mother. An effort is made to help the growth and perfection of all aspects of the child's personality—Physical, Vital, mental, psychic and spiritual. Great importance is given to develop various faculties of observation, judgement expression and other sense allowing the students to arrive at the right conclusions themselves.

Sri Satya Sai Institute of Higher learning, Puttaparthy follows the fundamental Sai Philosophy of Integral Education. Truth, Righteous conduct, love, peace and non-violence are the apex of Education for Human Values programme. This deemed university has a well drawn out teacher-training course. It includes a full paper on value based education and general foundation courses in both the semesters to provide the background of Indian culture, Indian Constitution world perspectives and relationship of spirituality and science.

Education for Value Development

The school curriculum has to include certain components that communicate essential values in their totality. Every teacher has to be a teacher of values. Every activity, unit and interaction must be examined from the viewpoint of value identification, inculcation and reinforcement and then deciding appropriate strategy for a balanced and judicious implementation. These values can be attained by stating clearly the school goals, evolving discipline through participation of staff and students, wherever necessary, ensuring two way communication for redressal, welfare services, help to needy students, remediation, re-evaluation and non-rejection of poor achievers, formulating rules that ensure participation of each student in the games, activities and programmes relevant to their interests.

At the Elementary Stage

- The school assembly, group singing, practicing silence and meditation;
- Simple and interest stories about the lives and teachings of prophets, saints, scientists, their discoveries etc.;
- Field activities like games and sports, social work leading to the attitude of service to humanity and other creatures, even to nature and to the precept work is worship; and
- Cultural activities plays etc., on appropriate themes.

At the Secondary and Higher Secondary Stages

- The morning assembly, reading from the books of wisdom great literature or an appropriate address by a teacher or a guest speaker;

- Essential teachings of the major world religions, discoveries and inventions of various scientists etc.;
- Social science during holidays and outside school hours;
- National integration camps, the National Social Services and the National Cadet Corps, Scouts and Guide programmes; and
- Cultural activities, plays, science exhibitions, debates etc. on appropriate themes.

Support Interventions

- Highlight the values inherent in different subject areas;
- Provide students with opportunities for questioning, sharing and respecting each other;
- Provide students opportunities for learning democratic principles and processes in the classroom transactions;
- Emphasise equality of gender, social castes, classes and religions;
- Underline human rights, children's thoughts, environmental protection, healthy living etc.; and
- Make the classroom atmosphere tension free and democratic to enhance values.

Inculcation of Values

Values are caught rather than taught. Values begin to develop early in life and this process continues at different levels of life. Values can be easily related to the Piagetian concepts of stages of learning, teaching and reasoning skills rather than only 'content' in values and are therefore of crucial importance. For example, it is one thing to learn to speak the truth and another to practice throughout one's life. Students should be furnished with a set of reasoning skills, which they would then use in the real world.

At the primary stages values can be introduced and inculcated and nurtured through interesting stories. At the secondary stage, there may be frequent discussions between the teacher and the pupils on the values desired to inculcate. An enquiry approach would help students in clarifying the nature and consequences of the values and to become thoroughly committed to their values. Moral education based on this conception involves the use of activities, exercises and procedures in the entire school programme that habituate children in right modes of conduct thus strengthening their character.

The inculcation of values among learners is more a matter of teaching learning rather than the matter of content. Value orientation is an inter-human process, which demands the creative role of the teacher and the participative role of the learner. The teaching of every subject should inherit value orientation. The methodologies employed to instill these values have also to be sensitive to individual sentiments and needs. Every teacher has to be made responsible for his/her undertaking inside and outside the classroom and for value education. The textbook material should be correlated with the learning of values by identifying areas in which the desired values may be promoted.

In the pursuit of values, the teacher has the most vital role to play. It is the teacher who is the guide, friend and philosopher and the first interaction of children, after the parents, is with the teacher. Teachers with vision, dealing with curricular subjects such as languages, science, social, science, music, work experience and co-curricular activities such as NCC, Scouts and Guide, can develop suitable strategies and methods which could enable proper transmission of values.

Value education can be achieved directly, indirectly or incidentally. Direct value inculcation refers to deliberate systematic instruction given during the time of formation. Indirectly, value education can be imparted through the regular subjects of curriculum, and co-curricular activities. Incidental, value inculcation can be given through events and incidents related to good values occurring around us thus relating value inculcation to concrete situations.

Thus for value—education to be effective, the three factors family, school and community should join hands together and get peace and happiness and procure truth, beauty and wisdom—the three pillars of value based education.

Value based education can be adopted in a multifaceted environment—a cooperative effort involving: (a) Value education through family; (b) Value education through teachers; (c) Value education through textbooks; (d) Value education through management and (e) Teachers with vision, dealing with curricular subjects such as languages, science, social, music, work experience and Co-curricular activities such as NCC, Scouts and Guide, can develop suitable strategies and methods which could enable proper transmission of values.

10

Value Crisis in Education

M. Venkata Subbaiah*

All thinkers supported that the school should be integral to society. Education should lead towards an understanding to strengthen national unity by maintaining work mindedness. Education should lead towards a high standard of living for the masses than the existed, without detriment to cultural heritage and national identity by maintaining dignity of labour. Epistemologically speaking, Life emerges out of "Super-consciousness". According to Einstein, "My frail mind is unable to perceive the superior reasoning power behind the entire universe that superior reasoning power is my concept of God". Where science fail to answer there starts philosophy. The best form of devotion to God is in the form of an image rather than in the form of a human being.

Even though values are caught, children need proper guidance from teachers during the process of nurture. School should at least be the starting point for effective learning of values by which children can be able to build a useful, scrupulous and in memorable character, characteristics of an ideal personality before the society for which parents, teachers as well as the society at large will be proud of the great personalities emerging out of the school.

Values are nothing but the social—amity and adjustability without causing any damage to others rights, whether they may

* **Jakkidi College of Education, Shamshabad, Hyderabad.**

be personal, social or intellectual or even spiritual values. All these values are to be developed because they are the core elements for moulding the individual personality at large. Though teachers are the elevated personalities to save the children in one form or other. The presence of super natural element should be involved, in teaching-learning strategies, i.e. omniscient, omnipotent and omnipresent. Temporal relations with the materials may or may not damage the finer elements of human values. Every aspirant should be directed and lined towards permanent values for realisation of the major goals to be achieved, i.e. knowledge about the Brahman and oneness of God should be realised through maintaining religious tolerance. Supremacy of God and development of optimistic attitude, giving away congested and narrow-minded ideals, which do cause damage to the finer elements of then "Summumbonum of life".

Values are not achieved through solitary process, its multi-dimensional facets should be considered, while developing by using different teaching-learning strategies, schools cannot alone develop values among the children, because children are exposed to different situations to complete their task with variety of personalities and materials like audio-video systems as well as interaction with the materials like computers etc. influence and use of hardware as well as software technology during the process of teaching learning strategies enable children to face the task in the desired way easily at their own speed in the modern society. We have moved from the era of certainty to an era of uncertainty and doubt.

Modernisation in the sense development and exploration of scientific knowledge greatly influenced the exchange of different cultures and integration among them will yield results in the positive direction and should not be a curse for the peaceful co-existence in preserving their culture among the races or communities or different countries at large. Development of science, exploration of knowledge should influence positively. Invention of aeroplane is to drop food packets, etc., to the people to evade unforeseen conditions due to natural calamities with humanitarian outlook. Out of frustration people find by ways leaving alone the interest of the inventor or scientist. Now-a-days due to advancement of science and technology and the bad influenced of the society or due to development of aggregative aspects leaving human values aside, people are using the airplanes for bombing and for the use of highly sophisticated lethal weapons to give enormous damage to our brethren without proper ideals. Invention of atom bomb and production of atomic energy should lead the countries in better use of inputs for better out-puts for the upliftment of the life of the people to meet the needs relating to energy in all walks of life but not with the interest of giving damage leaving human values. Rational thinking development of values, progressive ideals are for better production only to save the people from all these disasters to meet the challenging taskes more confidently.

Education, I mean, the challenging task for social modernisation in the desired way whether it is to drive the masses into hazardous situations or peaceful co-existence are in the hands of educational advisors, administrators, curriculum planners, teachers, non-governmental organisations at large. Through better execution of plans related to the value-oriented education inside and outside the school should be for the development of values among the children in the desired way.

Though personal and social values are varied from place to place, society to society, religion to religion etc., whereas in case of eternal values all should come round to the idea of oneness of God and realisations of Brahman. Contradictory to this there may be pessimistic attitude due to frustration. They should also at least accept the values related to personal as well as social values because the incumbent of the society. Value education should remedy the pessimistic attitudes. Value education in schools should focus more attention on the development of personal as well as social values, which in turn reaps the fruits of eternal values. There may be variations in personal and social values among the religions/countries. All these personal and social values have common objective of achieving eternal values and oneness of God. Irrespective of religion, caste, creed, race or nationality. Value education should be the remedy for the unrest among the masses in the development of optimistic attitude and for arresting the pessimistic attitude. Undemocratic way of dealing things to democratic way, selfishness to selfless service. Personal values like, regularity, punctuality, social values like adjustability, service motive wage war against anti-social acts and superstitions etc., will enable the individuals to attain the eligibility for the realisation of eternal values. Eternal values are nothing but the super goals to be reached by every human being. Education should lessen the time to realise the super goals through better learning comparatively. In case of Indian schools of thought Hindu system Visista-Advaita, realisation of Brahman through idol-worship is very easy, whereas Advaita system somewhat difficult to realise. Nirguna Brahman, through study and practice of certain sacred books and rituals to achieve values. In case of Islam realisation through certain other practices basing on the "Khuran" the holy book related to Islam and sayings of the prophet. In case of Christianity realisation through study and practice of the "Bible" the holy book and practices of sayings of Jesus Christ etc., should have access to achieve the super goals. All these sayings and practices, should have a common goal and function to develop certain values among the human beings and realisation of almighty. All our inputs in education should be pressed in to service for better outputs i.e. realisation of values related to personal and social which in turn paves the way for better understanding of Brahman with a final view to achieve the eternal values.

Not only the school but also parents, community and society at large will be responsible in facilitating the children to acquire the required key quaiities. Though schools plays a predominant role in developing the required qualities by providing suitable learning experiences. As a teacher there is every need to imbibe certain basic values. Experiences provided to them have an ever-lasting impact in molding their personality. NPE'86 stressed the need for promotion of values such as Indian common cultural heritage egalitarianism, democracy and secularism, equality of sexes, protection of the environment, removal of social barriers, observance of small family norms, inculcation of scientific temper, education should foster an awareness of the equality of all by removing prejudices. Teachers will have to depend greatly on personal observation of student's behaviour and infer about the development using suitable rating scale and structured interview. But emotional qualities never are manifested in isolations to draw inferences. Evaluation of the values developed is a continuous process. Acquisition of knowledge and mental skills, health habits work habits, cleanliness, co-operation and such other personal and social values aimed at helping the children in acquiring valuable personal and social behaviour and in cultivating health habits for their will being that form character and personality. Accountability of teachers is invited to achieve maximum outputs.

A.

	Personal Values	*Strategies for the Development of Values (Suggested Activities)*
	1	2
1.	Regularity and punctuality, self-respect	Attending prayers, school, and classroom activities on time, punctuality and regularly with self-respect.
2.	Cleanliness, health habits and sanitation	Maintaining personal, school, classroom, neighbourhood cleanliness with good habits. Maintaining good sanitation in and around for the welfare of the individuals and society. Cleaning the premises and preserving the greenery free from pollution.
3.	Industriousness diligence work-habits.	Attending the classwork, homework with devotion by improving working habits.
4.	Truthfulness, honesty, trust worthiness	Attending and helping the men at work with work mindedness, and participation in activities related to honesty and trustworthy.
5.	Sense of responsibility	Completing the work related on time and attending the developmental activities related to school home and society. Feeling the responsibility with proper care and sensitivity.
6.	Co-operation	Extending mutual support to peer group in school welfare activities, elders at home and society for their well being.
7.	Sense of duty and service	Extending help to needy, co-operation and participation towards social and welfare activities.
8.	National Identity and Integrity	Active participation in local festivals, national festivals in school and in the village, singing the National Songs, collection of national leaders, photographs, songs, coins, stamps, paper cuttings and preparation of albums and models, conducting exhibitions.

(Contd...)

1	2
9. Equality, sympathy towards needy people	Respect towards other sex and helpful to needy people giving equal opportunities to participate in developmental activities in and out of the school.
10. Service Motto, duty to God, duty to country and duty to neighbours.	Active participation in social service activities and respect towards elders and parents. Participation in cubs and Bull-bull activities, scouting and guiding in schools. Serving the old and needy people with humanitarian outlook.

B.

Social Values	*Strategies for the Development of Values*
1	2
1. Indian common cultural heritage, patriotic outlook	Active participation in school level functions related to nation and participation in cultural activities in and out of the school. Celebration of school-day, parents-day, old students-day, elocution and essay writing competitions on themes like national leaders, national integration, international understanding and about our cultural heritage.
2. Egalitarianism (welfare for all)	Through execution in curriculum children learns the welfare for all. Organising co-operative stores, honest post-office, small savings, maintaining school uniform, helping the needy at home and school.
3. Democracy and secularism	Running mock parliament, conducting of elections at school level, visiting the public offices like Panchayat office, M.D.O., M.R.O., post-office, Bank, Co-operate stores welfare offices, field trip to public services institutions and transacting with them.
4. Equality of sexes	Through better exposure of the curriculum related to family welfare and superstitions.
5. Protection of environment	Through execution of better curricular activities to understand the demerits of deforestation i.e. air pollution, water pollution, sound pollution etc., and remedial measures for the protection of environment through plantation, minimum use of water, electricity and other resources available.

(Contd...)

1	2
6. Removal of social barriers (religious tolerance)	Better participation in para-curricular activities like wage war against superstitions, early marriages, widow marriages, dowry system, untouchability. Through activities like role-play, dramatisation, wall writings, interviews, posters, use of mass media, essay writing, elocution etc. Encouraging the habit of religious tolerance.
7. Observance of small family norms (Economic way of Living)	Through execution of planned and prepared curriculum related to family welfare activities, like display, essay writing, elocution, drama, role-play, singing songs, wall writings, use of mass media etc.
8. Inculcation of scientific temper	Activities related to core-curriculum, field trips, excursions, exhibitions visit to industrial museum, factories, planetarium, public gardens collection preservation of plant and animal materials, taxi dermy and stuffing the birds and animals etc. Maintaining Herbarium, Terrarium, Aquarium participation in club activities, etc., will enable to children to develop values.
9. International understanding and peaceful co-existence.	Participation in UNO, Mock Parliament, Pen friendship, stamp collections, tours, excursions, etc. Participation in local festivals and prayers.
10. Social service.	Participation in social camps, watching the T.V. Radio and other mass media, Library, success stories, watching the real situations in daily life, active participation in social service activities, scouting and guiding, NSS, aspiration for the defence and civil services.

Personal and social values lead to spiritual values or eternal values. Through better execution of plans in relation to curricular inputs. Teacher can develop affective domain. Activities related to visits to religious places, inviting philosophers, saints, thinkers to give their valuable Theosophical ideas to nurture the children with spiritual ideals like kindness, non-violence, generosity, love, affection, tolerance, helping the needy, piousness, yoga, meditation, all religious prayers, sacred acts, visits to sacred places, study of sacred books, prayers, offerings, alms to poor and deserves, services to humanity, kind towards animals and nature, fasting etc.

Realisation of almighty as He target for every human being. Prayer can work all things, development of aesthetic sense involve so many contradictory problems. Even then every teacher should have inclination towards the development of values, which leads to achieve major goals of education to become life centred, and useful. Activities related to the development of spiritual values are nothing but summation and essence of the individual and social values. Without the completion of prerequisites of education, there is no possibility of all round development.

Teacher should be ideal and model before the class and should feel accountable for the development of expected values among the children. For this teacher should strive against to become ideal. Commitment on the part of teachers only improves the conditions of value-education in schools. Development of values solves the problems of student's unrest and paves the way for better understanding. Answer for all these maladies will be realised only through value education. Teaching learning strategies have no meaning if they are devoid of value education. Teacher should act as guide and able to rectify the defects during the process of effective learning by students only then students get maximum benefit out of schools. Well planned and designed curriculum better inputs related to value education will be pressed into service, for better output in school education.

Value education should not hamper fully the scientific advancements and rational thinking. Development of values synchronises children to live mentally stable, peacefully to continue their work dynamically, in the progressive society with optimistic outlook free from disastrous, frustrated attitudes and cursing nature. Teacher should be kind and generous in dealing with children to achieve maximum outputs related to value education, through better schooling.

11

Challenges in Science Education

Relevant to Value Crisis in Contemporary Indian Education

T. Rajyalakshmi*

Introduction

Values are generally considered as perceptions of socially avowed desires and goals actualised by internal processes by learning and adopting, conditioning and adjustments. Values represent philosophical paradigms and the general notion of values is integrated with the existence of man.

The crisis of values is therefore so pervasive in the contemporary Indian education that it impinges upon every aspect of our life. The advances in science and technology, explosion in knowledge and the crisis and dilemmas we face in life are engulfing the entire society and confronting us with many challenges.

Science and science education having a far-reaching permeating and recondite effects on the young as well as sensitive minds the need for revamping and reorienting science education to our contemporary situation is so essential, desirable and urgent as never before. The distinction between human society and humane society must be clearly conceptualised to transit into a progressive, visionary and emancipated educated society.

* **Associate Professor, Institute of Advanced Study in Education, Sri Venkateswara University, Tirupati.**

Whatever conflicts, dilemmas and paradoxes are confounding the prevailing social mind-set by the backlash, antithesis and over-weaning influences of science and science education, must be rectified, reformed and revitalised with right values, ethical concerns and humane, compassionate, benevolent and missionary zeal.

Classification of Values in Education

There are different methods of classification of values in education which are intimately associated with man. The following are examples of such classifications:

- Biological values
- Intrinsic values
- Instrumental values
- Health values
- Recreational values
- Spiritual values

Another system of classification

- Spiritual values
- Material values
- Intellectual values
- Social values
- Moral values
- Political values
- Economic values
- Cultural values

Whatever the system of classification all the values have inter-relationship with the different scientific systems and the educational implications of these values are best understood in the context of each branch of science which the science educator endeavours to teach. Some of these scientific disciplines are discussed in detail.

Ethical and Social Responsibilities in Scientific Education

A modern of society depicted below proposed by Frazer and Kornhauser is to relate it to ethics and social responsibility.

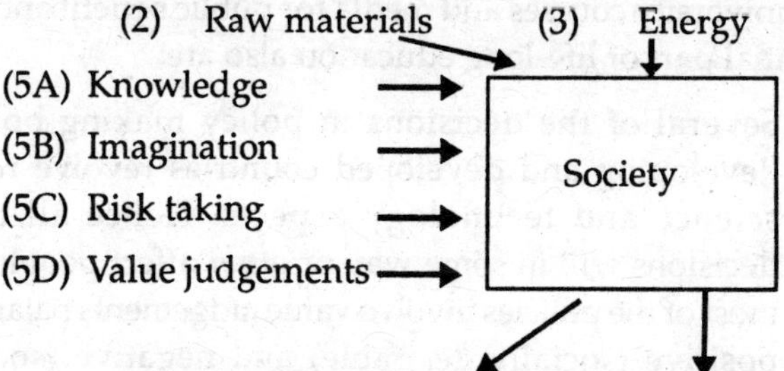

It is a systems approach model from production engineering which has an input-output understanding. The desires and needs of every society have to be provided through products viz., food, shelter, clothing, transportation, entertainment (TV etc.) as well as services e.g. health care, transport system. These products or services (1) are created out of raw materials; (2) and useful energy; (3) an unavoidable result of this process is the generation of wastes; (4) as for example slag from a coal mine, sulphur dioxide in the atmosphere, nitrogenous discharges into rivers, low grade energy etc. The inputs (2) and (3) and outputs (3) and (4) are in addition to another dimension—the people.

The knowledge and ingenuity of people are involved (5A and 5B) in the inputs being conversed to outputs. The eagerness to take risks (5C) and pupils' values judgement (5D) is the basis of the whole cycle of events. These value judgements constitute the social responsibility and ethical consideration. The crux of the problem lays in the fact that while everyone appreciates the need for increased production of food (desired product) their undesirable consequences like pollution from the manufacture and consumption of fertilizers and pesticides, over exploitation of natural, resources like fish etc., are harmful. This aspect is elaborated, while discussing about agriculture in later pages.

The Importance of Dissemination of Knowledge of Social Responsibility and Ethics in Education in the Context of Value Crisis

Three main reasons for creating awareness in education at school, in university courses and media for public benefit and also as an essential part of life-long education also are:

1. Several of the decisions in policy making both in developing and developed countries revolve round science and technology aspects. Hence all these decisions will in some way or other affect people and most of the policies involve value judgements balancing positive (socially desirable) and negative (socially undesirable) effects.
2. Public activism is proving to be too powerful a force to deal with. If they gain knowledge and insight into social, ethical issues of science and technology they have to be necessarily involved before taking public interest decisions.
3. The dichotomy of society into a minority of knowledgeable people understanding science and social issues and a majority of people not able to grasp science nor its concerns may feel that science is manipulating things. This feeling may become so strong that anti-science activists may emerge with irrational behaviour, causing harm to society. The ignorance of science produces fear out of which irrational behaviour arises, according to psychologists. The crisis in values is a manifestation of this type of situation.

Selected Issues of Value Crisis in Various Fields of Science

1. Agriculture/Food

The green revolution, white revolution and blue revolution are great biological values of science and science education that are meeting the challenges of human needs of food, ensuring food safety and nutritional requirements. With the ever increasing population growth in the country, shortages of food, bottlenecks in public distribution system and exploitation of toiling agriculturists by unscrupulous middlemen, traders and antisocial elements are becoming everyday happenings. The values of honesty, hardwork and ethical concern for society are taking a beating at the hands of ruthless, unprincipled and opportunistic people. Spurious seeds, adulterated fertilizers and pesticides, lack of proper storage facilities usurious money lenders are contributing to degeneration of values and suicides by farmers. Apart from this overuse of land, unending cultivation practices and indiscriminate tapping of ground water resources, irrigation facilities, energy resources, unbridled use of fertilizers, pesticides, destruction of natural species of insects, birds and other coexisting creatures in the ecosystem by disregarding values of non-violence, tolerance and respect for nature, is the major cause of crisis in values. Science education plays an important role in highlighting the social and ethical issues and values related to production and distribution of food products. The balance between providing sufficient food and environmental protection must be emphasised in agriculture, and also awareness of safety in use of dangerous, hazardous, toxic chemicals like pesticides, fumigants and poisons must be spread to prevent intentional or unintentional deaths by farmers, laymen and criminals who may use them for killing fish, valuable wildlife or even humans.

GM Foods

In recent years genetically modified food including corn, vegetables and fruits are being promoted through GM plants produced by genetic engineering of identified gene/genes for increased productivity, resistance to insect damage, harmful diseases etc. Enhancing meat production in animals by the same means for example GM sheep, cattle, pigs and other animals is also another case in point. These GM foods have raised questions of ethical concern about promoting such customised plants and animals. As genetically manipulated plants/animals they become succeptible to diseases, infection and other ecological disasters. Commercial GM crops including Bt cotton, have ruined farmers who were initially encouraged by the spectacular results shown by scientists, in selected field trials. However, when adopted on large scale in Nature under natural conditions huge losses due to lack of resistance of such crops to new diseases, insect/viral bacterial attacks and natural enemies dealt a death blow to cultivators. The crises in values between adopting GM seeds and unconcionable promotion of such varieties against nature is a serious ethical issue. The students must be properly educated in understanding the implications of GM foods. Environmental activists, conservation and other interest groups like Vandana Shiva and like minded people are crusading against large scale introduction of GM crops in the country and they are also advocating organic farming practices against excessive use of fertilizers, pesticides and harmful chemicals in modern agriculture which have damaged soil fertility, rendered soils into wasteland and created ecological degradation.

Fast Foods

Fast foods which have become the craze in younger generation, children and vast majority of people are lurking dangers to them in future. Traditional nutritious, nature foods, home made snacks are given to go by due to changing life styles, faster mobility by modern transport vehicles from scooters to cars, and working women unable to spare more time in households. The fast foods are cooked in oils rich in saturated fatty oils, milk products and harmful food colours also added in some foods. As people age the saturated fatty foods, sugars and starchy food and harmful colours give rise to heart problems, diabetes and complicated diseases including cancer which will be described in more detail under the topic health and medicine. The traditional values of eating natural foods, products and hand pounded rice, ground flours, germinated seeds, and so on have yielded to faster methods of food making and consumption. Science education and instruction must make children understand the harmful effects of fast foods, lack of exercise by moving in two wheelers, cars, etc., and sedentary habit of watching TV for hours together and spending time before computers for long periods. They have to be enlightened about values of recreation in walking, jogging, adventure sports and nutritive values of eating natural foods like sprouting seeds, nuts, fruits, fibrous vegetables salads, green and leafy vegetables, more frequently rather than endangering their health by eating fast foods, chocolates, icecreams etc. The recent discovery of pesticide residues in soft drinks like cocoa-cola, and presence of DDT in milk samples are all examples to be brought to the attention of school going children so that they may not hanker after soft drinks. The society may take notice of indiscriminate use of pesticides like DDT which has now been banned.

2. *Biology*

Biological organisms from nanno-or pico-level to mammoths, DNA/prions to cloned plants and animals and from microcosm to biosphere level are valuable resources to us for their role in the food chairs, importance in hidden yet unknown biological molecules for our welfare either as curatives or their potential to cause harmful diseases, infections and other ailments like the recent cases of SARS, dengue, fever, bird-flu to name a few, against which we have to keep on fighting, researching for new drugs to develop vaccines or remedies and in yet unknown ways either to harness them for our benefit, or eliminate them for our survival or strive to maintain their possible role, in the ecosystem.

Biology educator must teach students the need for making peace with Earth, so that they may know the values of earth, critical problems facing water, forests, land and biodiversity and the concept of ecowatch. As a result of globalisation, liberalisation and loosening of imports, permitting of foreign businesses like Cargil and Monsanto, to name a few 8,47,000 ha of forests were diverted for non-forests purposes, human and animal populations affected, killed and coastal safety zones have been abused for industrial, tourist, aquaculture and other purposes destroying the pristine natural beauty and resources given by nature as well as our great heritage of nature worship, value system and respect for environment.

Environmental Problems

The dangers to the environment by pollution of land, water, air and upper atmosphere resulting out of the activities of man are well known like the Bhopal gas tragedy, the chlorine leak in a factors in Adilabad recently and Chernobyl nuclear disaster in Russia and Kodamkulam nuclear establishment, radiation risk in our own country which have been widely reported. It is imperative these aspects need to be placed in proper perspective in science curricula. Even if it is possible that some people die through accidental use of pesticides this needs to be contrasted with the reality that many more can be saved from early death or disability from the evil of suicides, homicides, crimes, by proper education. The equilibrium between desired and undesired products is illustrated. There are no absolutes about the state of balance in knowledge at school or of public. The level of pollution may be temporarily acceptable in relation to economic development in one place while it may not be so in another place. For example the pollutants discharged into a river or sea at particular places are accepted against public outcry and activism because of larger economic considerations, in reality it is a crisis of values. In teaching such instances must be explained. If all the rivers in the country are connected for the sake of irrigation and agriculture and other purposes the danger of pollution spreading throughout the country is a challenge greater than we cannot escape from.

Pollution does not recognise national boundaries when "Acid rain", Aerosols and atmospheric pollutants raise an important ethical problem. The countries providing energy by burning fossil fuels must have enough information to understand that they are "exporting" sulphuric acid to other countries with disastrous effects on forests and lakes in neighbouring countries. Aerosols and other gaseous pollutants also pose identical problems. Such issues can be tackled by lowering consumer's demand for energy and mentally preparing consumers to pay more for energy. The dumping of chemical, biological, radio active wastes, plastics and used batteries, tyres etc., by public as well as industry is a social responsibility created by the excessive production of energy, consumer goods, luxury items and so on and so forth. The important part of science curricula should deal with the conservation and improvement of eco-system and promote awareness that man must live in balance with the environment to overcome crisis in values.

The Genome Riddle

According to Roger High-field (2001), recent research suggests that human genetic code may contain fewer genes (30,000) only as against earlier estimates of around, 1,00,000 gene. New evidence also debunks the notion that genes are responsible for our behaviour and instead environmental influences are more crucial on determining our behaviour. The book of human kind reveals an extraordinary mine of information about human development, physiology, medicine that will lead to personalised medicine.

Studies of genetic variation in human population may become easy to abuse in terms of using the data as "scientific support" for racism or other forms of bigotry. However, such studies may also have the opposite effect because prejudice, oppression and seggregation on colour, race, and caste feed on ignorance, but the riddle of genome reveals that all human beings have the same genes. Ethical delusions of discrimination by insurance companies, immigration authorities apart, "genetic hypochondria" wherein people may keep on anticipating disease which may never arrive, may became a vague. We will discuss about how discoveries in genetic understanding will play a role in health care in the next topic on Medicine and Health. So far as Biology Education Curriculum is Considered, students should be familiarised with relevant values while dealing with aspects like DNA finger-printing by which people committing crimes are nabbed, through genetic probing methods. Use of drugs, alcohol, cigarette smoking which affect our neural mechanisms, behaviour and expose us to risks or health hazards early in life, like heart diseases, lung cancer, Parkinsonism etc., should be candidly exhorted.

Biodiversity

The growing interest in natural environment is marked by intensive scientific studies and active involvement of younger generation in preserving our great heritage. Biodiversity with which the country is richly endowed needs more active participation by students in saving it from destruction. Scientists are alarmed that the clandestine stripping of biologically rich flora and fauna in the Western ghats, Eastern ghats and North East for commercial exploitation would be leading species to extinction before they are even discovered. The National Biodiversity Action Plan which was recently notified as the Biodiversity act involves the states and local communities in salvaging many threatened areas including wet lands, and oceans from permanent destruction. The International Union for Conservation of Nature and Natural Resource (IUCN) has listed no less than twelve thousand species of plants and animals faced with the extinction from the planet.

The challenges of biology education lies in imparting and disseminating knowledge of natural habitats around the children and how they should save the rich biodiversity.

Medicine and Health Care

Medical science and health care are complementary to each other in many ways. Though medicare is to reach the common man, drug production is becoming mainly commercial and market oriented. Over one billion people suffering fro tropical diseases and because they represent a poor market, there is insufficient development of appropriate drugs. It is a social responsibility of all nations to ensure the prevention and cure of all diseases in all parts of the world and public opinion through well-informed education is a most important factor.

The number of old people are increasing as nations develop and mortality rates decline. Positive values of respect, extending courtesy and help to old people should be created in younger minds to facilitate the old generation to enjoy an active life. Education has an important role to play in developing an attitude of responsibility towards the aged.

Experiments in the development and use of drugs and new medical methods and techniques either with animals or people have both negative and positive values. They should be weighed in the context of humaneness. It is possible to prolong life with medical advances and while no one wishes to see a life destroyed at the individual level, the use of resources which might have been utilised for treating many other patients also poses a great challenge of crisis in values. The high costs of heart, transplants, dialysis machines balanced against the need for curing and preventing illness in the population as a whole presents harsh realities of value crisis and the dilemma should be openly debated and discussed.

Euthanasia (termination of life) of the terminally ill is a controversial issue in the value system, just as human fertilization through experiments on human embryos sperm banks and surrogate motherhood are at the other end of the wide range of issues concerning our welfare. Unless people are properly enlightened through education and public debate such highly sensitive issues cannot be tackled through value judgements, wisdom and objectivity. The dangers of drug addiction, alcoholism, smoking, permissiveness, lesbianism are too well known to be reiterated but they have to be priority areas in school education to wean away students from falling victims to such perils in life.

HIV/AIDS education is already going on through governmental programmes may also be given impetus in school education to enable adolescent groups gain necessary knowledge as well as realising age old values of abstinence from harmful practice, developing healthy habits and leading hygienic life.

Genetic diseases and disorders also need urgent educational efforts to develop right understanding of consequences of consanguineous marriages which can cause birth of defective children with mental retardation, hemophilia, sickle, cell disease etc. More and more researches are revealing many life-threatening diseases including heart disease, diabetes, Alzheimer's disease, epilepsy etc., are found to be hereditary, warning us to sacrifice old customs and values such as marriages among blood relations, pre-marital genetic counselling for people carrying genetic disorders for taking proper decisions before marriages.

Family planning for checking the explosive population growth, which is affecting the economic emancipation of people, food shortages and social instability is also a value crisis, particularly in secular democracies like ours where religious faiths do not allow family planning. Only through science education and explanation of reproductive physiology, its positive/negative effects on population and economic welfare we can ameliorate to some extent the portents. In the same way problems of infertility, female child foeticides, test tube babies and modern artificial reproductive measures have both negative and positive aspects. While on one hand it is necessary to promote these techniques to help cope up with their lives, the challenges in science education lies in fighting against unethical practices like manipulative or custom made child births, abuse of genetic engineering technologies to create monstrosities. There is a major controversy in advanced countries over the issues of reproductive cloning and therapeutic techniques of embryonic stem cell culture or autologous stem cell culture from the patient's own bone marrow or muscle stem cells to repair damaged vital organs like heart, liver, pancreas, kidneys etc. The problem of human values involved and controversies raging among scientists, politicians and business groups, on the issues are challenges to science and science education.

Information Technology

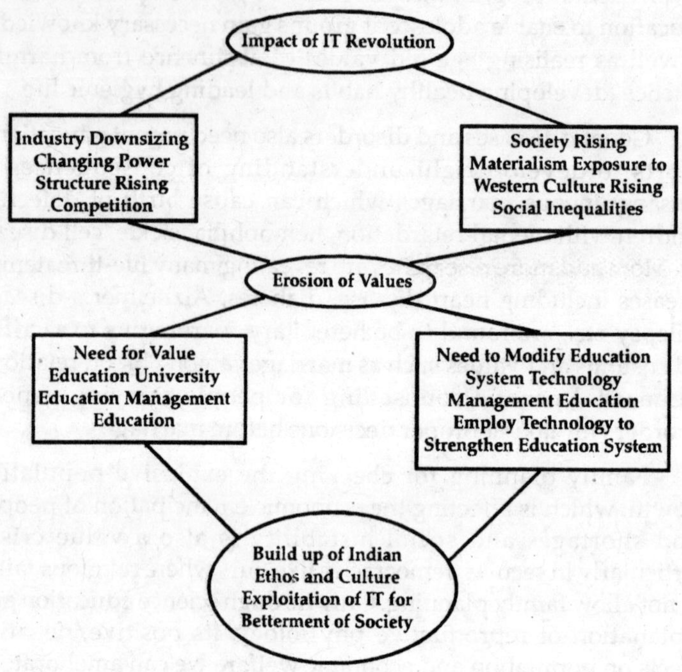

At a lower level even animal sacrifice practices, experimental animal killing or exposure of animals during drug trials, physiological experiments and other areas of investigations are matters of grave concern to society against the backdrop of value crisis. Human organ donation, harvesting of organs from brain dead patients in accidents or cadavers for saving others' lives is looked from ethical point of view as a socially unacceptable practice and as an abuse of value system. Science education must disseminate information, knowledge and fresh thinking by society in humane terms, whenever such dilemmas arise.

In addition to raw materials and energy for producing desirable products needed by the society, waste products also become an unavoidable end result. Information technology acts as an important intervention as knowledge, imagination etc., playing a crucial role in the production model. It ultimately becomes the basis for public debate and decision-making.

Computerisation is endowed with positive aspects like more efficient storage of information, search and retrieval of the same and generating new, information. On the other hand there are also inherent dangers in computers like centralised control over the population, misuse of information, loss of privacy and spurring opportunities for crimes.

Access to scientific and technological information is restricted not only by costs but also by political policies. This reduces the chances of third world countries to overcome the development gap and results in an ethical contention.

The abuse of information technology by hackers, fake stamp and currency producers, video piracy, pornographic websites, terrorists, blackmailers and attacks on peaceful, democratic, developed nations through internet, email and websites in recent times have thrown up such massive crises in values to cope with, that they require endless efforts and continuing research to deactivate, neutrialise and counter all such pernicious erosion of values.

Information technology on the positive side has given a veritable source of impetus in knowledge quest like Bio-informatics, space technology, robotics, medical sciences and various other areas. In the development of new drug molecules and understanding of human plant and other animal genomes as well as in many other cutting edge areas, IT is playing an irredeemable part. It is important that the society should the better informed about results of scientific research, emphasising the fruitful value of such research to mankind rather than making it appear that scientific research is inaccessible to people at large. Ethical issues like experimental animal research, and genetic engineering as already stated, need to be addressed by public who must be well informed about the risks and potential benefits only with this information via science education to give public opinion a powerful and objective voice.

Road Map in the Resolution/Redemption of Diverse Values Vs. Crises

Harrison (n.d.) has stated that societal issues almost invariably have scientific engineering and technological component in their origin or their resolution or in both their origin and resolution.

The quality of life is dependent on societal interfaces and hence social issues involve necessarily value judgements for taking proper decisions. In contemporary society value judgements especially on the quality of life are the prerogative of the public and representatives of the public who are elected by them are responsible to them including those who are elected by public election. This creates an inherent dilemma. Though scientists and engineers are part of the society they are the custodians of scientific, engineering and technological knowledge vital to the identification, assessment and resolution of many social issues. The public frequently through their representatives take the responsibility for decision making based on technical as well as values considerations. Such decisions may have far reaching effects on the quality of life of the present and future generations.

In the words of Rajput (2000) science cannot replace wisdom. The vulnerability of our planet is a reflection of this truth. Our mindset is stultified. Even as we have become closer in a global village, and we are each others neighbours, we are not neighbourly. Medicines and medical science have alleviated physical pain but we are not able to overcome from inflicting pain on each other.

Intellectual perception must be transformed into a human agenda with a conformist outlook and understanding that we are guardians of future generations assets. The individual, society and nation have to integrate themselves through attitudinal changes reinforced by insight into human endeavours and their outcomes in terms of science and technology that could lead to a peaceful world sooner or eventually. The challenges of science education lie therefore in this direction of change of mind, heart and soul for well being of all.

REFERENCES

1. Frazer, M.J. and A. Kornhauser (1986) "Ethics and Social Responsibility in Science Education; An Overview."; In *Ethics and Social Responsibility in Science Education* (Eds) M.J. Frazer, Vol. 2, Perganon Press, pp. 31-36.
2. Roger Highfield (2001) "The Genome Riddle", *The Hindu, Weekly,* Edn. Magazine, February 16.
3. Usha Rai Negi (2000), *Value Education in India*. Association of Indian Universities, AIU House, 16 Kotla Marg, New Delhi–110 002.

12

Value Education and Social Reconstruction

Dr. P.N. Nataraj*

Values are the guiding principles of life which are conducive to all round development. They give direction and firmness to life and bring joy, satisfaction and peace to life.

Value Education

Value education means inculcating in the children a sense of humanism, a deep concern for the well-being of others and the nation. This can be accomplished only when we instill in the children a deep feeling of commitment to values that would build this country and bring back to the people pride in work that brings order, security and assured progress.

Value education teaches us to preserve whatever is good and worthwhile in what we have inherited from our culture.

All-round development of the child its head, heart and hand is emphasised in basic education proposed by Gandhiji. He identified certain values as the basis for the establishment of a new social order in India. They are truth, non-violence, democracy sarvadharma, equality, self-realisation, self-discipline and cleanliness.

* Sr. Lecturer in Education, Department of Education, Annamalai University.

The National Policy on Education 1986 document has given the following justification for value education:

1. The growing concern over the erosion of essential values and an increasing cynicism in society has brought to focus the need for readjustment in the curriculum in order to make education a forceful tool for the cultivation of social and moral values.
2. In our culturally plural society education should foster universal and eternal values oriented towards the unity and integration of our people. Such value-oriented education should help eliminate obscurantism, religious fanaticism violence and superstition.
3. Apart from this combative role education has a profound positive content based on our heritage national goals and universal perceptions.

Various committees and commissions set-up by government of India before and after independence have been highlighting the urgent need for incorporating appropriate programmes in our educational system that would directly or indirectly develop among the students an integrated growth of body mind and spirit.

Condition of the Present Society

We are building a purely economic society which seeks security in money and not in concern for social harmony and social well-being. Wherever we go we hear people talking of corruption which has become so widespread that it is at the root of many other evils like injustice, exploitation and violence.

It is a fact that religious fundamentalism, language and regional chauvinism and caste and communal feelings are raising and threatening the very existence of our nation.

Importance of Value Education

The present educational system, with all its complexities has proved to be deficient in so far as it neglects or does not give the deserving importance to values in human life. Thus human sufferings and sorrows are for ever on the increase in spite of the phenomenal explosion of knowledge. Values have become the neglected lot in the current educational system and consequently the maxim "Education changeth man" ceases to be meaningful or has almost lost its 'value'. "Education without vision is waste; education without value is crime; education without mission is life burden" Education in our life enables us to become comfortable and to look after our family well. But so far as the social progress is concerned, value-based education is an unavoidable necessity. If a nation is to be strong, then the character of the people of that nation needs to be elevated.

Inculcation of Values

The inculcation of values is by no means a simple matter. Value education with all its comprehensiveness involves developing a sensitivity to values; an ability to choose the right values, internalising them, realising them in one's life and living in accordance with them. Therefore it is not a time-bound affair. It is a life long quest.

In inculcating values, all human faculities such as head, heart and hand should play a role. Thus role education covers the entire domain of learning, the cognitive, affective and psychomotor.

Inculcation of values is influenced by a complex net work of environmental factors such as home, school, peer group, community, the media and society at large. Home takes the higher position in the hierarchy followed by school. As the home, so the society and within the home—as the parents so the children and within the school—as the teacher, so the taught are common sayings.

In the pursuit and promotion of values, the teacher has the most vital role to play. It is the teacher who is the guide, friend and philosopher and the first interaction of children after the parents, is with the teacher. Teachers with vision, dealing with curricular subjects such as languages, science, social science, music, art, work experience and co-curricular activities such as NCC, Scouts and Guides community service, Red Cross, field trips, sports and games can develop suitable strategies and methods which would enable proper transmission of values.

Value could be integrated properly with different subject areas and educational programmes. Through physical education emphasis on health, strength, agility, grace and beauty can be laid. One would also develop right attitudes friendliness, self-control, acceptance of victory or defeat, discipline, obedience, order and team spirit. Likewise, work experience will help in perfecting skills, utilising materials, tools and processes of work, dignity of labour etc.

Conclusion

Values are influenced by the changing philosophical ideologies, sociological perspective social conditions doctrines. In modern India there has been a revolutionary change in the field of values due to many factors in addition to the influence of the western culture, industrialisation, moderanisation urbanisation and other international transactions. It is necessary for us to preserve our traditional values. It is also necessary to make efforts to present a new scheme of values in a clear and complete form. One of the chief tasks of the contemporary Indian society is to bring about a synthesis of the traditional social values and the modern social values.

The present situation in India demands such a system of education which apart from strengthening national unity must strengthen social solidarity through meaningful and purposeful constructive value education by adopting the inter-disciplinary approach.

13

Value Education for Social Reconstruction

Dr. R.R. Madankar*

Introduction

Almost permanently haunted for centuries by the socio-economic inequality and the resulting oppression, subjugation, exploitation and fracturisation of the being, it is very evident that human society has been throwing up human beings with very inhuman qualities such as cruelty, violence, greed. This state of affairs has thrown to the winds the most highly valued value, social justice, though directly or indirectly all the religions, philosophers, preach social justice. For several centuries the religions have held a strong on the minds of the followers, through their basic perception that all human beings are equal has not had any effect. Sectarianism and communalism have an appeal and create conditions of violence.

Hence, the crisis in modern society has a long history as the problem of social reconstruction demands that we take stock of the problem in all its complexity. In this connection value education is most important in social reconstruction.

Value

A value is a relationship between a person and an environmental situation which evokes an appreciative response in the individual. Frequently values are divided into types such

* Senior Lecturer, P.G. Department of Education, Karnataka University, Dharwad -580 001, Karnataka, (India).

as bodily values, economic values, social values, moral values, aesthetic values, religious values etc. To the extent that any activity increases or diminishes the worth of human life it takes on a moral significance. Value are thus both individual and social.

Education

Education is one of the most powerful agencies in moulding the character and personality of the individual and in determining the future of individual and nations. Education is a process of acquiring skill and dexterity in some fields of work. Education in its true sense is a process of aiding the all-round development of an individual—physical, intellectual, social, moral and spiritual. Education is a strong instrument of social change.

Social Reconstruction and Value Education in India

Value education means inculcating in the children a sense of humanism, deep concern for the well being of others and nation. This can be accomplished only when we instill in the children a deep feeling and commitment to values that would build this country and bring back to the people price in work that brings order, security and assured progress. Value education is a broad framework of sensitising the educational community towards human excellence based on personal experiences. It gives inner direction to man for his all round development centered in moral and spiritual consciousness. It involves three components of human personality viz., cognitive related to thinking; affective related to emotions; feelings and sentiments and; conative related to action, physical manipulation. Further value education has three bases:

1. *Philosophical or metaphysical:* Faith and ideal/aim of life and directional and operative concepts for development of values.
2. *Psychological:* Self awareness based on needs, motivation, inner capacities, self perceptions and reflections determine the nature of values.
3. *Socio-cultural:* Societies cultural heritage, wisdom and ethos enrich the value system.

Value education is a process which provides personal experience to the learner; valuing is the central concept which leads to development of values while internalising one's experience. Valuing i.e., process of value development follows specific behavioural operations—choosing freely, choosing from among alternatives, choosing after thoughtful considerations of the consequences of each alternative, prizing, cherishing, affirming, acting upon choice and repeating. Value education is a total programme to bring out the best in the learner while inculcating awareness through (a) value judgement strategies; (b) integration of course content; (c) development of personal vision; (d) resolving value; (e) study of Indian Ethics and culture; and (f) comparative study.

Social values refer to those values concerning society. These values are cherished and practiced because of our association with others, the practice of social values necessitates the interaction of two or more persons. Social values are always practiced in relation to our neighbours, community, society, nation and the world. For example, accountability, brotherhood, concerns of environment, courtesy, dialogue, dutifulness, forgiveness, freedom, friendship, gratitude, hospitality, justice, love, respectability, service, sharing, sportsmanship, sympathy, team spirit, tolerance etc., among all irrespective of caste, community, creed, race and sex.

Objectives of Social Reconstruction

Reconstruction of social systems signifies elimination of social scum pollutants and horror system defects to prevent the production of social filth and pollution. It implies removing their vulnerability to decay deterioration and disintegration. It signifies restoration of their capability for facilitating the social existence of man. Human needs are both existential and developmental. Social systems are meant to meet both types of needs through inter-human acts and relationships. Developmental needs consist of man's creative potentialities and spiritual urges. They are reflected in the maxim: man does not live by bread alone. But bread or material needs are also existentially important. The objectives of social reconstruction hence be seen as the fulfillment of man's material needs, creative aspirations and spiritual urges. Social systems are the only entities in and through which such fulfillment is possible.

Social system comprise patterned human interactions and therefore their reconstruction can meaningfully be appraised from this perspective. Human relationships and interactions in delaying and collapsing social systems are characterised by egotism, instability, dishonesty, greed, distrust, jealousy, selfishness, manipulation, tension, antagonism, opprobrium, chauvinism, disorder, conflict, violence, exploitation, destruction, loneliness, depression, helplessness, misery, suffering and sorrow. In reconstructed social systems, these characteristics should be replaced by hope, goodwill, benevolence, understanding, help, regard, respect, sympathy, friendliness, kindness, trust, stability, harmony, satisfaction, grace, sharing, sacrifice, joy, emotive fulfillment and love. Social reconstruction thus involves a polar transformation of existing characteristics of human relationships and interactions.

Values and Social Reconstruction

1. *Truth:* Provides mankind with a common super ordinate identity based on divinity. Realisation of his unity with God becomes the prime goal of man. The appreciation of shared common identity by man thence in principle serves to eliminate socially divisive based of his self-concepts and images, caste, class, community, creed, culture, language, race, religion, sect and political ideology become irrelevant as the cohesive forces of human groupings. The whole mankind is seen as belonging to a single caste of humanity. All persons become kin through their common fatherhood in a loving God.

2. *Love:* Love orientation begins to permeate social relationships and interactions. With its growth and extension, the social orbits of individual come to be increasingly pervaded by love. Social relationships and transactions come to be characterised by the positive symptoms of warmth, mutual, regard, sincerity, kindness, co-operation, help, supportiveness, benevolence and soon under such conditions, individual motivations for crime, cruelty, exploitation,

enmity, violence and destructions etc., are smothered. Love orientation also helps in effective repair and restoration of damaged and broken inter-personal relationships. Expansion and mutualisation implied by love transmutes the very nature of bonds between man and man.

3. *Inner Calm:* This orientation protects the mental and physical health of individuals. It also prevents the deterioration of inter human relationships. An internally serene person can withstand situations of great psychological stress without being mentally damaged. Sustained psychological stresses involving frustrations, failures and crisis usually turn people into neurotics and psychotics.

   Inner clam orientation also helps to halt an aggravation of worsened social relationships. An internally peaceful person does not react to perceived provocations, harm and humilitations in terms of hate, rage expectations of others who anticipate similar and matching actions from him.

4. *Righteous Action:* This consists of quiet and selfless service to others. Its other major component is doing one's duty sincerely without expectations of recognition and reward. The potential impact of these conative orientations is tremendous. If everyone renders loving, unselfish and silent service to others, it would generate an unprecedented upsurge of inter-human goodwill and co-operation. It would also materially contribute to the task of social amelioration i.e., meaningful help to the poor, deprived, infirm, sick and miserable.

5. *Duty:* Sincere performance of one's duty without thought of reward would revolutionise the function of organisation in every sector of society. Economic development, effectiveness of administration and efficiency of public services would benefit tremendously from such a perspective. Production productivity and benefits from development

programmes would be enhanced dramatically. They would thence substantively contribute towards the removal of poverty and backwardness.

Freedom, equality and dignity of human life have been emphasised in the beginning of the nineteenth century. Socialism in a comprehensive sense is a social order based on freedom and equality and charged with the spirit of co-operative life. Social unity, fellow feeling and brotherhood are the necessary outcome of such a social system. The idea of socialism is very significant for social reconstruction. If it is implemented properly through education. All healthy social changes are the manifestation of the spiritual forces working within and if these are strong and well adjusted, society will arrange itself accordingly. Each individual has to work out his own solution, there is no other way and so also with nations. Again the great institutions of every nation are the conditions of its very existence and cannot be transformed by the mould of any other race. Today's society would be reconstructed by rising humanity to the level of ultimate reality. First thing of social reconstruction is recovery of peace, education is this way is very significant for total human race to generate into the spirit of divinity.

Finally, National and International state policies regarding economics, politics are of the course essential for a hopeful change of society in the future but education invoking values in man would be constant focus of light to remove darkness of society from all aspects. If society would be a growing institution of providing opportunities to the individuals to enjoy freedom in manifesting creativity, harmony and their cultural attitude would sure make an ideal global society and it would be challenge against individualism and state.

Modern educational thought in India depicts the values of democracy, secularism, socialism and dignity of work on the one hand, justice, equality and fraternity on the other. Further, scientific and technological development poses a challenge to educational practice to inculcate temper, scientific insights and inquisitiveness among younger generations, besides preparing them for democratic citizenship. In order to inculcate these values among younger generations, modern classroom practices have become more sophisticated and technologically-oriented and this is the area where exactly the ancient system of education is believed to be inadequate. However much an attempt is made to transact scientific, technical and professional education to younger generation, it must be kept in mind that Indian students must be educated in an Indian way.

Conclusion

The problem of social reconstruction should be founded on the principles of social justice, the most important of which is the establishment of socio-economic equalities. This means the implementation of all the truth, love, inner calm, righteous action and duty. No piece-meal social engineering would help solve the crisis of modern civilisation. Education while attempting to inculcate the values of social justice through teaching etc., should develop general social awareness that the problem of social reconstruction is for deeper and more complex than that what is required in this context is a system approach i.e., realisation of interconnectedness of preaching and action and the necessary implementation on the concrete plane what is preached.

REFERENCES

1. Gupta, N.L. (1986) *Value Education Theory and Practice*, Krishna Brothers, Ajmer.
2. *Problems and Perspectives of Social Philosophy* (2000).
3. Ruhela, S.P. (1990) *Human Values and Education*. Sterling Publishers Private Limited, New Delhi.
4. Sorokin, P.A. (1958) *The Reconstruction of Humanity*. Bharatiya Vidya Bhawan, Bombay.
5. Taneja, V.R. (1986) *Inculcation of Human Values. Educational Approach and Strategies in Human Values and Education* (ed.) Ruhila, S.P. Sterling Publishers, New Delhi.
6. Venkataiah, N. (1998) *Value Education*. APH Publishing Corporation, New Delhi.

14

The Role of Value Education in Social Reconstruction

M. Pramod Kumar*

Education has been gradually recognised as a "Human Right" with the socio-economic and political evaluation of mankind and its growth in consciousness. The 1948 UN "Universal Declaration of Human Rights" thus proclaims: (1) Everyone has the right to education; (2) Education shall be directed to the full development of the human personality and to strengthening of respect for human rights and fundamental freedoms; (3) Parents have a prior right to choose the kind of education that shall be given to their children (Art. 26). The 1966 "International covenant on Economic Social and Cultural Rights", adds among other things, that "education shall enable all persons to participate effectively in a free society" and that secondary and higher education—the later, "On the basis of capacity"—shall be made accessible to all "by every appropriate means, and in particular by the programme introduction of free education" (Art. 13).

In its "Directive Principles", the Constitution of India acknowledges the right of all to education (Art. 41) and sets up the target of universal elementary education by 1960: "The state shall endeavour to provide, within a period of ten years, for free and compulsory education for all children until they complete the age of fourteen years (Art. 45). The Constitution also requests the

* Research Scholar, Dept. of Education, S.V. University, Tirupati, (A.P.)

state to "Promote with Special Care the educational and economic interests of the weaker sections of the people (Arts. 46 and 15.4), and to "Provide adequate facilities for instruction in the mother tongue at the primary stage of education to children belonging to linguistic minority groups" (Art. 350A).

The forms and length of relevant education however evolve with history and linked with people's capacities. Vatican II thus declared: "All men of every race, condition and age, since they enjoy the dignity of a human being, have an inalienable right to an education that is in keeping with their ultimate goal, their ability, their sex, and the culture and tradition of their country, and also in harmony with their fraternal association with other peoples in the fostering of true unity and peace on earth. This is why the UN declaration spoke of higher education "on the basis of merit" and the Radhakrishnan commission tersely stated that "intellectual work is not for all, it is only for the intellectually component".

The task of providing such an education is undoubtedly difficult, especially in third world countries, with their meager resources and exploding population. The World Bank pinpoints five major issues or problems facing their world education system. (1) Development of skills; (2) Mass participation; (3) Equality and Justice; (4) Efficiency; (5) Planning and Management.

To elaborate appropriate policies in this sector of limited resources and unlimited demands, third world countries should therefore answer the following questions:

Who shall be educated? How? At whose expense? And at what expense?

The major educational values can be variously described and classified as the utilitarian or practical value, moral value, aesthetic value, disciplinary value, intellectual value, cultural value, international value and social value.

Education helps in the proper organisation and maintenance of our social structure. Society is the result of the union of individuals. It needs various laws, morals and traditions for its perpetuation. Education helps not only in the formation of laws but also their compliance. In fact the harmony, law and order dynamicity prevailed in our society are all because of education. The world transaction exchange, commercial trade and business depend on education. The means of transport, communication and the so many scientific inventions and discoveries that have knitted the world into a family, owe their existence to education.

Moreover, one can lead a normal society life only where he is able to adjust himself in the existing social set up. Today our social setup or social existence is totally governed by the scientific and technological knowledge which can only be attained by education. In fact the ignorance about the education is the stumbling block in the progress of a nation or society. In this connection the great Napoleon once said, "the progress and improvement of education is linked to the prosperity of the state".

Bread and butter value of education can hardly be denied. Directly or indirectly, education does not only help everybody earning but also helps in wise spending. In the modern era of Science and Technology almost all the vocations have been dominated by the knowledge and skill of science and technology. Education helps in learning this essential knowledge and skill and thereby its study has earned a valuable place in one's life.

We have functioned as a nation in spite of the cultural, social, political, economic and religious diversities. We are a unique nation with unity in diversity and diversity in unity. We have built a vibrant democracy, an independent judiciary and a diversified and widespread industry.

In spite of all that we have achieved, several formidable challenges remain: exploding population, wide spread poverty, illiteracy, raptures, and cleavages based on religion, language, water and gender threatening the social fabric, urban congestion, wounded eco-system, critical power and energy situation. Almost half of Indians are below the poverty line and illiterate in the entire population of India.

In order to meet this challenge and build the new India of our dreams, we will have to create a major national agenda for action based on education.

If the Indian society has to become a knowledge centred society, then it is important that every Indian becomes a knowledge worker, be it a farmer, a rural woman, a mediaman, an artisan and so on.

A farmer can be a knowledge worker provided he understands the soil that he is sowing his seeds in, he understands the why and how of the micro nutrient and pesticide addition that he makes, he lives in an information village, where he has the benefits of short and medium range weather forecasting to plan his farming activity and so on. Innovative experiments for creating much knowledge workers are already on the anvil. Computer-aided information systems are operated on local languages, formers are being trained to maintain soil health cards to monitor the impact of farming systems on the physical, chemical and microbiological components of soil fertility and so on. We need Indian customers to be knowledge workers. They will change the market dynamics dramatically.

But let us remember those early days, when some producers began diluting the milk and customers could not determine its quality before buying it. It was empowering the customers with knowledge with simple lactometres that put emphasis on quality, and that led to the qualitative and quantitative growth of milk production. Knowledge can get encoded implicitly in the products.

For instance, insistence of ecolabeling is nothing other than insistence on the customer being empowered with knowledge about the environmental and ecological impact of the products he is buying and using.

Enlightened citizens, who are knowledge workers will not be guided by misinformation fed by the vested interest groups. In a knowledge society, the knowledge workers will perform different tasks. Some of them will generate knowledge, some will acquire knowledge, some will absorb knowledge and some will communicate knowledge. Absorbing knowledge will involve ensuring universal basic education, creating opportunities for lifelong learning, supporting tertiary education in science and technology etc.

For building true knowledge societies, extending education to girls and other disadvantages groups will be crucial.

True knowledge societies of tomorrow will make a creative use of modern information and communication technology. Access to information and knowledge will therefore assume a different dimension altogether. This will mean that the poor will have an access to information as much as the rich have it. This is good news for India.

Many societies in the developing world have nurtured and refined systems of knowledge of their own, relating to much diverse domains as geology, ecology, botany, agriculture, psychology and health. We are now seeing the emergence of terms such as 'parallel', 'indigenous', 'traditional' and 'civilization' knowledge systems. Indigenous knowledge systems must be sustained through active support to the societies that are keepers of this knowledge, their ways of life their language, their social organisation and the environments in which they live. In particular a strong linkage between the indigenous knowledge holders and scientists is needed to explore the relationship between different knowledge systems.

If it does not promote self reliance, critical transitive consciousness and resourcefulness, the future generation instead of being reflective will be only reflexive. Hence education should be oriented towards the creation of a self-reliant and reflective youth force that transforms.

In the years to come, in order to improve the system, we must raise above ad hoc, short range and statistical educational planning; utilise the available resources wisely; utilise the human resources to the maximum; give greater attention to elementary and secondary states for at least twenty years to come; socialise school education; provide facilities of life long education; reorient the system and interlock is structurally with the rest of the economy; constantly go on evaluating and reevaluating the educational ideas and objectives.

REFERENCES

1. *Pivotal Issues in Indian Education*—S.K. Kochhar.
2. *Education for Social Change*—John Desrochers.
3. *The Pursuit of Equality and the Indian*—Beteille.

15

Empowerment of Women and Value Education

Dr. (Smt.) Shahataj Begum*

Values are core to the development of human society. It is not mandatory for any other species to be born within the purview of values, perceive values, grow with values, develop values for self, society and the welfare of universe at large.

We humans cannot eat, live, procreate, develop, interact, believe or do any activities like other species. We are different from other species because we possess the domain of intelligence, therefore humans are considered as the crown of all creations. But, within human we have male and females who are intellectually proved equal.

The role of women in the past was limited only for the procreation of the race and maintenance of the home. But today women holds a significant position of distinct character in every sphere of life. As a result of modernisation and social change and liberal education, the empowerment of women has become a symbol of continued trend and movement since the beginning of 20th century.

Women gradually began to step out of the four walls of the home into the social and public life. Today they have emerged

* (M.A. (Socio.) M.A. (Eng.) M.Ed., M.Phil, Ph.D., Dip in Teaching PGDHRM), Karnataka Uuiversity, College of Education, Dharwad-580 003, Karnataka (India).

shoulder to shoulder with men and claim equal rights in every sphere of life, but the number has not reached the hallmark of the zenith of its glory. The above argument provides an insight into women and her status till the recent past.

Women today are assuming different roles besides the role with in their homes. The traditional family model, the husband as bread earner and the wife as homemaker in becoming a vestige of past society (Hall and Hall, 1980). As women are emancipating and emerging in all walks of life, they are faced with many gender related conflicts. Hartley (1960) found that working women considered their work as an aspect of their nurturing formation. Blooks and Wolfe (1975) have shown that there were some differences in the dimension of labour, when wife was employed. Modernity has created certain conflicting and anxiety situation among women due to the laxity in shedding traditional outlook and at the same time in assimilating the modern outlook. The incompatibility in women's outlook has put them into a problematic situation at various levels. Modernisation of women has to a very great extent been able to break the shackles of tradition and opt for employment which has brought about dramatic and drastic changes in their belief, attitude and values (Nishol, 1975). Employment has brought about socio-economic emancipation of women pushing equalisation and egalitarian values to forefront (Rappaorty and Rappaport; 1969, Chakroborty; 1977).

Equal opportunity in employment is supposed to be extended to people irrespective of sex, race, place of birth etc. Most of the problem in our life is due to non-acceptance of realities. Gender justice is a reality and necessity but it should never confused with wrong notions and wrong values, but it is to be pursued vigorously, certain attitudinal changes that are urgently called for. These comprise change of contract, change in relations and change in values. Without such a comprehensive change in the existing value judgement of the present consumerist culture, value education is far flung perception and not a reality.

Women in India constitute to about 48 per cent of the population, in the interest of creating a balanced humanhood based on gender justice, scientific outlook, logical and rational thinking humanitarian attitude should be inculcated among men first. Therefore the following steps had to be taken at different levels.

The curriculum, syllabus, reference material, textbooks, teacher guides etc. should be written with due respect for gender justice, gender sensitivity, women empowerment and special treatment for women's issues.

The behaviour of the traders in the educational institutions should be fair to the women teachers.

The ill-treatment meted to others half of the humanhood i.e. womanhood being a historic needs to be erased through a special education, legal measures, political empowerment, economic empowerment, cultural refinement and change in behaviour in action. The suppression and regressive meted out to women should be replaced by emancipation and actualisation of women's potential.

There is urgency in attitudinal change of men. Men colleagues need to realise that women colleagues are competent and efficient in doing the job assigned to them.

Certain top officials and bureaucracy are of the opinion that the sex work must be legalised. Instead of legalising sex work as a profession women must be rehabilitated into different skilled and unskilled professions and if they are found in bad state they must be punished like another citizen.

Women must be projected as mother, wife, daughter and with different kinship relations than in a bad state and taste. They must be projected as efficient, successful and intelligent career-oriented and simultaneously leading a normal family life.

The present government should table the Women Reservation Bill in the parliament and pass it.

There must be a code of dress for every department, that must be dignified rather then explosive of women physique.

The punishment for offences against must be made stringent and uniform irrespective of the social status of the culprit.

The guardian, of law, the police force, lawyers, NGO must be fair enough in understanding the severity of the situation and deal with reality, with the problems associated to women.

The value orientation and dissemination must be refined rather than polluted.

Women from individual level to organised level themselves need to have a sense of self esteem as women.

Women who deveiop affairs with married men or married men who develop affairs with unmarried girls (whatever may be the situation), their must be a stringent law to deal with.

Women's organisations must be set up at every organisational and institutional level.

Religious instruction and moral education must be made compulsory at all levels.

Instruction related to health and hygiene and sex education must be made compulsory upto the secondary school level.

Above all like how Karl Marx had given a call to the workers of the world to unit. I say *"Women of the world unit"*.

16

Value Education and Empowerment of Women

Dr. K. Jayaraman*

K. Vanitha**

Introduction

The most important and the central problem of modern philosophy in the theory of values. They are important because, every human action is the reflection of an individual value and every human institution the outgrowth of the social values.

Anything or everything which for instance is of significance and importance for education contributing to its constructive side and serves as a unit in its formative aspects of value.

Value education is to enable pupils to explore values of values. Value education should therefore be closely related or linked with values aesthetics which again can only be caught and can hardly be taught. Education for values primarily demands on inquisitive search for the true concept and role of the self. He must explore and examine each value concept in terms of Truth, Goodness, beauty. Value always demands a positive role which in operation either in case of an individual or a group.

* Department of Educational Technology, Bharathidasan University, Thiruchrappalli.

** Department of Educational Technology, Bharathidasan University, Thiruchrappalli.

Education for values is a psychological affair. It is concerned with the world of emotion and expression, analysis and appreciation, interpretation and evaluation. Values as values often remain abstract and ambiguous.

In education, values are directed towards motivation where excellences awaits a closer reach towards perfection in all directions virtuous, well-bred in the strictest possible maintenance of discipline added to ingenuity.

Status of Indian Women

There are major areas of discrimination against women in India.

1. **Mal Nutrition**

India has exceptionally high rates of child mal nutrition, because tradition in India requires that women eat last and least throughout their lives, even when pregnant and lactating.

2. **Poor Health**

Female receives less health care than males. Many women die in child birth of easily prevented complication.

3. **Lack of Education**

Families are far less likely to educate girls than boys and far more likely to pull them out of school, either to help out at home or from fear of violence.

Now, education for women has been recognised as the central issues determining the status of women. National Commission for Women was set up by Act of Parliament in 1990 to safeguard the right and legal entitlements of women.

Women's Empowerment and Values

It is the term most widely used at present often with an emphasis on the social rather than on the psycological in other words. On the freeing of women from the constraint of traditional women's role.

The consequent programme of Action (POA, 1992) in the section, "Education for women's equality" states that education can be an effective tool for Women's Empowerment.

The Government of India has declared 2001 as the year of Women's Empowerment. The empowered women should be able to participate in the process of decision-making. Education will be the only factor which would play most conical role in empowering women.

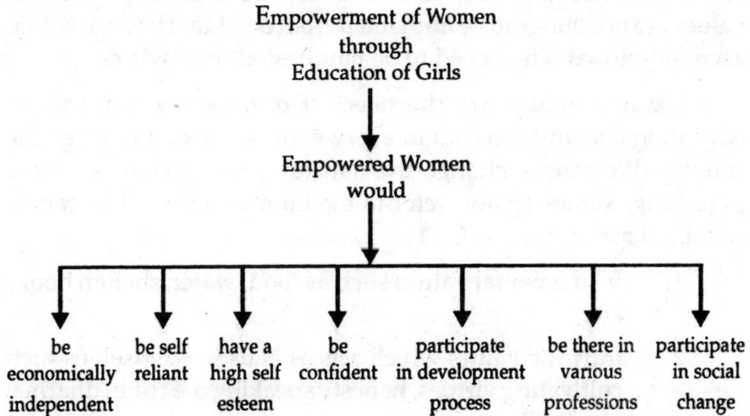

Women's empowerment also would mean the propagation of total literacy in the society among the women but the literary is increasing as compared to men's illiteracy which creates an alarming situation in the country. One has to fight all these problems in a meaningful way.

Education, is a life-long process and is essential for human resources development at all levels. Education should help intellectual, social and emotional development of human beings. Education also brings about reduction in inequalities in society presuming that education levels leads to equalisation of status between individuals coming from higher to unequal socio-economic strata of the society.

The National Education System would play a positive role in the empowerment women and contribute towards development of new values. In the recent years, the empowerment of women has been recognised as the central issue in determining the status of women. The National Commission for Women was set up by an act of Parliament in 1990 to safeguard the rights and legal entitlement of women.

Lack of Imparting Value Education

It is pertinent to mention here that value education is an integral part of our education system that we offer to both boys and girls. "The essence of education is service to one's fellowmen. There is no greater occupation than service to society". Human values are not things to be implanted from outside. They are within each individual. They need to be manifested from within.

Human values are the need of our society not only in educational institutions but in every walk of life and through the country. We cannot change the nature of the persons be mere preaching. Values always refer to the human needs. They can be classified as:

1. Instrumental values such as food, water, shelter, books etc.
2. Intrinsic values which acts as ends in themselves such cultivating virtues, honesty speaking the truth, dharma, goodwill, etc.

Value education also implies that teachers should generates a feeling of awareness among the students and try to develop a sense of maturity of the mind. Girls when they become teachers should take the profession seriously so that they are in a position to mould the character of the students, students interaction should have no barriers between them. The students need to take interest in sports, games, social work and self reliance programmes. They should follow the principle of "Love all, Serve all" have also ruled the country for sometimes. As we move into the new millennium, we can see the crucial point in the long history of the human race on the planet earth.

According to National Curriculum for Primary and Secondary Education (1985), the crisis of value our society is passing through, demands more explicit deliberate educational efforts towards value development.

Globalisation

Globalisation has presented new challenges for the realisation of the goal of women's equality. The gender impact of which has not been systematically evaluated fully. However, from the micro level studies that were commissioned by the Department of Women and Child Development, it is evident that there is a need for reforming policies for access to employment and quality of employment. Benefits of growing global economy have been unevenly distributed leading to wider economic disparities the feminization of poverty, increased gender inequality through often deteriorating working conditions and unsafe working environment especially in the informal economy and rural areas strategies will be designed to enhance the capacity to women and empower them to meet the negative, social and economic impacts, which may flow from the globalisation process.

Education has been an important factor of development, which has helped in raising the status of women and their role in society since independence when there has been an accelerated rate of expansion of women's education among girls and women. Articles 15 (1), 16 (1) and 16 (2) respectively states that, "The state shall not discriminate against any citizens on grounds only of religion, caste, sex, place of birth or any of them" and that there shall be equality of opportunity for all citizens in matter relating to employment or appointment under any office under states".

Conclusion

Value education which is essential for devoting positive values and attitudes towards women must start in the family which is the most basic and fundamental school for educating its members. In schools also value education with ourselves that we can really radiate values in our students. So women's education is must and it will educate the whole family. According to 2001 census, "Literacy rate for Men—82.33 per cent and Women's 64.55 per cent. Empowerment of women in education will bring achievement to chance their discovery by every young person.

REFERENCES

1. Usha Sharma, *"Women in South Asia Employment, Empowerment and Human Development."* Himalaya Publication, 2001.
2. *National Policy for the Employment of Women*, 2001.
3. Promilla Kapur, *"Empowering the Indian Women"* Publication Division, 2001.

4. Joshi Kineet in "Value Education and the Girl Child" Chapter by Vandana Sachdeu, in the Book *Urgency of Value Education and Primacy of Girls Child National Agenda for Educational Reforms* Edited by Subhash C. Kashyap, 1998, p. 74.

5. G.S. Yonzone, "*Higher Education and Development*" Himalaya Publishing House, 2002.

6. Jaya Indire son, "*Education for Women's Empowerment Gender Positive Initiative in Pace Setting Women's College*".

17

Role of Parents, Teachers and Students in Strengthening Value Education

Dr. K. Chandrasekhar*

In Ancient India, religion had a dominating influence in every sphere of human activity. In fact, the development of character of learners was a significant aspect of the educational system in India during the Vedic, Post-vedic and Buddhist period. Learners used to undergo rigorous character training and value education during their stay in *Gurukulas/Ashrams/Viharas*. They were required to lead to life of strict discipline, austerity and observe strict code of moral conduct. A great deal of emphasis was laid on their spiritual development. Education was primarily value-oriented.

Present Scenario

With the beginning of the modern education in the country, there has been a gradual erosion of values in our society. This is because character training and value education have been ignores altogether in our educational system. In fact, education stressed acquisition of knowledge and its testing through examinations. The stress on habit formation, attitude development and value inculcation as a goals of education were totally discounted. This had led to erosion of values. The erosion of values is causing havoc in our society. Cases of embezzlement of public funds, adulteration

* **Lecturer, DEME, NCERT, New Delhi.**

of food and other commodities, kidnapping, forgery, murders, adultery, eve-teasing, youngsters humiliating their elders, private medical practitioners cheating their parents, killing of brides for inadequate dowry are on the increase. Justice Ranganathan Misra mentioned that "all of us are experiencing to our horror degrading human behaviour in society everyday. The deterioration is gradually becoming sharper and unless this fall is immediately arrested and a remedial measure found out and enforced, the situation would not improve" (MHRD, 1999).

Are these happenings taking place now or were they taking place earlier too? The obvious answer to this question would be that some of these happenings were taking place earlier too, but their incidence was very low and some others did not exist at all. Things are now deteriorating relentlessly to the level that one fails to perceive as to where these would stop. One of the significant factors contributing to the present situation in our society that 'contentment' one of our long cherished value is losing ground. We are in the rat-race of accumulating wealth and gaining power. This strong urge has polluted climate in the country and has resulted in widespread corruption in all walks of life.

Need for Strengthening Value Education

Should we allow these happenings to take place? Should we allow things to drift the way they are drifting? The obvious answer to these questions would be that we need to check the trend and rather reverse it in order to live at peace and harmony. Without values, one floats like a piece of drift-wood in the swirling waters of a river. The whole world cannot be a place worth living if there are no values to be realised.

The happenings cited above can hardly be checked effectively through coercive measures by the government. There is no doubt that coercive measures may put a check on these happening but it would be very difficult to reduce them to a significant level. The most suitable intervention to remedy the situation would be to strengthen values among our people. This process of strengthening values need to start right from the primary education level. In other words values need to be incorporated as an integral component of the entire educational system. This aspect had gained the attention of various high powered Commissions and Committees in the Post-Independence period. Secondly Education Commission (1952-53) observed, "religious and moral instructions do play an important role in the growth of character". Education Commission (1964-66) recommended that "conscious and organised attempts need to be made for imparting education in social, moral and spiritual values with the help where possible of the ethical teachings of great religious".

Acharya Rama Murthi Committee reviewed NPE, 1986 and stressed that education must provide a climate for the nurture of values. The Parliamentary Standing Committee on Human Resource Development (1999) observed, "it is disappointing that well concerted efforts made during the last four decades have failed to achieve the desired results. Well chalked out plans and strategies for making our education value-oriented still remain on paper". The National Curriculum Framework for School Education (2000) proclaims "A Comprehensive programme of value inculcation must start at the very earliest stage of school education as a regular part of school's daily routine. The entire educational process has to be such that the boys and girls of this country are able to 'know good', 'love good' and 'do good' and grow into mutually tolerant citizens. The comparative study of the 'philosophies' of religion can be taken up at the secondary and higher secondary stages".

Value education being the need of the hour in the country today requires an emphasis for actualisation of vast human potential. The parents, teachers, students, school and community are in a great way responsible for the value inculcation in children, thus they become central figures in the value education programme.

Role of Parents

Family is the first school where good habits and values are nurtured in a child. The foundation laid in the formative years of a child play a significant role in determining the personality of a child and making him a good citizen. It is in the family where a child learns different values, such as love sharing, living together, tolerance, respecting elders, obedience, discipline, sincerity, kindness, etc. Therefore, parents must ensure that right values are developed in children. Parents must also volunteer themselves to initiate such efforts that could contribute to the process of inculcating values in society. The parents may do the following to inculcate values in children:

- Love the child to inculcate the feeling of love.
- Ask the child to share things with others.
- Promote the value of living together through plays. Teach the value of respecting elders.
- Develop the feeling of kindness in a child through your actions. Tell stories that promote different values in children.
- Develop the habits of discipline and obedience.
- Promote honesty, sincerity and faithfulness through your actions.

Role of Teachers

The teachers must be accorded an honoured place in the society. This is quite consistent with the Upanishadic dictum: *Acharya Devo Bhava*. Today a teacher will not be venerated simply because of his noble profession. It is the traits of a teacher that count. Who will have regard for a teacher or a lectures who demands higher fee for private tuitions during the months of February and March? Who will adore the principals who indulge in frauds and issue false certificates to youngsters? Scams in academic institutions are serious challenge to the credibility and responsibility of educational institutions. Heads of such institutions, the leaders of teachers' unions even teachers and professors and concerned members must do something to stop this rot.

The teacher has the most pivotal role to play in the pursuit and promotion of human values. According to an estimate in India, in the year 2001, the number of teachers will be around 63 lakhs. Through dynamic interaction with nearly 20 crores of students, who will form a very significant proportion of the emerging population of 100 crores, teachers will play a dynamic role in giving shape to a vibrant India. All over the world, it is accepted that the future will be the product of what is being done in the present day schools. This depends largely on the competence as well as dedication of teachers.

Value education starts not with the student but with the teacher. If the student has to be taught values, first the teacher has to be taught values. If the teacher is not sound in himself, how can he teach others? He would be like a blind man leading other blind men. Even academically he should have sound and correct knowledge. If a teacher, who is otherwise, gives wrong information to his students, he is spoiling the students, and these students, when they themselves become teachers, in their own turn further spoil the students. Thus a chain reaction of wrong knowledge is established and we can see that a wrong teacher can harm not only his immediate students but he can harm generations. So, top priority should be given to the appointment of right teachers.

Real, good and dedicated teachers, who are able to provide proper and overall guidance to the students, have to be identified, professionally trained, promoted and provided appropriate economic status, which will attract the best and most talented persons to the teaching profession. It is also very important that during the teacher education programme, the teachers are introduced to the concept of value development and also made aware of the methods and techniques keeping in view the physical and psychological development of the students to promote human values. It is important to develop the vision of the teachers in such a way that they can incorporate suitable strategies and methods while teaching any subject, be it science or humanities.

Thus, we see that it is the true teacher who can change the students and produce right citizens. If the teacher himself is morally unsound, he cannot induct mortality in his students, if the teacher does not change himself, he cannot change the students. If at present the teachers are not able to control the students, this is because of the moral and spiritual bankruptcy of the teachers.

So the real problem is not of correcting the students but of correcting the teachers. This is an open secret of education. But how can the teacher be corrected? The teacher changes the students, but who can change the teacher himself? Nobody else can change the teacher. The teacher can change as and when he himself chooses to change himself. So it is requirement of the teacher that he should become ideal teacher.

The following steps ought to be taken to inculcate and strengthen values in students:

- Frequent workshops under the teachers' training programme should be held and it should be impressed upon the teacher trainees that it is their duty to import values to the students, and that it is obligatory for them to become value conscious and practise values themselves.
- Theoretical and practical courses of values education should be given to the students in creating value consciousness.
- Providing interaction opportunities with persons of unimpeachable character, sacrifice, creative abilities, literary tastes or scholarly attitudes whose mere presence motivate others.
- Making the institutions responsive to emergencies like fire, floods, drought, etc. This would strengthen mutual relationship with the society.
- Visits to institutions, establishments, centres of creative arts, zoos, museums and homes for the aged and handicapped not only to enhance knowledge and understanding, but also to generate appreciation and empathy.
- Cleanliness within the institution helps in a big way. Development of aesthetic sensibilities in a basic imperative of individual preparation.
- Asking the pupils to read good literature. Reading of auto-biographies, biographies which is known as 'success literature' could pave way for the young minds to plan for their life in the right path with positive attitude.

- Teach students the importance of unity among people.
- Deliver a talk during the assembly on common fundamentals of all religions.
- Deliver a talk on a selected value during the assembly.
- Deliver a talk during the assembly on exemplary personalities, such as Mahatma Gandhi, Bhagat Singh, Subhash Chandra Bose, etc.
- Each student may be encouraged to speak on a selected value.

Role of School

Value acquisition by children in fact goes on constantly within the school environment and also outside through a variety of organised activities like classroom instruction, innumerable interactions between teacher and pupil, pupil and pupil, parents and the child and also through participation in variety of curricular and co-curricular activities. The school ethos silently transmits through the general tone of the school and its curriculum a number of values to its students.

Role of Students

Students can play a very significant role to accelerate the process of inculcating values in society. Students being young and enthusiastic, ought to serve the society exemplifying various values, such as dignity of labour, help, compassion, duty, honesty, sincerity, obedience, etc. They can work for removal of social evils through awareness programmes and through literacy campaigns. In some of the Universities National Social Service (NSS) scheme was introduced to motivate students to serve the society; however, not much work has been done and this scheme needs to be revitalised. This scheme may be made mandatory for all students to motivate them to work for society. National Social Service may be made compulsory for all students and they may be asked to carry out some social work before awarding the certificate to them. This will create a sense of responsibility among the students for the society.

Joint Responsibility of the Teachers and Parents

The term 'teacher' has a wider connotation. It means not only the school teacher but also the parent, the guardian, the religious and spiritual Guru. The teacher alone is not responsible for the value education of the student. Value education continue to be joint responsibility of the teacher, parent and community. Of course, the task of moulding the students primarily rests upon the school teacher. But the problem before the teacher is that he cannot succeed in imparting values to the students without the collaboration of the parents and community who play a major role in the life of the student. Therefore, teacher-parent collaboration is essential for the value education programme to achieve success.

REFERENCES

Ambasht, N.K. and Singh Ajit (2001). 'Inculcation of Values at Secondary Stage—A Promising Approach'. *Journal of Value Education*, 1(1), pp. 44-54.

Dhokalia, R.P. (2001). 'Significance of Inculcation of Human Values in the Quality of Life', *Journal of Value Education* 1 (2), pp. 15-25.

Kamalakar Mishra (2003). 'Value Education: A Suggested Programme for Teachers and Parents' *Journal of Value Education*, 3 (1), pp. 27-38.

Khandelwal, B.P. (2001). 'Values for Human Excellence'. *Journal of Value Education*, 1 (1), pp. 120-125.

Meganathan, R. (2002). 'Value Learning through Success Literature'. *Journal of Value Education*, 2(2), pp. 129-134.

Ministry of Human Resource Development (1986). National Policy on Education, Government of India, New Delhi.

NCERT (2000). The National Curriculum Framework for School Education—2000, New Delhi: NCERT.

Rajput, J.S. (2000). 'Values in the Context of School Education in India'. *Journal of Value Education*, 2(2), pp. 5-19.

Rajya Sabha, Parliament of India (1999). Development Related Parliamentary Standing Committee on Ministry of Human Resource Development: Eighty-First Report on Value Based Education, New Delhi: Rajya Sabha Secretariat (Mimeo).

Sen Gupta, M. (2001). 'Personal and Professional Values of an Effective Teacher—Students' Perception'. *Journal of Value Education*, 1(2), pp. 98-109.

Soni, R.B.L. (2003). 'Inculcating Values Through Values Actions'. *Journal of Value Education*, 3 (1), pp. 97-105.

18

How Parents, Teachers, Students and Administrators can Strengthen Value Education

Smt. M. Padma Kumari*
Dr. V. Dayakara Reddy**

The main aim of education is to produce citizens with sound character, a health personality and to help individuals make necessary adjustments towards a constant changing environment. Education can be viewed in one sense as the transmission of values and accumulated knowledge of a society.

Swami Vivekananda says "Education is not the amount of information that is put in your brain and runs not there, undigested all your life. We must have a life-giving, man-making and character making assimilation of ideas. If education is identical to information, libraries are the greatest sages of the world and encyclopaedias are rishies" (Ibid).

Values are principles which direct our actions and activities. They are in-built in our society common to not only all the communities but also to all religions at all times. There are many definitions of values given by many philosophers and educationists.

---

* Research Scholar, Department of Education, S.V. University, Tirupati.
** Head, Department of Education, S.V. University, Tirupati.

There are personal values, community or social values, cultural values and institutional values. We need a value imparting education which not only given a shape to one's own personality or character but also imparts a certain amount of real joy to life and work. Schools, colleges and universities are vital instruments for the preservation of spiritual and moral culture. Especially a university stands for reasons, for progress, for experimentation of ideas and for search of truth i.e. centre for cultural and academic excellence. It is true that we must redesign our education all levels to stress the importance of human values in human relations as well as in social development. Parents, teachers, students and administrators are the four pillars for strengthening the above value in education. The child's character is developed only on these four pillars.

Role of Parents

The role of parents are very important in character building of a child. Character is not ready made but it is created bit by bit and day by day. This character building first starts from home itself i.e. from parents. Hence parents follow moral and ethical values and stands as an example for their childrens. Inculcate among children values, ideals, proper moral conduct, life based upon good principles.

Role of Teachers

The role of teachers in education is very important for preparing the students as good citizens who will shoulder tomorrows responsibilities. Therefore Guru is considered *"Gurubrahma, Guruvishnu, Gurudevo, Maheshwara, Guru Sakshat Parabrahmaha, Tatmaishri Guruvennamah"*. Whatever may be the religion, region and race, the essence is that Guru is everything and supreme. It shows the respect and status given to the real guru in the society, because Guru alone can take an active part in strengthening value education in students.

The success of any education system depends on the quality of the teacher which, in turn depends on the effective reaching learning process in a classroom. Teachers performance is the most crucial input in the field of education. Whatever policies may be laid down in the ultimate analysis, these to have to be interpreted and implemented by teachers as much through their personal example as through teaching learning process. Teachers must "glow in" their profession. They should never "glow out" and become "burn outs". Teachers are to awaken the lives of others and work as supermen for the creation of a sense of human values. Teachers should be committed to their job and perform the same with integrity and devotion. Teachers should be inject curiosity among their students and become model teacher and think education as a challenge.

Role of Students

The role of students is also very important in strengthening value education. They should maintain strict discipline, peace and devotion towards their duties. Students maintain self control. Because self control is key to peace happiness and success. The conditions to become great are self control and moral behaviour. Even if you have failed for a thousands of times, make efforts again, you will definitely become successful, do not lose heart, keep adopting a small routine, keep taking a small pledge towards self-control everyday and move on towards becoming great. Students to work religiously towards the accomplishment of their determined objectives through a chain of it's survival, success, stability and significance.

The Role of Administrators

The role of administrators is also having an important role in promoting value education. They have to arrange special lectures by persons actively involved in social work, encourage extra-curricular activities, organise, symposia and seminars by the students on moral values, include a few value oriented items in the admission tests.

Conclusion

Values cannot be forced, even if conveyed with good intentions. No real integration or internalisation of a value can be achieved unless the learner agrees with it. Communication is the key in this. The classroom should send message to the young people, messages of love, safety, security, belongingness, warmth, messages which says that this is the place where the individual is respected and trusted. Let us provide opportunities to our young ones to "learn, live and flourish" in our classrooms like perfect human beings. Education must develop sensitivity to environment and must foster human ethos for the enjoyment of the fruits of progress.

19

Importance of Parents, Teachers, Students and Administrators in Strengthening Value Education

Dr. G. Narayana Rao*

According to Prof. Emile Durkheim, education is a "socialisation of the younger generation". Since education is something that takes place. 'For the society', 'By the society', and 'Of the society', to meet the changing needs and cultural aspects of the society. The action and reaction of human being, or the environment has created a rich heritage, through ages in the name of culture. This great culture accumulates knowledge and experiences, are nothing but a sort of an education, which would mould human life. The ethical principles of olden days such as adherence to truth, non-violence, tolerance and spirit of charity etc. lost their ground.

In this article, an attempt is made to analyse the three keys areas of importance; to assess the value in education, through the role of: (1) Parents, teachers, and students to strengthen the Value Education. Secondly, the author has also expressed; (2) India's rich and varied cultural traditions should be bridged through an enrichment of the curricula and making education a forceful tool for the cultivation of social and moral values, in the school and college education system. Finally, it was held, that; (3) Sincere

* **Associate Professor, Department of Special Education, Andhra University, Visakhapatnam.**

efforts of the central, state and local self governments can implement the values in education by strict vigil on the practices of values in education through the classroom teachings. The national unity programmes, and participation will strengthen the value education inputs into meaningful education, was exhaustively elaborated in this article.

Introduction

Education is a process, by which people's abilities and talents are developed. People become educated, thus acquire knowledge skills not merely by attending schools and colleges. They learn from parents, teachers, friends and self learning, from institutions, schools, colleges, libraries and social agencies. In this presentation, the importance of education, value and the role of parents, teachers and students was analysed.

Value in economics, the power of a commodity or service to command other commodities or services in exchange. Economists have advanced many theories about value. The theory most widely accepted states that value depends upon desirability and scarcity. Desirability may be based on utility, aesthetic quality, or any other factor that makes a good or service wanted. But, this article, speaks about the rich heritage and culture. The culture accumulates knowledge, is nothing but an education. The enrichment of curricula, in education, a forceful tool for the cultivation of moral values in education.

Education: In this broad sense, is also everything that is learned and acquired in a lifetime; habits, knowledge, skills, interests, attitudes, and personality. From the standpoint, people become educated not merely by attending schools but by the total experiences of life. They learn through direct experience, imitation and self-teaching. They learn from parents and friends, form such institutions as temples and libraries, from recreational and social agencies such as clubs, and from the press, motion pictures, radio, television, etc.

In a narrower sense, education is the systematic, organised process of teaching and learning that centres largely in some form of school. It is with this definition of education that the remainder of this article deals. Schooling is usually divided into stages or levels: elementary, secondary and higher education. Adult education is often considered a fourth level. There are two main types of education: (1) Liberal, or general education—the non-specialised education that is concerned with activities that all people have in common regardless of occupation; (2) Vocational and professional education, the training that prepares persons for specific jobs or professions.

Teacher: An attempt is made to identify the qualities of a teacher whether developed by training or by inheritance. However, the nature of the educative process is shaped in considerable measure by the kind of person the teacher is, particularly in his relationships with his students and colleagues. A teacher, performing in a position of leadership and guidance, is expected to be able to establish an empathic working relationship with students based on mutual acceptance of one another's role. On the basis of these basic components, the present study framed the following objectives.

Objectives

1. How the parents, teachers, and students will help to strengthen the value education.
2. To study, how the students inculcate the social and moral values in the school and college education.
3. To study the role of central and state governments in implementing the values in education.

Methodology

This study is a descriptive and theoretical, based on the latest reviews of literature on the selected areas of the value education. The primary and secondary sources are consulted, and studied the feasibility, and how to implement them achieve the value education in schools and colleges. The government efforts through commissions, committees, and the traditional principles and practices of value education was analysed to implement these methods and models to arrive the conclusions on value education in this article.

1. The Role of Parent, Teacher and Student

In olden days, the children had such great regard and love for the parents that they were both to go away from them. They should be careful how they themselves behave in the presence of children for young people have to learn a lot from emulation. A spirit of understanding and sympathy has to be pervade at the home, create a sort of value education and knowledge. From the age of two to five the children looks up to its mother, and so the mother's behaviour, has to be very proper. So you reach the children 'we must always speak the truth', provides a way of ethical education.

Prof. Humayun Kabir, has stated that the teachers is the key to any educational reconstruction. The teacher is the real maker of history, writes H.G. Wells. John Adams describes the teacher as a "maker of man". He is the torch bearer of race and guardian of the future of mankind. He plays an important role in shaping and moulding the personality of a child. The teachers are expected to play two important roles in relation to: (i) the students; and (ii) the community. Regarding the student, the teacher build the character, learning, observing the individuals, classroom management, reporting pupil performance and curriculum development and implementation. In regards to community, participation in parent-teacher interaction community, affairs, available to parents, sympathetic and understand attitude and supporting community behaviour will help to achieve the value education.

2. Moral and Ethical Values

There has been a steady deterioration in the value system in society as a whole over the past two decades. It is increasingly becoming clear that several of the ethical principles of yesteryears, such as adherence to truth and non-violence, temperance in speech and conduct, tolerance and spirit of charity, etc., are losing their ground in value education system. The author felt that the National Policy on Education (NPE-86) urged, that Indian's rich and varied cultural traditions should be bridged through an enrichment of the curricula and making education a forceful tool for the cultivation of social and moral values. Hence, this study felt, that the values and moral education in schools/colleges, should have a new start to tone up the value education system. It should be implemented, imparted with a sense of mission, and dedicated with a clear vision of value education. The 'Simple living and high thinking', have become feature of the past, but now, the crippling aspect from the modern day is 'less thinking and high exhibitive living'. The evils like academic corruption, among the academic staff, is a basic cause, to demoralise the value education system. Hence the government and the administration must act judiciously to improve the quality and value education system.

3. Government Efforts

The Kothari Commission has rightly observed, that the knowledge explosion, strengthen the sense of social responsibility, through appreciating the moral and spiritual values. We would like to emphasise the need to pay attention to observe the good values in the students at all stages of his education. The University Education Commission (1948) considered both its philosophical and practical aspects, and made certain valuable proposals for reforms. In 1959 the Central Advisory Board of Education appointed a special committee on Religious and Moral Instruction, popularly known as, Sir Prakasa Committee. The Committee Report has been present before the educational system for many years, but response from educational institutions has been neither active nor enthusiastic. It has, therefore, become necessary and urgent to adopt active measures to give a "value oriented education". From this point of view, we make the following recommendations:

1. The central and state government should adopt strict measures to introduce education in moral, social and spiritual in all institutions under their control, on the lines recommended by the University Education Commission on religious and moral instruction.
2. The privately managed institutions should also be expected to follow the same.
3. To inculcate values in among the students, some periods should be allotted, apartment from the regular timetable for this purpose. There is also a proposal, that the

university departments in comparative religion should be concerned, with the ways in which these values can be taught wisely and effectively to the students at all levels.

This, 'Mahatma Gandhi', 'Indira Gandhi' — and some other great leaders, thought and inspiration and their ideals towards the social justice and democratic values, will inspire the students and improve the values in education.

The present paper strongly felt, that the school programmes like; community prayer, health and cleanliness, citizenship, social service and socially useful programmes, celebrations of national festivals, unity of religions, harmony among the communities and national integration, will entirely improve the value in education. The NCERT in its publication, 'Documents on Social, Moral and Spiritual Values in Education', published in 1979, wherein the values are classified in alphabetical order, may be strictly implemented in all the schools and colleges, to create awareness among the students develop values in education and studentship.

This paper also take note of the governments' efforts, through the Ministry of Human Resource Development (MHRD). The Ministry decided to make it more meaningful, and thus, a revised scheme of education was approved, with two broad components: (1) Strengthening cultural and value education inputs in the school and non-formal education system; (2) Beefing up the inservice training of art, craft, music and dance teachers. The government has taken note of this value added education, and adopted above two components to streamline the value education system. Lastly, it may be stressed that the teachers, educational workers, educators, supervisors, the administrators and above all the parents must try their best to promote value-oriented education.

Conclusion

The author felt that the value in education will be achieved through strict academic discipline, which inculcate good habits, regularity, politeness, time-sense will shape the student through value education. Another important focussing area, is that, among the parents, the academic background of the parents play a significant role in moulding the child with values in education. It was also held that the interaction between the student and the teacher within the classroom or outside the classroom on academic activities will contribute a lot to value education, thus it shapes the student development. The study felt that the meaningful and academic initiative between the parents and the children may contribute to the overall growth of the student through value education. This article suggested a "Parent and Teacher Interface" model to improve value education system through the following observations of both parents and teachers:

1. Parents should inquire about the progress and overall performance and behaviour of the student in the school.
2. Parents should inquire about the regularity, sincerity and honesty, towards the homework, assignments and other academic routines.
3. The teachers should observe, whether the student is regular in all the academic, culture, extra-cultural and moral activities of the school/as per time-table.
4. Students may be encouraged towards the participation in NCC, NSS, Redcross Sports, and national functions.
5. The parents expectations about the development of the student, and the duties of the teacher should be balanced to achieve the value in education and development of the student career.

REFERENCES

1. Burrows Loraine: Sathya Sai Education in Human Values, Prasanthi Nilayam, Anantapur Dt., A.P. India, 2001.
2. Johnson, Walter P., Stefflre, Bufford and Edelfelt, Roy A. *Pupil Personal and Guidance Service*, New York: McGrew-Hill, 1961.
3. Lowe, Raymond N. "Parent—Teacher Education Through Family Council," *The Family Life Coordinator*, XI, No. 4 (October, 1962).
4. Taba, Hilde, Curriculum Development, Chap. 10, "Social and Cultural Learning", New York: Harcourt, Brace & World, Inc., 1962.
5. Preston, Ralph C., Teaching Social Studies in the Elementary School, Part Two, "Social Studies Unit", New York: Rinehart and Company, Inc., 1958.

20

Can Teachers, Parents, Students and Administrators Strengthen Values?

C.V.V. Prasad*

M. Chandra Sekhar**

Value Oriented Education

It means including in the children, a sense of behaviourism a deep concern for the well being of others and the nation this can be accomplished only when instill in the children a deep feeling of commitment to value that would build this country and bring back to the people pride in work that brings order, security and assured progress.

Through value-oriented education we would like to develop the social, moral, aesthetics and spiritual sides of a person which are often underlines within formal education, value oriented education teaches us to preserve whatever is good and worth while in what we have inherited from our culture. It helps us to accept respect the attitude and behaviour of those who differ from us. Value does not mean value imposition.

* Department of Education, S.V. University, Tirupati.

** Department of Education, S.V. University, Tirupati.

Value Crisis in Education

Lack of proper value in educational system is responsible for value crisis. The contradictory values that govern the present day life are baffling the minds of educators and educators as well thc effect of the value crisis in the present day life is witnessed in the following.

The democratic ideology that has been accepted by our state is yet to be actualise in the form of social and economic democracy so as to realise the democratic values guaranteed by the constitution of India.

A new impersonal social order that is developing fast, has been unduly ignoring the ancient ideational values and concepts without attempting to replace them suitable ones.

The individual is becoming a prey to the contradictory values and ideologies and is being converted, as a consequence, as on extreme racial, are actionary, a septic or a cynic.

The present Indian educational system is reflecting more or less borrowed ideologies and philosophies, and the national values are really neglected.

The teacher educators and teachers are not being clearly oriented as to the national values and ideas, ideals and ideologies that they have to inculcate to the students. Hence they are not able to play their due role as value education's.

Our curriculum is also reflecting the same valuational confusion. Human values are not property, upheld by the present form of curriculum. It should be reflecting the values that are truly are truly Indian.

Value—Definition

The value of an act or object may be considered as its worthiness to be chosen by the people for various purposes. Usually, we desire certain things and to not wish some other things. We prefer to act in certain way and do not like act in other ways.

The concept of values is very important in education. It is only what is valuable that is transmitted. To the younger generation by the elder generation. The concept of education is to be visualised as nothing but a set of value in essence.

According to idealist, values are the supreme ends foreseen, planned, desired, and willed by god, the cosmic mind and gradually realised through the world. As saying goes "values are not taught but caught". They are not "existents" but "subsistents" real and unchanging. R.S. Peter had stated in his 'Ethics and Education the following has one of the criteria for education. "Education implies the transmission of what is worthwhile to those who become committed to it.

Types of Values

1. Values According to Western Philosophy

Values are commonly known as two broad types according to Western Philosophers.

(a) Absolute values; and

(b) Pragmatic values.

(a) Absolute Values

Absolute values are the contribution of idealisation. Absolute values have universal validity. They represent true reality. They are not bound by time and space or other physical limitations. They may be stated to have been derived from Plato's concept of absolute ideas. Kant's philosophy contributed to the categorical imperative of 'doing good'.

Absolutes are through of the determining the behaviour of men. Hence they determine the content of education, according to idealists.

(b) Magnetic Values

The idea of values of pragmation are quite different from that of the idealism. Pragmatic values are some times known as the instrumental values too.

For Dewey absolute ideas are not the governing factors but the personal experiences of men to govern their behaviours. The experiences of the person, dictate their decisions. Hence experience is quite important according to him both in morality and education. So he described education as the "continual reconstruction of experience" whatever works is right.

2. Values According to Indian Philosophy

According to Indian philosophy, has two functions:

1. *Theoretical:* i.e. revealing the existence of some object (artha—paricchitti).
2. *Practical:* i.e. helping in fulfilment of a purpose in life (Phala—prati).

According to Harry Schofield value is "What a particular society value so high that it finds it important to pass it on to each succeeding generation".

According to Jules Henry in "Culture agains Man" (1963), values are something that we consider good such as love, kindness, quietness, contentment, fun, honesty, decency, relaxation and simplicity.

According to Louis E. Raths, Merill and Harmin and Sidney B. Simon in "Values and Teaching" (1966) values are due to the out of experiences may come certain and guides to behaviour. These guides tend to give direction to life".

Value simply stated, are the determiners in the man that influence his choices in life and that decide his behaviour.

Value System

Dorck Rawntree is a dictionary of education quote, "the set of beliefs, principles and standards of a person has in relation to a particular subject example comprehensive schools, it is a system so for as the belief etc., are relates to one another.

A Value System Contains

- A set of beliefs about the nature of men
- Beliefs about ideals about what are good or desirable or worthy or pursuit for its own sake
- Rules laying down what ought and what ought not to be done
- Motivates that include us to choose the right and wrong course.

Source of Values

- Religion
- Philosophy
- Science
- Literature
- Social customs

The first one is known as 'fact' and the other, as 'value'. Both are inter-related because knowledge of fact leads to persuit of a value.

3. Indian Classification of Values

According to Indian philosophers values are classified into four classes:

- Dharma (Virtue);
- Artha (Wealth);
- Kama (Pleasure); and
- Moksha (Self-realisation)

Of the above values, dharma is a moral value; kama, a psychological value; artha, an economic value; and moksha, a spiritual value.

(i) Dharma, A Moral Value

Dharma is a moral value spoken in case of human beings only. It is superior to the other two values of artha and kama. Speaking truth, kindness; purity, etc., come under dharma. Yagnavalika in his smrit; speaks of nine virtues—non-injury, sincerity, honesty, cleanliness, control of senses, charity, self-restraint, love and forbearane. All these virtues have social bearing.

(2) Artha, An Economic Value and Kama, A Psychological Value

Dharma is related to kama and artha as well. Artha is means for kama, dharma furnishes the necessary criteria for kama. It helps to discriminate between good and bad kama. Dharma is the regulative philosophy of life. Hence dharma is a means as well as intrinsic.

(3) Moksha, A Spiritual Value

Moksha has two shades of meaning.

1. Absence of all pain and suffering; and
2. A state of bliss. It is based on the conception of self.

It is also considered as 'Jivan mukti' or liberation when one is still alive, though this was not accept by all systems. Others feel that it is only. 'Videha mukti' spiritual freedom to be attained after physical death.

Trinity of Values

Satyam, sivam and sundram—the trinity of values satyam like truth

Sivam like goodness and

Sundram like beautiness

In generally, values maybe classified as spiritual, personal social, moral and behavioural values.

(a) Social Values

The social values can be explained as the relationship between the individual and a group of individuals; or between a group of individuals and an other group of individuals. If the individual satisfies the needs at being a member in a particular group his behaviour is said to be socially valid. If deviates from the established norm of the behaviour, then individual does not behave in approved way then said to be antisocial.

(b) Moral Values

The moral values concern the relationship between the individual and other fellow individuals. If the membership is accepted by many people in the society then it is said to be moral. If deviates from the 'norm' or standard opinion, then it is said to be immortal.

1. Spiritual Values

Spiritual value is the relationship between the individual and his own self. The activities of the individual should be in accordance with the needs of the individual. Each individual possesses certain abilities, certain desires, certain aspiration and certain expectations. He discharges his duties and plays several roles.

2. Aesthetic Values

Aesthetic value is the main concern of beauty. The individual should appreciate the beauty of the nature. He should enjoy the varieties of aesthetic senses in the world. He should enhance the beauty of the world through his effort of skills.

3. Economic Skills

An economic value, it commands a money price. It is a common place that we don't value money as material things for thus own sake; but rather for enjoyments they make possible. Economic value is instrumental rather than intrinsic, although the miser get a genuine and perhaps unique satisfaction from the more handling of his money.

Role of Teacher in Strengthening the Value—Education

Studies related to values of teachers:

Every one of us has good inherent in the soul, it needs to be drawn out by the teachers and only those teachers can perform this sacred function whose own character is unsullied, who are, always ready to learn and to grow from perfection to perfection.

—*M.K. Gandhi*

The function of the teacher is of vital importance. He must be a committed man, committed to faith in the future of man, in the future of humanity, in the future of this country and the world. He must work with this implicit confidence in the power of humanity, in the recuperative power which it has and by which it can cleanse and purity itself. Unless he has faith in that, he will never be able to advance higher.

—*Dr. Radhakrishnan, Sarvepalli*

Bowic and Morgan (1962) conducted a research on personal values and verbal behaviour of teachers. In this study, it was noted that the teacher who were high on religious value were making more supporting statements than the teachers who were high on political value. The teachers high on social value laid down more emphasis on school rules and regulations than the teachers of high social value.

Anderson (1966). studied the personal and situational factors affecting the choices of college and secondary school teachers found that secondary school teachers scored higher on economic and lower on aesthetic value than the college teachers.

EMERGING VALUE—PATTERN OF TEACHERS

Characteristics of the Emerging Value—Patterns of Teachers are Described Below Under various heads:

(a) Humanitarian Value

The teachers have given their main preference to Humanitarian value. In a democratic country like India it is heartening thing. Our Constitution guarantee each individual the right of his own opinion, and the right of his own opinion, and the right to disagree. The top property of Humanitarian value, indicates that the teachers do not like to discriminate on grounds of caste, creed, religion or membership. The teachers showed faith in humanity, and were considerate for the welfare of the students in the schools. They looked upon the students as socially equal, and considered it important that all pupils should get their rights without any discrimination, and the school should provide all the avenues and opportunities to all the students according to their capacities and abilities. They thought that their profession should be loaded with the humanistic ideals.

They loved their students, and wished to be loved by them. They considered that the best aim of education, and society was to develop the spirit of love for humanity.

(b) Distinct Strengthening of Professional Value

Value stands for dominant interest in learning and discovery of truth. The teachers had shown a desire to get and impart knowledge. They endeavoured to give all the important importations regarding the subject-matter to the class. They felt the necessity of seminars, discussions and symposia for the improvement in their efficiency. They considered that school should aim to develop the sincerity and honesty in teachers for their profession. They had the feeling that a teacher could influence his students, if he was prepared thoroughly for the topic to be discussed in the class. They believed that excursions and tours for educational and professional purposes, should be frequent in schools, they should able taken to the places of higher learning where noble thoughts may be inculcated in the minds of the pupils. They utilised the leisure time by studying the literature and preferred to participate in educational seminars etc. and were willing to take various responsibilities in this connection.

(c) Emphasis on Social and Progressive Values

The responses of the test items, indicated that teachers believed in mutual respect and recognition in their professional work. These teachers believed in the values of professional work. These teachers believed in the values of charity, kindness and sympathy. They liked to inculcate feelings of "brotherhoodness" in schools. They liked to evaluate the things on the basis of their manifested sociability. They seemed to be interested in improving the human relationship between parents and teachers. They loved "togetherness" and wished that the education should be the cultivator of this feeling. They stressed the importance of working together in a spirit of mutual help and cooperation. They considered the school as a motivating force which enabled students to participate in social and national activities. They liked people, and wished never to remain alone. They preferred the social students who should mix easily everywhere. If they were to be given opportunities they would prefer to give awards to those students of the school who were social and cooperative. In their view, school should lay more emphasis on the social behaviour of the students. They had a feeling that if they play important role in social functions, they could be more popular in the school and society.

The progressive teachers possessed positive attitude towards search for new ways of living. New ideas for their work and modifications in status quo. They felt satisfaction and happiness on the performance of some new experiment by them, or on getting some new ideas. They believed in new form of education i.e. the 'child-centred' education and considered education for all-around development of the child. They had faith in psychology and laid more emphasis on psychological principles in education. They preferred to go on excursions to the places where some new social experiments were being done.

(d) *Emphasis on Aesthetic Value*

Aesthetic value indicates that teachers emphasis aesthetic aspect of life and take care of decoration of the home, school, community and surroundings. It is also the common observation that some teachers care much for accuracy, punctuality and attractive manners and they seem to be alter, smart and conscious of personal habits and hygiene. The scores on Aesthetic Value showed that some teachers believed in good habits and traditions. They wished to have decorative well furnished houses. They liked the places of natural beauty and loved artistic things. They liked systematic work and put emphasis on clear and good handwriting and blackboard work.They wished to be tip top and remained conscious about their appearances and about showing their happy and sweet nature. They loved art and read the biographies of artists and were ready to take the responsibilities for organising aesthetic and other literary activities. They laid emphasis on the beauty of every article, in the school.

(e) *Economic Value*

There were some teachers who were found exercising economy in their expression, communication habits and some aspects of teaching. They were found economical in the utilisation of time. They were also economical in the spending of their money and planned in the direction of minimising their expenses. They preferred the persons like Tata and Birla. They believed in equal pay for equal work. They made efforts to become self dependents and considered the development of the feeling of self-dependence as one of the main functions of the school. If they were given evaluation work, they did not evaluate on the basis of the number of pages the students had written but tried to assess them on the quality of the subject-matter presented by them. They believed in pragmatism and judged everything from this view point. They did not like to give more freedom to the students than what was needed.

(f) Authoritarian Values

Authoritarian teachers aimed more at the status, prestige, dominance and power in school affairs. They were characterised by craving for unquestioning authority, not permitting anyone to share in the decision-making process in their class, school, or outside. Such teachers were more interested in their prestige and wished to read and write about the authoritarian personalities. They considered that the schools principal should be the authoritarian and dominant person. They did not want to discuss the problems but wished to impose their decisions on others, including the parents and the students. They had positive feelings towards accepting an idealised person or institution, and did not wish to deviate from the norms. They treated the students strictly. They placed of teacher was most important in their view and they had appreciation for authoritarian personalities like Hitler and Napolean. They aspired for power and dominating place in teaching. They did not want interference from the students in their class while they were teaching. They did not believe in the secular policy. They liked the teachers who could sacrifice everything for their prestige and position.

ROLE OF 'EDUCATIONAL' ADMINISTRATION IN STRENGTHENINGVALUES

1. About Administration

Administration is Art

Those who regard administration as an art believe that administration literature (painting, dancing, sculptures) belongs to those who have the natural gifts, traits, abilities for it. This 'trait' paint of view holds that only those who have the personality qualities and traits for the practice of the art of administering succeed as administrators not by training or the mastery of any special techniques of administration but they possessing the essential traits of administrators. As one prominent university administrator argued "The successful administration has skill which have not been reduced to order and codified administration is on un-codified art, therefore the only sure way to learn administration is to administrators. This implies that good administrators are not trained in education, instinct, rather than they are born administrators.

The problem of organisations, therefore is how to identify and select good administrators and many studies on administration tend to show that "successful" administrators today need more than inform personality traits to manage modern complex organisation.

Administration As Science

The view that administration is a science and not an art emanated from the organisation of administration as a "technology" a matter of applying administrative principle and rules to the structure of management or organisation problems. The administration must know and apply the rules—the do's and don'ts of administrating. That the administrators must know what action leads to what result and what results fits what action in developing values in students in value-oriented education.

Valuing: A Complex Process in Education

Educational administrators can seldom clarify the "if" part of the valuing process. The variables in a socio-political situation are incompletely defined and seldom completely understood. Theory to help us understand the relationships among the things we observe and to help predict what will happen und r given conditions is not well developed. The alternative valu choices are fuzzy and their implementations seldom produces the results desired. Finally, valuing involves intensive efforts to anticipate and measure scientifically the consequences of the various alternatives.

The analysis of court and political activities on school busing by Bolner and Shanley indicated that as pressure was applied to use buses to provide racial balances in schools, more political action was taken (and subsequently, more court decisions were made) to render racial integration more difficult. Frequently mentioned by some politicians was the possibility of a constitutional amendment to prohibit busing across school district boundaries. Those who have proposed uncontrolled voucher plans have been confronted with the prospect that their implementation might destroy public education for all except the poor. In many decision-making situations, one faces the awesome possibility that deciding on the basis of what appears to be a better value may, under the conditions given, produce consequences antithetical to another desired value.

If these foregoing propositions about valuing are relevant to administrative behaviour in decision-making, there are some important implications for those preparing to be educational administrators. One rather obvious implication is that administrative valuing in decision-making should not be an armchair exercise. The aspects of "what ought to be" are interrelated. The decisions made are as good as the objective data one has about "what is" and the clarity in which those deciding understand alternative values and their massive interaction with "what is". If the prospective educational administrators are relatively ignorant of cultural values, of their own value system, and of the nature of value held by others, they could become Dr. Strangeloves at the control of educational system. Being an intelligent, responsible educational administrator involves much personal study of one's own value system and of the nature of valuing in decision making. Valuing in Educational Administration involves such important considerations as the nature of truth, the nature of reality and other philosophical considerations.

Influence of Dualism Upon Knowledge

A school of thought referred to as idealism accepts a dual concept of reality consisting of (1) the perfect world of ideas and (2) the imperfect world of everyday existence. The real and true knowledge is in the perfect world of ideas, which can only be grasped by mind. The material existence is an imperfect manifestation of the real world of ideas. True knowledge is a deductive process of mind and is nonmaterial idea. Dualism is deeply ingrained in our culture, and all of us are influenced by its streams of thought processes.

Many practical-minded educational administrators would scoff at this discussion as philosophical mumbo jumbo. On the other hand, let us examine how relevant it is today. As one example, school administrators are forever reorganising. A fairly typical way to recognise is to engage consultants to assist key administrators in generating alternative structure for the operation of the school system. In many instances this is an ivory tower exercise, although, in all fairness, the participants may have years of experience as a foundation for making decisions. What those involved finally come to is to select the organisation that at the time and in that particular group seems to be the most rational way to recognise.

This preferred rational model is consciously or unconsciously assumed to be the perfect model for the verbally described situation. Yet there is no experimental evidence that would indicate this perfection. The next step, of course, is to adopt the rational alternative. When problems arise in the functioning of the model, the idealist-oriented educational administrator assumes the two-world stance. The problems are not with the rationally designed model but with the irrationality of teachers, principals, parents and others who did not accept it as a basis of organisational behaviour. Thus the two-part (ideal and imperfect, unreal) worlds are expressed as rational-irrational perspectives. This was a good organisation, but the people would not accept it. Why was it good? Because a group of our best minds got together and decided that it was the best-the exercise of pure reason.

The Real World and the Empirical Verification of Truth

The growth of scientific inquiry eventually precipitated what white referred to as warfare of theology in the Western world with science. As indicated previously, the truths of pure reason cannot be tested in an imperfect, unreal world. Galileo, sometimes referred to as the founder of modern experimental science, was subjected to inquisition, publicly humiliated, and imprisoned by Church authorities for extolling the Copernican theory. Nevertheless, the triumph of science and its methods for determining true knowledge eventually ended in a rout of pure reason. The naturalistic philosophies, such as realism, became popular. A 1912 publication entitled *The New Realism* was the manifesto of scholars bent upon founding a new and distinctive philosophy of realism.

Mankind: The Only True Reality

What reality is without man's existence in it can only be surmised, it cannot be know. Man is the definer, nothing has meaning except as man gives it meaning. Reality is precisely what man, as a result of his existence in it, says it is. Except as choosing human being with nothing to impinge upon his absolute freedom of choice if he is to know true reality. To the extent that man relies on factors outside himself, science, God, Government, or social conformity, as determinants of his choices, precisely to that extent, does he fail to know reality.

Educational administrators facing crises or difficult problem situations are frequently heard to say, "If only I had enough facts to go on!" Having the data necessary to conceptualise given conditions is one of the greatest needs of practitioners. The uneasiness of making decisions is as much a result of no empirical understanding as it is unsureness of where we ought to be going. When we are forced to combine lack of evidence and unsureness of purposes in making decisions, which, unfortunately, is so often true, the prospect of having to decide is frightening. Within recent years the prospects of storage and retrieval of knowledge through management information systems have given hope for relief. However, few enthusiasts of this view have considered the nature of knowledge that should be collected, stored, and retrieved. This is the question at hand.

Truths from Empirical Reality and Discovery

Empiricist or positivist concepts of truths or knowledge grew with the acceptance and growth of science. Most early scientific thought followed realist assumptions. Logical positivist epistemology is much more demanding than that of the realists. Although not expressly stated by positivists, knowledge somehow exists in the complex rubric of the universe independent of values. Through a rigid application of scientific method one can empirically verify that which is to be exalted as knowledge. Knowledge is the end state of scientific inquiry independent of the non-confirmed intellectual activities of persons.

Educational Programmes for Developing Secular, Moral and Social Values

The programme of value education should be pre-planned. All the curricular and extra-curricular and co-curricular activities of the schools should appropriately be geared to achieve the desire goals these educational programmes are strengthly arranged by educational administration and fulfilment of aim of these programmes are developing values.

Method of Value Education

The method of value education involve the formal, internal and non-formal method of teaching.

The above values secular, moral and social are implicit in any good educational programme. For moral and religious values, there may be separate curriculum and syllabus in case of Andhra Pradesh.

1. Direct and Indirect Methods of Teaching Values

(a) Direct Method of Teaching

When there is a separate subject, there will be scope for undertaking direct method of teaching the values in the periods allotted to be subject direct method of teaching has it own defects, sometimes, it may be result in reaction formation or contra-suggestions being formed. Which will be detecting the purpose of instruction.

(b) Indirect Method of Teaching

Indirect method of instruction will be fruitful many a time, students will learn the related values as concomitant learning. The desired values have to be inferred as a result of stories, story—poems or anecdotes that are taught.

2. Curricular, Co-curricular and Extra-curricular, Approaches to Teaching Values

(a) Curricular Approach

In this, there will be separate syllabus prepared for value-education. Definite number of teaching hours will be allotted to it is in the case of all academic subjects. Here the subject will have its own identity.

The curricular approach may also involve incorporating the contents either in the language subjects or non-language subjects. This is an integrated approach, wherein the subject will not have individual identity.

(b) Co-curricular Approach

The co-curricular approach activities can be well exploited for the development of secular, moral and social values.

Debates and essay writing competitions, story telling and writing story-poems etc., can be associated with the teaching of values. Dramas, songs, dances, etc., can also be associated with value-education.

(c) Extra-curricular Approach

Extra-curricular activities like organisation of social service, common celebration of different religious festivals in the schools, mutual greeting on the different religious celebrations, organisation of visits to temples, mosques, churches, gurudwaras, etc., will be helpful for developing some of these values.

3. Formal, Informal and Non-formal Methods of Teaching of Values

If the values are taught through classroom teaching directly with the help of textbooks or supplementary reading materials, it comes under formal method of teaching values.

If the students learn about different values incidentally by their own experiences by living in the community or school programmes in out-of-school hours casually, it becomes an informal method.

If the students are taught values through non-formal methods like utilising leisure periods for studying books on values in the library or by organising discourses by eminent scholars on the subject, or through radio and T.V. lessons or utilising other mass media, organisation of Burra Kathas, Hari Kathas, or folk ballads representing secular, moral and social values in comes under non-formal method of teaching values.

Thoughtful Educational Administrators: Concerned with their Personal Beliefs

Preoccupation with "what is" to the exclusion of the values used as a basis for goals in nonsense. To survive and help educational organisations thrive demands personal attention to what one believes. Indeed, there is some evidence that belief consistency, as a basis of behavioural consistency may be an important element in attaining prestige or leadership in groups. Thus all of us should search our belief systems for internal consistency. Again, we do not recommend a pure exercise of reasons for this process. Dewey wrote that mind is "the power to understand things in terms of the use made of them".

Setting up dual concepts of personal values and administrative knowledge has caused many school leaders problems. This inevitable makes one's values completely subjective and empirically irrelevant. For example, through scientific processes we know that smoking tobacco is related to cancer. The dualist in valuing would accept this as truth but attach no value to it. Value to some persons is a personal feeling of the worth of a thing or idea regardless of empirical consequences. Thus one may both accept the truth that smoking is harmful to health and also value smoking.

This dualistic things may result in nonsensical administrative practices in schools. True values of the individual are seen in personal action. If one values knowledge as a basis for solving problems and achieving personal aims and objectives, knowledge and value are continuous with each other. Personal values run much deeper than how we feel about educational procedures and purposes.

The moral factor in any choice-situation is proportional to the consequences which follow from the alternative course of action. To discriminate and anticipate such consequences is an intellectual act of the highest quality. Decisions that are thus related to all aspects of our complex social experience cannot be safely taken merely on the basis of what "feels right" in the situation as immediately experienced.

The school administrators in the new era of educational administration must know what they believe and understand the basis for their beliefs. Through constant attention to consequences of alternative choices (and anticipated consequence of choice) and through using the scientific evidence and experience of others, personal values may be reconstructed and confirmed to one's personal satisfaction. These values are not universal. Thus confirmation of personal values is continuous.

Ostrander and Dethy emphasised the importance of the administrator developing and understanding his own value system. "The individual educational leader must develop his own value system and his own philosophy of education. He should be continuingly examining his position in terms of new evidence and changing conditions.

As the authors have indicated, tremendous gaps in empirical research exist in our field. Much of what we call knowledge is borrowed from other disciplines, and every little has been done in developing these concepts to observe the consequences of their uses in educational organisational. Thus there is quite a way to go in achieving a high degree of expertise in valuing.

21

Necessity of the Role of Parents, Teachers, Students and Administrators in Strengthening Value Education

A. Muniraja Reddy*

B. Ramachandra Reddy**

Concept of Values

According to the Oxford Dictionary, value means 'worth'. The encyclopaedia of social sciences refers to value as 'interests, pleasures, likes, preferences, duties, moral obligations, desires, wants, needs and many other modalities of Social Orientation (Williams, 1968)".

Mukerjee (1964) defines values as, "values as integrated experiences that simultaneously touche all the dimensions of human adaptation; organic, social and cultural, and transcend them in all their 'propitiate', forward orientation".

The hope of the world as well as our country lies in value based education for the younger generation. The present generation has lost the meaning and purpose of life due to the

* **Department of Education, S.V. University, Tirupati–517 502.**

** **Department of Education, S.V. University, Tirupati–517 502.**

western type of education in India as a legacy of the British. There is steady deterioration of values not only in the field of education but in all spheres of activity. Education should help us to discover lasting values so that we do not merely cling to readymade, formulas or repeat slogans. It should help us to breakdown the national and social barriers, instead of emphasising them, for they breed antagonism between man and man. Unfortunately the present system of education is making us subservient, mechanical and deeply thoughtless; though it awakens us intellectually, inwardly it leaves us incomplete, stultified and uncreative.

Since our independence, an increasing amount of stress is being laid on the formulation of objectives of education that aim at uniting science and humanism, ethics and aesthetic and material welfare with spiritual welfare.

The University Education Commission (1948-1949) was of the opinion that the great virtues of loyalty, courage, discipline and self-sacrifice may be used as means of good or bad cause as such spiritual training should be included. Hence the commission recommended certain practical measures at different levels of education stating that while at school level, stories which illustrate great moral and religious principles are used, at college level, ideas, events and leading figures associated with religious monuments should be studied. The University Education Commission ascertained: "No amount of actual information could make ordinary men into educated and virtuous men unless something is awakened by them; an innate ability to live the life of soul.

Secondary Education Commission (1952-53) headed by Dr. A. Lakshmana Swamy Mudeliar, considered healthy trends arising from three sources.

(i) The influence of home which is dominant factor.

(ii) The influence of the institution through the conduct, the behaviour of the teachers themselves and the life of the students as a whole.

(iii) Influence exercised by the public of the locality and the extent to which the public opinion prevails in all matters pertaining to religious and moral codes of conduct.

The committee on religious and moral instruction–1959 under the chairmanship of Sri Prakasa considered the recommendations of the Central Advisory Board of Education (1956) which states the religious education should be the business of the home and the community.

Education Commission (1964-66) headed by Prof. D.S. Kothari noted the negative response to the recommendation of the Sri Prakasa Committee. It therefore, felt the need to adopt the active measures to give a value-based orientation to education, it recommended that:

(i) Central and State Government should adopt measures to introduce education in moral and spiritual values on the lines recommended by the secondary education Commission and Sri Prakasa Committee.

(ii) Some periods should be set apart for moral instructions.

(iii) The university department in comparative religions should be considered in the ways in which these values can be taught widely and effectively and also prepare literature for use by the students and the teachers.

The Need for Value Oriented Education

I may be permitted to quote the following sub-paragraphs under value education on page 36 of *National Policy on Education 1986* modified in 1992.

8.4 The growing concern over the erosion of essential values and an increasing cynicism in society has brought to focus the need for readjustments in curriculum in order to make education a forceful tool for the cultivation of social and moral values.

8.5 In our culturally plural society, education should foster universal and eternal values, oriented towards the unity and integration of our people. Such value education should help to eliminate obscurantism, religious fatalism, violence, superstition and fatalism.

8.6 Apart from this combative role, value education has profound positive content based on our heritage, national and universal goals of perception. It should lay primary emphasis on this aspect.

The National Policy on Education (NPE-1986) has slightly pointed out the crisis in values in all aspects of life. Therefore it has recommended a special thrust on inculcation of values at all stages of education.

The *Programme of Action* (POA) Document, 1992 which has dealt with value education has widely interpreted value education as a broad cultural education leading to removal of superstition, obscurantism, religious fatalism and all other narrow loyalties. It has stressed the importance of the positive approach in which the roots of the Indian culture have to be highlighted along with the development of scientific temper and unity and national integrity having a special focus.

Values are to be caught and not taught is a very old saying. It was perhaps true in days goneby when parents at home and leaders in community in various walks of life were all value-based people. Therefore younger children and growing adolescents could catch values of elderly people either by imitation or by special efforts and developed appropriate values accepted and respected in society. There is a grave deterioration both among parents and community leaders in terms of being value models for the younger generation. We cannot therefore expect values to be caught from undesirable situation and persons in society. In today's world therefore *values have to be taught in addition to being caught* from selected situations and personalities.

The document Education for Our People (1978-79) prepared under the chairmanship of Justice V M Tarkunde suggests programmes to bring about educational transformation. He states that "the value system underlying education should emphasise social objectives, cooperation and team work, complementarity of intellectual and manual work, development of skills and building of character. The ethics of the existing system are highly authoritarian where values such as equality, love of truth, or spirit of enquiry cannot be fostered. Great emphasis will have to be placed on promoting a scientific outlook on life and the basic values of pursuit of truth, equality, freedom, justice and the dignity of the individual".

Pandit Jawaharlal Nehru, during 1959 in his Azad Memorial Lecture says, "Can we combine the progress of science and technology with the progress of the mind and spirit also? We cannot be untrue to science because that represents the basic fact of life today. Still less can we be untrue to these essential principles for which India has stood in the past throughout the ages. Let us then pursue our path to industrial progress with all our strength and vigour and at the same time remember that material riches without toleration, compassion and wisdom may well turn to dust and ashes."

The UNESCO sounded an almost similar note in 1972, which stated the inadequacy of education in these terms. "Education suffers basically from the gap between its content and the living experience of its students, between the system of values that it preaches and the goals set up by society, between ancient curricula and the modernity of science. Link education to life, associate it with concrete goals, establish a close relationship between society and economy, invent or rediscover an education system that fits its surroundings, surely this is where the solution must be sought..."

"In the present system of education there is no place for ethical *dharmic*, or spiritual studies, with the result that the students do not make any attempt to understand the purpose of life."

Role of Parents in Strengthening Value Education

Parents are the first teacher even as the teachers are the second parents. The foundation of knowledge, the skills and the attitudes which children display in later life, is laid in the impressionable period in the home which is a world in itself, providing varied and numerous opportunities for learning through observation, suggestion and influence.

The parents must improve themselves, for the sake of their children. Example is more profitable than percept.

Joshi (1981) says, "Today if several youngsters deviate from the path of dignity and decorum, to a large extent is due to the lack of sober influences in their own house. They should not be seen by the children worried, disconnected and distressed. When the parents behave in an undefining manner, the youngsters who watch them shrewdly imbibe the unhealthy tendencies and display them in their activities in larger life outside. It is unfair to blame teachers when the young do not behave properly, the parents having neglected their training in their plastic period. Great men like Shivaji, Vivekananda and Mahatma Gandhi whose lives well served as a model to others, have acknowledged with reverential gratitude the value of the wholesome training they received at the hands of their parents while young".

Parents have to exercise a very vigilant control over their children, meeting all their legitimate wants and giving them evidence of the affection by positive acts of love, not necessarily by placing too much money in their hands and impressing upon them that indiscreet behaviour will meet with a stern rebuke.

Fisher (1948) studied the correlation between the value scores of college students with the value scores of their parents as shown below:

Relation Between the Values of Parents and Their Children

Values	*Mother* *Daughter-son*		*Father* *Daughter-son*		*Median*
Religious	.49	.40	.60	.45	.47
Economical	.32	.27	.31	.27	.29
Theoretical	.30	.15	.25	.18	.24
Aesthetic	.38	.16	.13	.26	.21
Median	**.35**	**.22**	**.29**	**.27**	

The religious, economic, theoretical and aesthetic values of both son and daughter resemble the values of both mother and father. Specific religious, economic and other types of attitudes of children were even closer to those of their parents.

Children must closely resemble their parents in religious values. The median correlation shown at the right of the table which given a rough measure of overall resemblance between children and parents, is much higher for religious values (.47) than for any of the other value areas. Wives also most closely resembled their husband in this area.

Daughters were more influenced by the values of their mothers. Sons were more influenced by the values of their fathers. In general, women have higher religious and aesthetic values, for numerous investigators have consistently verified them.

Role of Teachers in Strengthening Value Education

The role of teachers is quite significant in the development of society. Teachers are the real nation builders. It is the teacher community who moulds the future society. Teachers are the section of society who can influence the future generation towards a positive attitude with a healthy value base. The extent of the influence, which a teacher casts upon the students, is well known and understood. The teacher is the role model for the student and what they imbibe gets multiplied subsequently in the society.

A conference was held in Shimla in May 1981 to ponder seriously on the meaning and scope of value oriented education and to formulate practical guidelines for governmental action. It recommended, that value orientation should be the central focus of education and that the teacher should be given the necessary training in the effective methods of development of values among students.

The national policy of Education (1986) begins its sections on 'The Teacher' with a very comprehensive and meaningful statement, "The status of the teacher reflects the socio-cultural ethos of a society; it is said that no people can rise above the level of their teachers".

A teacher easily inculcates values if he has professionalism and love towards his profession and student. There is no need of prescribing any method to teach values for a devoted teacher who loves his students.

A teacher, once he accepts teaching as profession cannot make compromises with life because he has to realise that he is playing with the future of the nation. Though the mastery of his subjects and primary role is to build character. The products of the institutions will be future decision-makers and they can hardly forget the source, which has made them what they are.

Teachers themselves should not be ignorant of basic human values. In fact, they should be the living embodiment of all the human values, both preaching and practicing, more the latter than the former. It is the teacher who can lead us from darkness to light, thereby, from untruth to truth and finally take us from the stages of death to immortality. Guru is an incarnation of God in human form for students. While God is universal, the guru is said personal in relationship. Kalidas, the ancient poet, speaks of the guru as, "He converts darkness into light and makes the invisible God visible."

Gandhiji also highlighted the pivotal role of teachers in the following words "... Of textbooks, about which we hear so much, I never felt the want. I do not even remember having made much use of the books that were available. I did not find it at all necessary to load the boys with quantities of books. I have always felt that the true textbooks for the pupils is his teacher. I remember very little that my teacher taught me from textbooks. But I have even now a clear recollection of the things they taught me independently of books..."

"Teachers in colleges have themselves to be examples of what they require the students to be. Men in authority who exhort others to follow the path of love and cooperation have themselves to practice those virtues. Teachers should put into practice what they preach to the students. They should guide the students properly, as they are the most important assets of an educational institution. The ultimate factor in education for all times and in all places is the teacher".

Teachers should identify their role and their responsibilities. For example: "When the tap is turned water flows only if the overhead tank is full; the quality of tap water is the same as that of the water in the tank. The teacher offers, the student receives. The teacher is like a tank, the student is like a tap. Pure water in the tank gives pure water in the taps." (Baba 1978).

The examples of teachers have to hold before them should be of those men and women who have learnt and practiced spiritual education. Unless the teachers transform the knowledge into wisdom and help the wisdom to express itself in character, the educational process would be utter waste. If education could confer this gift of transformation, then surely life will become peaceful, happy and full of mutual help and cooperation. Teachers reveal the direction and the goal, whereas students lay the road and journey into the future.

The teacher is trusted by the students, parents and the society as a guru with all the hallowed association of that word and this trust must be repaid by honest service. He should discharge his duty of instructing and inspiring the students so that they develop their talents and advance in the perfection of their skills.

Teachers have to be ever inspiring models. In fact they are life long students engaged not in mere study but immersed in practice too. Only a lamp that burns can light another lamp. It may be worth-while here the views of some educationists who have spoken on similar line. The report of the working group for for preparing a scheme for Revitalisation of Teacher Education (1986) also says that the teacher should practice values in his own conduct and behaviour. The practice of values by the teacher is more important than their mere inclusion in the syllabus. Likewise Ramji (1973) writes that "above all, personal example of the teacher who endeavours to practice fundamental values such as truth, universal love and service to humanity and who creates loving and healthy atmosphere in the classroom by his gentle and kind behaviour is perhaps the most important factor in any value-oriented education in the education institutions".

There are a large number of studies, which highlight he role of the teacher's expectations in the development of the s udents. Students achieve what the teacher expects them to achieve, for example Rosenthal and Jacobson (1966) found that teachers' expectations determined pupils I.Q. gain. This phenomenon was termed by them as a 'self-fulfilling prophecy'. Likewise, Nagalakshmi (1987) found that students' academic achievement' corresponds to their teachers' expectations. The teachers' place in a society is that of a visionary architect whose mission evokes universal respect.

We want our teachers value-oriented because we want them to be rightly equipped as vehicles of values for the benefit of our children and youth. By this very nature, the teacher is a transmitter, a messenger, a carrier. Our determination of what he has to transmit will depend upon what we determine to be valuable for our children and youth."

It is no wonder why there is a shift in favour of value-orientation for teachers in the new education policy. Teachers have an influential position and definite role in value-orientation to our youth today.

In our country and culture a teacher is still held in great honour and respect. He is considered as a fountain of all knowledge and a source of great ideals. He is the torchbearer to society. Students look up to him with faith and hope and they seek his counsel in matters temporal or transcendental. Hence if the teacher has a keen sense of values and has faith in the higher purpose of life, he can guide the whole generation through his versatile personality.

Dr. Radhakrishnan and Rabindranath Tagore are examples of great teachers who influenced this country with their philosophy of value-oriented education. Radhakrishnan (1965) states "what the teachers do, the students follow, so they set the example. Teachers by their conduct should be an example to the student".

All knowledge comes from the teacher is the belief of students in the class. Since our children are not turned to independent study from childhood, they believe whatever the teacher says as absolute truth and nothing less than truth. They do not question the authority of the teacher. Hence, if good ideas and values are to be perpetuated and inculcated in the younger generation, they must come from the mouth of teachers in their classes at all the levels of education. Whenever the teacher finds that these values are violated he should point out the dame to the pupils and guide them in changing their behaviour. He should also evaluate the behaviour of the students in relation to the values from time to time, but he should use this evaluation not for grading the pupil but for guiding them for better development of values. The practice of the values by the teacher is more important than mere inclusion in the syllabus.

In the works of Gokak (1985) "Teacher's life-style, manner and substances of his teaching should coincide. The student has a right to expect his teachers, to lead a good life. A teacher-educator may be specialist or a scholar, but these are not central to his personality. The centrality lies in the fact of his being primarily a seeker of truth who is eager to share his passion for truth with the young, and to make them familiar with the mode of living which helps to be in tune with such a pursuit."

Some of the recommendations, which are relevant to our study made by *Kireet Joshi Report (1981-82).*

(i) Provision for value-oriented education should be made throughout the country with due regard for flexibility of approach.

(ii) It should be regarded essentially as an education for self-actualisation.

(iii) All teachers should be regarded as teachers of value education and all subjects should be used for the inculcation of right values.

(iv) Special teacher-orientation programmes should be taken up at the state level.

(v) There should be foundation courses at the universities aiming at giving the students basic knowledge about India, its people and cultural traditions.

Role of Students in Strengthening Value Education

I may be permitted to quote some of the preachings of Sri Sathya Sai Baba in this connection:

"One should enter into the society to serve the society and to serve the nation: make your life an ideal one, give up selfishness and self-interest. Only when the society is happy can you be happy. All your joys and sorrows depend upon the society. If society is not happy an individual can never be happy. Therefore you should continuously aspire for the welfare and prosperity of the society".

"You (students) should undertake service activities which can give you self-satisfaction. There is nothing greater than service. Enter into society and undertake service activities. Do this continuously. *Paropakaram Idam Sareeram*. When you undertake such a sacred service, your education gets sanctioned."

"When you (students) clamour for rights, you must bend your shoulders to carry the obligations too; finish your studies; develop the skill to distinguish between what is good and what is not, and the means to secure the good and avoid the evil. Instead, if you plunge into the streets behind the leaders who use you for their ends you are harming your career and harming politics too".

Students union can orient students about customs and traditions, rules and regulations and the culture of the institution. It can provide consultation regarding career development, improving classroom interaction, interview etc. It can take part in academic and non-academic activities like guidance and counselling. Students can easily influence their fellow-students in following values.

Role of Administrators in Strengthening Value Education

Sri Sathya Sai Baba (1973) says, "It is clear to every thinking person today that our educational institutions which have been established to impart to the prospective citizens of our country. The strength and ability to fulfil their responsibilities properly in every sphere of life are fast declining and are sunk in chaos. This is proved by the number of problems facing our educational institutions". He also says, "discipline which should illuminate our path of learning is now like a remote lamp already shattered in the dust. Virtues like renunciation, integrity, justice and truthfulness, which should be natural attributes of man are nowhere to be found even in a small measure".

He also says, "An educational institution is assuredly sacred place where a holy task is being put into action—the shaping and moulding of the fortunes of many generations of the country." (Baba 1971)

Defining the goals of Education the NPE (1986) document says that emphasis must be laid on the socio-economic well being, competence and creativity of the individual, which encompasses:

(i) Physical, intellectual and aesthetic development of the personality.

(ii) Inculcation of scientific temper and democratic, moral and spiritual values.

(iii) Development of self-confidence to innovate and face unfamiliar situations.

(iv) Fostering a healthy attitude to dignity of labour and hard work.

(v) Creation of an awareness of the physical, social and archaeological, economic and cultural environment.

(vi) A commitment to principles of secularism and social justice.

(vii) Dedication to uphold the integrity, honours and foster the development of the country.

(viii) Promotion of international understanding.

Teacher training in values should be a strong component and the curriculum in value education should be related to the present practical needs of society rather than the ideals based on *puranic* stories or philosophical treatises by great scholars which may not have a direct bearing on day to day life of students.

This therefore emphasises the need for development of appropriate curriculum and the relevant training course for the teachers to enable them to handle value education in a practicaal way.

Religious places may take care of value education. But as we all know the present situation has resulted in religious feuds. Hence value education cannot be fully entrusted to religious institutions.

Secular educational institutions are to evolve a non-sectarian, non-religious but ethically and morally strong value-curriculum to be practically implemented in all educational institutions there by creating at least a resisting force against the onslaught immortality in society.

Therefore values have to be both *caught and taught*.

The NCERT listed 83 values. The Sathya Sai Organisation has classified and grouped these 83 values under five well-known prime values of the Education of Human Value (EHV) Programme.

These are: *Sathya* (Truth), *Dharma* (Righteousness), *Prema* (love in its broadest sense), *Santhi* (Peace) and *Ahimsa* (Non-violence in various forms and actions, thoughts, feelings etc.)

The core principle of value is:

(a) To enjoy life

(b) Help others to enjoy it

(c) Without harming anybody

Administrators and policymakers should prescribe graded series of textbooks to achieve the above mentioned values in students and through them in the whole society.

Administrative authorities in education can be classified into a few levels, namely secretariat, directorate and district or inspectorate level. Higher education comes under secretariat and directorate levels. In this context the possibility of interface between the decision-making bodies and the college system is more contextual and dynamic in nature.

Extending different kinds of data and feed-back on different aspects of college system to authorities is a major area of interface. In return such a kind of cooperation facilities decision-making leading to quality improvement of the institution. Through the participation of educational personnel at different levels of planning, curriculum design and renewal, continuous and comprehensive assessment, organisation of training and development activities the authorities can foster the values-oriented education at their respective levels to build value oriented society.

Morris (1956) found intricate but direct relationships between values and institutional structure and behaviour. It is argued that democratic institutional procedures can inculcate responsibility and autonomy. Teachers, caught between the hostility of their pupil and the guilt displacement of their headmaster and having to adopt what Webb (1962) calls the "drill-sergeant" role with discipline, punishment and custodial routines as their weapons in a repressive system, may well wonder how moral education can be conducted in such a milieu.

Sharma (1968) found that schools, having open and autonomous climate have high achievement index as compared with close climate school. His study revealed that the organisational climate with academic motivation and found that the total influence of the staff and the principal in creating good atmosphere which is conducive to the attainment of academic results play an important role.

Mishra (1968) studied the leadership behaviour and values of principles and teachers. The value-orientation scale as developed by Ansari was used. The value-orientation scale consists of sixty statements and covers five dimensions—conservatism, liberalism, fatalism, scientism, herediterianism, environmentalism, authoritarianism—non-authoritarianism, economic and altruism. The study showed that:

(i) On teachers' value-orientation scale, the values, authoritarianism and non-authoritarianism have almost the same value index. Almost all teachers tend to be fatalistic.

(ii) The scores of teachers about the perception of principles' initiation is positively related to the score of principals' on value orientalism.

(iii) The score of teachers about perception of the principals' consideration is positively related to the scores of principals' value liberalism.

Some of the recommendations evolved from the four weeks All India Workshop on 'Methods and Techniques for Value Development' in 1988 for teacher programmes:

1. System approach through different agencies towards value teaching/value development and the whole process of education should be oriented towards value education.
2. The central and state governments should take immediate steps to introduce value education in all institutions.
3. Voluntary organisations may conduct value orientation programmes for the students, teachers and parents and prepare teaching learning materials for value education.

4. UGC and NCERT should make provisions for value-oriented education throughout the country with a flexibility on approach. However, the UGC should take a lead in introducing value education programmes for teachers at higher education belonging to all the faculties.
5. Research in value education regarding prioritisation of values, curriculum development, methodology and evaluation strategies should be given priority.
6. A foundation course in value education at higher education level should be introduced.
7. Teacher orientation programmes should be taken up at the national, state, regional and district levels to train teachers in effective methods of development of values among students.
8. SCERTs universities and voluntary organisations should be given responsibility of producing literature and teaching learning materials especially designed for value education programmes in regional languages.
9. College and university management should plan and provide activities having social relevance during the academic year, as well as during holidays with a real spirit of social service. It should be made obligatory to students to participate in at least three activities and a certificate may be awarded. The environment of colleges and universities should be designed in such a way, which may help students, and teachers to identify, understand and internalise the relevant and desirable values.
10. Parents should invariably be involved in value education programmes at higher level. They should also be informed about various value activities/value programmes to be undertaken at college and university.
11. UGC, AIU, NVC, NCERT, etc. should be called upon to organise training courses for preparing, adopting and using value kits effectively.

Conclusion

"Education must enable a person to discriminate between light and darkness. It must foster and promote the precious wealth of moral strength and spiritual victory. It must purify the inner impulses of man. Mere mastery of books does not entitle a man to be known as 'educated'. Without the mastery of the inner instrument of emotion no man can be deemed to be educated. The talent has to be cleansed so that the patent can flourish".

In the Indian setup, the transformation of education must be a collective and democratic enterprise involving the active participation of all concerned mobilising the energies and faith of teachers, teacher-educators, parents, students and administrators. It needs deep vision and dynamic leadership to make Indian education relevant to our times and capable of meeting the challenges of the emerging future.

Parents and teachers now ignore the real purpose of education. Parents wish that their children must secure a University Degree, by hook or crook, takes it is a status symbol. Teachers wish that a high percentage of their pupils must pass the examination without giving them any bother while teaching, or while not teaching! (Baba 1980).

REFERENCES

1. Fisher S: *Relationship in Attitudes, Opinions and Values Among Family Members*, California, California University Publication, 1948.
2. Gokak, V K and Rohedikar, *Teachers Handbook for the Course in Human Values*, Prasanthi Nilayam, Sri Sathya Sai Bal Vikas Trust, 1982.
3. Ministry of Education Government of India:
   - (a) Report of the University Education Commission, Govt. of India, New Delhi, 1948.
   - (b) Report of the Secondary Education Commission, Govt. of India, New Delhi, 1952-1953.
   - (c) Report of the Committee on Religious and Moral Instruction, Govt. of India, New Delhi. 1959.
   - (d) Report of the Kothari Commission, Govt. of India, New Delhi, 1964-1966.
   - (e) Report of the Indian Education Commission, Govt. of India, New Delhi, NCERT, 1971.

(f) The Challenge of Education—A Policy Perspective, Govt. of India, 1986.

(g) Report of Working Group for Preparing a Scheme for Revitalisation and Modernisation of Pre-service Teacher Education, New Delhi, NCERT, 1986.

(h) Report of the Working Group for the Teacher's Training Programmes and Inculcation of Ethical and Social Values in Education, Recommendation of the High Level Seminar on Value Orientation Education, Simla: 1981.

4. Mishra H. in M B Buch, *Second Survey of Research in Education*, Baroda, Society for Education Research and Development, 1979.
5. Morris C., *Varieties of Human Value, Chicago*, University of Chicago Press, 1956.
6. Mukerjee R K., *"Social Structure of Values"*, London, MacMillan and Co. Ltd., 1964.
7. Ramji, M T., *Value Oriented School Foundation*, New Delhi, NCERT, 1973.
8. Radhakrishna S., *The Present Crisis of Faith*, New Delhi: An Orient Paper Back, 1965.
9. Rosenthan R and Jacolbson W., *Teacher's Expectations and Determinants of Pupils IQ Gains, Psychological Reports*, 1966.
10. Sharma M S., in M B Bush, *Second Survey of Research in Education*, Baroda, Society for Education Research and Development, 1979.
11. Sri Sathya Sai Baba, N. Kasthuri (Tr) *Sathya Speaks* Vol. VII, Bangalore: Sri Sathya Sai Education and Publications Foundations, 1971.
12. Sri Sathya Sai Baba, N Kasthuri (Tr) *Sathya Speaks* Vol. X, New Delhi: Sri Sathya Sai Gulab Singh and Sons Pvt. Ltd., 1980.
13. Sri Sathya Sai Baba. V K Gokak (Ed) *A Value Orientation to Our System of Education*, New Delhi: M Gulab and Sons, Gulab Bavan, 1973.
14. Sri Sathya Sai Baba, In *Sai Autar* by Krishna Moorthy, Calcutta: C J Gandhi Welfare Trust, 1978.
15. Tarkunde V M. *Education for Our People—Citizens for Democracy*, New Delhi, Allied Publishers, Ltd., 1978.
16. William, R M., in *Encyclopaedia of Social Humanist Ethics*, 1968.

22

Parents, Teachers, Students and Administrators and Strengthening Value Education

T.I. Nagarjuna*

Dr. V. Dayakara Reddy**

Value education being the need of the hour in the country today requires an emphasis for actualisation of vast human potential. Value education on very basis of other developments—economic, social, political and so on. Even the material development of the country will be thwarted if there is no culturing of the masses. The teachers, parents, students, administrators are in a great way responsible to the value education in children, thus they become the central figures in the value education programme, making it necessary to impart the teacher and parents lessons in values.

Values are the principles which should make our lives happy and prosperous and also they should lay solid foundation for a civilised and caring society. Thus, a value is something that has its own intrinsic work and one ought to cherish it for its own sake.

Meaning and Purpose of Value

The term value' has different connotations depending on the context in which it is used. Value may mean principles, ideals,

* Research Scholar, Department of Education, S.V. University, Tirupati.

** Principal, IASI & Head, Department of Education, S.V. University, Tirupati.

standards, morals, ethics and worth. It is something that has its own intrinsic worth and one ought to cherish it for its own sake. The value does not depend upon its being experienced by some one; rather, its intrinsic worth by itself is self evident. Value may also connote price, desirable, useful, quality etc.

Value Education

The present formal methods of education are lying extra-territorial stress on the economic welfare of man, ignoring that true education has to aim at the full rather all-round development of human personality, by bringing out the best of him and burning up all dross that might be his psychological inheritances. Man-values education is a sacred triangle, where education is a vital medium of imbibe, foster and perpetuate values in man. Education is capable of developing strong and abiding values. Everywhere all times, education has been built on values system conducive to the development of physical, intellectual, moral and spiritual life it activates the latent capacities of the individual, enabling him to recognise 'truth', duty and goodness. It transforms man from animal, that man to authentic and autonomous human being, who is conscious of his role-play. It seeks to secure for him the right things and activities.

Value Education as the Topmost Need of the Country Today

Value education starts not with the student but with the teacher. If the student has to be taught values 'first the teacher has to be taught values, and the teacher's value training programme should be given top priority for the success of value education. This is because the student learns values mainly from the actual behaviour of the teacher who lives values himself/herself, the theoretical teaching of values works only a little.

The purpose of this paper, as the very title suggests, is to present a programme proposal for the teaching of educating the teacher, parents, student and administrators with regard to the value education of children. The purpose is also to point out the theory of philosophy that works behind this programme, so that we may become clear as to what are the conceptual grounds upon which the programme of value education is based. Moreover, since the teacher and parents are mature and not just young students or children. They must understand the sublime philosophy of value education, if they are to become value educations.

If we take education is the above sense, it becomes clear that it is not only the so-called educational institutions like schools and colleges that impart education, but there are other places of education also like home, neighbourhood and society, which directly or indirectly impart good or bad education. The purpose of this type of education is to bring out integral development of the inner personality and help attain self-actualisation of the person.

Teacher, Parents, Students and Administrators are the Central Figures in Strengthening Value Education Programme

When India became independent, the most pressing problem before the country was that of poverty, and so the economic development was given a high priority. The Government of India responded to the economic problem, but education was given a low priority. Education even in the sense of academic and vocational knowledge was not given proper attention, much less the case of education in the sense of culturing of personality. Cultural education, can it value education or moral education, should become one of the top priorities, for value education is not merely an 'ideal' but is the very basis of all other developments—economic, social, political and so on. Even the material development of the country will be thwarted if the sense of values is absent in the peoples or, in other words, there is no culturing of the masses. The present Indian scene where we find skewness in work, lack of the sense of responsibility and wide spread corruption in every walk of life, amply proves our point. It is a happy development to note that the government of India to day is trying to introduce and promote value education in the education institutions.

At the very start there is an important question can we impart value education (or moral education) to the students merely by training a theoretical syllabus and given formal education by way of lecturing in the classroom! Although difficult, the answer is not impossible and it lies in the personality of the teacher himself/

herself. The teacher is the centre around which the entire education system revolves or in other words, the teacher is the foundation on which the edifice of education is concerned. The student learns the values not from the oral teaching in the classroom but from the living example of the teacher. When the teacher lives the values in his own person, he is able to directly and indirectly transmit the values to the students. Just as a lighted lamp can light other lamps.

What is true of the teacher is true of the parent also parent is the first teacher, perhaps the most effective of values. The children learns the first value-lesson from the parents. Moreover there is band of love between the parents and the child and so the transmission of values become easier. Therefore, the parent too has a very important role in the programme of value education.

In the same way administrators also play an important role in the development of strengthening value education in children if they maintain strictly the values in the educational institutions. Thus, they develop the values in children.

23

Place of Teachers in Promoting Value Education

Dr. G. Visvanathan*

Dr. M. Govindan**

This chapter is mainly focused on the role of teachers in promoting value education. It explains the concepts of education, values and value-oriented education. It also deals, why the teachers should inculcate the values among the students. Finally suggestions are given in what way the teachers can inculcate the values among the students.

Introduction

We are living in the globalised, liberalised, privatised, modernised and digitalised world. And also we are living in the corrupted, bureaucratic and unhuman world. The social life is swallowed by tension, violence and conflicts. These problems can be eradicated only through providing proper education and inculcation of desirable values.

Education and Values

Education and values are the two sides of the same coin. They are interrelated. Education is the key that opens the doors of life. Education is widely accepted as the essential tool for the attainment

---

* **Professor of Education.**

** **Lecturer in Education, Annamalai University, Annamalai Nagar–608 002, Tamil Nadu.**

of desired goal. It is the principal instrument in awakening the child to cultural heritage. The NPE (1986) rightly stated that, "education is an unique investment in the present and for the future". Education has an acculturating role. It refines sensitivities and perceptions that contribute to national cohesion, scientific temper and independence of individual spirit—thus furthering the goals of socialism, secularism and democracy enshrined in our Constitution.

Values are the windows of understanding society. It justifies action. Allport (1950) define "anything that yields a satisfaction (or provides a means for such satisfaction) is designated as value". Values are what people like or dislike, need, enjoy, desire or what their culture prescribes for them.

Values are imbibed by an individual through a process of conviction. Values contain the judgemental element in that they carry in an individual's ideas about what is right, good or desirable. Values are necessary not only for individuals but also for organisations, societies and nations for their sustenance and growth. Values are relative in nature. They differ from individual to individual, from organisation to organisation and from country to country.

Values are determined and influenced by the values cherished by the society. Values are not static, but change according to the changing society. There are two types of values.

1. Instrumental values like interests, wealth, prestige, etc.
2. Intrinsic values like health, honour, purity, etc.

Instrumental values cause confrontation, while intrinsic values caused harmony.

Value-Oriented Education

Education without value is equal to praying deity without Bakthi. Man, values and education is a scared triangle, where education is a vital medium to foster and perpetuate values in man. While teaching of science makes man wise, the teaching of values makes man a cent per cent human.

Value-oriented education does not imply only moral education, it has wider connotation and includes all the objects and all the teachers who can correlate teaching to values in their respective fields. In other words, value oriented education comprises all types of education, aesthetic, ethical and spiritual education.

Report of the Committee on Religious and Moral Instruction (1959-60) indicate that "anything that helps us to behave properly towards others is of moral values, anything that takes us out of our self, and inspires us to sacrifice for the good of others or for a great cause is of spiritual value.

The National Policy of Education (1986) stressed the need for fostering the value education in the following ways.

"The growing concern over the erosion of essential values and increasing synicism in society has brought to focus the need for readjustments in the curriculum in order to make education forceful tool for the cultivation of social and moral values. In our culturally, plural society, education should foster universal and eternal values, oriented towards the unity and integration of our people—such value education should help eliminate obscurantism, religious fanaticism, violence, superstition and fatalism".

Ramamurthi Review Committee (1990), observed, "value education is to be constructed as a continuous process which is to be sustained throughout the process of growth of the individual from childhood to adolescents, then to adulthood and so on.

It is also the role of value education to bring out integration of the hand, head and heart to ensure that education does not alienate the students from the family, community and life. One of the key role of the education should be creation of work culture at all stages of education, so that the individual develops in to a socially and economically human being with respect for welfare of all living beings. It is the package of values which will help the creation and sustenance of an enlightened and humane society in the country".

Why Value Education?

Bundestage (German Constituent Assembly) in 1993 declared that "Germans have been humiliated not because they are under-educated, but because they are over-educated without values".

Nidhi Sachdeva (2000) viewed that, in future "social relations will become mere weak. The tendencies of cheating, bluffing, and robbing grow fast and they will grow further. Moral values decline more. Obedience on the part of the youngsters towards their elders is fast disappearing. Feeling of cooperation will be no more. Good manners, gratitude's, humanism, kindness, peace, sympathy will weak and more in next few years".

The universities are the nurseries of the values and ideals of life in every country. Without values and ideals the universities with its hundred classrooms, laboratories and museums remain but an impressive scaffolding, not an edifice of civilization". (Mukerjee, R.K, 1969).

Teachers Role

The Kothari Commission (1964-66) viewed that "the destiny of the India is being shaped in her classroom". What it implies is the future citizens of India completely depends on the role of the schools and the teachers.

Right from the vedic period the teachers are responsible for developing the knowledge and moulding the character of the students. Teachers are capable of opening of the young minds to realise their ability and capacity. They are dedicated to the task of national development and human welfare. They assume a new role of nation-builders and social-welders besides being experts in their subjects.

The present formal education system in India has failed to provide a balanced blend of scientific knowledge and spirituality to promote better life. It has failed to promote better quality of life, character and culture among students. Most of the teachers spend their time only for teaching material and neglect the spiritual values.

Teachers may motivate, communicate, illustrate, activate and inculcate the values among the students either by curricular or co-curricular activities.

— Todays youths are worried and depressed about their unemployment. The teacher should guide them to select a right vocation for their future development.

— Good manners verily are likely the oil that helps to keep the machine of the human society running smoothly.

— Cleanliness is next to Godliness. So, teachers should stress this concept through proper examples.

— The NPE (1986) puts a target of division of 10 per cent students in vocational stream in the total enrolment by 1990 and 25 per cent by 1995. But the Operations Research Group (ORG) evaluation results shows that, the actual enrolment is only 4.8 per cent. The reason for this slow progress is that there is a wrong attitude towards manual work and vocational education. Therefore the teachers should develop the positive attitude towards manual work among the students.

— The teachers should advise the students to eradicate the social evils like purdha, dowry, child marriage, untouchability, begging etc.

— The teacher should give greater emphasis on peace, love, secularism, unity, cooperation, cultural enrichment, national unity and creativity.

— The teacher should allot more time for work experience, music and art and socially useful productive work.

— The teacher should develop leadership skills and responsibilities and promote positive leisure activities.

— Worship and prayer important activities of the daily work of the school. Teaching of moral instruction should be made so interesting and effective that students would be able to accept the subject voluntarily.

— Yoga and meditation programmes should be encouraged by teachers.

- — Teachers can develop a sense of self-respect and esteem their pupils by respecting them as individuals of unique abilities.
- — Teachers may give opportunities and scope to implement innovations and new ideas.
- — Today most of the students follows the hedonistic principle of obtaining maximise pleasure with minimise work. Teachers should create positive work ethics among the students.
- — The teachers should emphasise on "man-making" and not "money-making" education.

Conclusion

The year 2010 will be not like the year 2000. The future society will be completely different from what is today. Materialism and modernism will have a great influence on Indian society. Nalini Saksena (2000) predicted that, in future, the terms like "Satya" (truth), "Dharma" (right conduct), "Shanti (peace), "Prema" (love) "Ahimsha" (non-violence) will be replaced by the terms, like, Computer, Science, Technology, Electronics, T.V., Radio, Nuclear bomb etc... in the field of education. For any nations development both the material and spiritual values are essential. If we consider the development is like a child, the material and spiritual values are like father and mother of the child. For the healthy development of the child both the mother and father's cooperation is very essential. Similarly for the healthy development of nation both the material and spiritual values are very important. So, in future, the teacher should try to inculcate both the material and spiritual values among the students.

REFERENCES

Mukerjee, R.K (1969), *Social Structure of Values*, S. Chand, Delhi.

Nalini Saksena (2000), *Indian Society and Education in 2010*.

Report of the National Policy on Education (1986), Ministry of Human Resource Development (Dept. of Education), Govt. of India.

24

Teachers and Strengthening of Value Education

Dr. K. Sudha Rani*

P. Manohar Reddy**

It is admitted on all hands that the chief objective of education is overall development of the student's personality. The personality may be defined as integration of an individual's modes of behaviour, interests, attitudes, capacities, abilities especially when considered from reactions to social and other situation. It is an inner system of beliefs, motives, aspirations and values, which organise and control a person's observable behaviour. It is an undoubted fact that more and spiritual education focuses on the value system, which provides the basis for right conduct of the individuals and right relations between the people. But, as a result of quick economic growth, influence of western culture, over mechanization, urbanisation are carving for materialistic life there has been a loss of values and of the value system at the individual level and in the country as a whole. Dr. Radhakrishnan stated that "Both in ancient India and Greece education was regarded as initiation into the values that Govern human life, which enables the initiated one to raise himself above the external conditions of existence. It is very essential to understand and recognise the role

* **Associate Professor, Department of Adult Education, S.V. University, Tirupati.**

** **Research Scholar, Department of Adult Education, S.V. University, Tirupati.**

of the teacher is giving such a type of value education to the students and to inculcate values.

Concept of Values

Values are described as the socially defined desires and goals that are internalised through the process of conditioning, learning and socialisation.

Values are goals set for achievements and they motivate, define and colour all our activities cognitive, affective and conative. When education builds up true values in the life of our students, it has equipped the ship of students with radars and compass to sail clear in the stormy sea of life.

Value, reflect different philosophical positions. The concept of values is closely associated with the concept of man.

Value, in education are classified in different ways. One such classification is as follows:

- The biological values
- The intrinsic values
- The instrumental values
- The health values
- The recreational values
- The aesthetic values
- The spiritual values

Another Classification

- The spiritual values
- The material values
- The intellectual values
- The social values
- The moral values
- The political values
- The economic values
- The cultural values

and like this.

Value Crisis

Erosion of moral values in all aspects of life and the crisis of values experienced in modern times. There is no doubt that technological development however little it might be, compared to the western societies, in one of the factors that the Indian society is facing today. There are also other factors like personal greed, meanest, selfishness, indifference to other interests and laziness that have brought about large scale corruption in almost all spheres of life personal and public, economic and political, moral and religious. The mind of man has been lociniated in to small fragments, which makes the value concept of human life diminishing factors in modern times. The reappearance of barbaric qualities of selfishness, clashes and conflagration and other destructions force give a clear indication of the process of degeneration of human society. We see on all sides a sadistic unconcern for human values and it has shattered their idealism.

Value crisis of the present day life is baffling the minds of educators and the students as well. The effect of the value crisis on the present day life is witnessed in the following:

The democratic ideology that has been accepted by our country is yet to be actualised in the form of social and economic democracy so as to realise the democratic values guaranteed by the Constitution of India.

The individual is becoming a prey to contradictory values and ideologies and is being converted as a consequence into an extreme radical, a reactionary, a sceptic or a cynic.

The present India educational system is reflecting more or less borrowed ideologies and philosophies and the national values are being relegated to the background.

The teacher educators and teachers are not being clearly oriented to the national values and ideas, ideas and ideologies that they have to inculcate in the students. Hence they are not in a position to play their role as value educators.

Our curriculum does not reflect human values and value system. Hence our schools and colleges have become examination centres and not value centres.

The problem with value education appears to be that while everybody is convinced of its importance. It is not clear as to what it precisely means and what it involves.

In our educational reconstruction the problem of an integrated perspective on values is pivotal, for its solution alone can provide organic unity for all the multifarious activities of a school or college curriculum and programme. An integrated education can provide for integrated growth of personality and integrated education is not possible without integration of values.

Concept of Value Education

The Phrase 'Value Education' as used in the area of school education refers to the study of development of essential values in pupils and the practices suggested for the promotion of the same. In its full range of meaning, value education includes developing the appropriate sensibilities—moral, cultural, spiritual and the ability to make proper value judgement and internalise them in one's life. It is an education for 'becoming' and involves the total personality of the individual. Value education is essentially 'Man Making' and 'Character Building'.

Value education forces on the value system, which provides the basis for right conduct of the individual and right relations between the people who interact with each other. The development of human personality cent red in a sound value system is expected to fulfill the three principal objectives of education: (1) Man-making; (2) Nation-building; and (3) Service-mindedness.

Health and happiness signify desirable physical and mental condition. Patriotism, love, freedom, justice, respect and friendship are held high in every nation. Moral values such as thoughtfulness, generosity, honesty, impartiality, courage, love of truth and self-control are ideal qualities. These two sets of values and traits are not only important in themselves but interlinked with health and happiness. The role of education is to preserve and transmit these basic human and cultural values of society.

Recommendations of Various Commissions on Value-Oriented Education

It is gratifying to note that all the committees and commissions on education appointed by the Union Government made a categorical recommendations in favour of value-oriented education. Eminent educationist gave their unstinted support to this worthy cause. Let us examine the views expressed by some of them.

1. Wardha Education Conference 1937 under the Chairmanship of Mahatma Gandhi Adopted the Following Resolution

"That the truth that are common to all religions can and should be taught to all children."

"The truth that all religions are the same in essentials and that we must love and respect others 'faiths as we respect our own, is a very simple truth, and can easily be understood and practiced by children of seven. But, of course, the first essential is that the teacher must have this faith himself.

2. Dr. S. Radhakrishnan Commission (1948-49)

Recommended:

"The fundamental principles of our Constitution call for spiritual training. There is no State religion. The state must not be partial to any one religion. All the different forms are given equal place, provided they do not lead to corrupt practices. Each person is at liberty to approach the unseen as it suits his capacity and inclination. If this is the basis of our secular State, to be secular is not to be religiously illiterate. It is to be deeply spiritual and not narrowly religious".

"The absolute religious neutrality of the state can be preserved in state institutions. What is good and great in every religion may be presented, and what is more essential, the unity of all religions must be stressed. It is in the detached atmosphere of an academic institution that we can study, analyse and eliminate the prejudices and misunderstanding, which disfigure inter-religious relations.

3. Dr. A.L. Mudaliar Commission (1952-53)

Recommended:

"Moral instruction or value-oriented education in the sense of inspiring talks given by suitable persons selected by the headmaster and dwelling on the lives of great personages of all times and of all climes will help to drive him the lessons of morality".

4. Shri Sri Prakash Commission (1959)

Recommended:

"Suitable books should be prepared for all stages from primary to university which should describe briefly in a comparative and sympathetic manner the basic ideas of all religions as well as the essence of the lives and teachings of the great religious leaders, saints, mystics, and philosophers. These books will be suitable to the various age groups in different classes of schools and colleges, and should be a common subject of study for all. Collections of poems and selected passages from Sanskrit, Persian, English and the religion languages should be made for young people".

5. New Education Policy (1986)

It is heartening to note that our New Education Policy stresses the acculturating role of education and totally endorses the programme of value-oriented education. In pursuance of this desirable scheme, the universities in Andhra Pradesh have already introduced two new subjects for the Degree classes (1) India's Cultural Heritage; and (2) Modern Science. It is also proposed to introduce moral instruction at high school level. For this purpose books for students and teachers guidance and commissioned to be written.

Students see a lot of difference between the world of books (what they are taught in the classroom) and what they actually see happening around them in practical life. They should be told that life will not be a bed of roses for good people who pursue values. They have to travel on a lonely road. The lessons of Christ's crucifixion and Mahatma Gandhi's assassination are examples. For those who put spiritual inputs in their lives there will not be material outputs!

Importance of Being a Teacher

The teacher has a vital role to play in our effort to relate education to national development and social changes. It is the responsibility of the teacher to guide and inspire his students, to enrich his discipline and to inculcate value, which are inconsonance with our cultural heritage and our social objectives.

Of all the different factors, which influence the quality of education and its contribution to national development, the quality, competence and character of teachers are undoubtedly the most significant. The most important factor in education reconstruction is the teacher, his personal qualities, his educational qualification. His personal training and the place that he occupies in the school or college as well as in the community. The reputation of a school or college and its influence on the life of the community invariably depends on the kind of teachers working in it.

As the Ministry of Education documents *Challenge of Education:* A policy perspective (1985) has mentioned. "Teacher performance is the most crucial input in the field of education. Whatever policies may be laid down, in the ultimate analysis. These have to be interpreted and implemented by teachers as much through their personal example as through teaching-learning processes" (p. 54). The National Education (1986) has similarly said, "The status of the teacher reflects the socio-cultural ethos of a society; it is said that no people can rise above the level of its teachers. The government and community should endeavour to create conditions, which will help motivate and inspire teachers on constructive and creative lines. Teachers should have the freedom to innovate, to diverse appropriate methods of communication and activities relevant to the needs and capabilities of and the concern of the community".

Role of Teachers in Strengthening Value of Education

Morals and values cannot be superimposed from above. They are to be cultivated from within and practiced in a voluntary manner. What is important is to realise that morals and human values are not to be promoted by direct instruction. The students should be made to discover them for themselves. Teaching is external and learning is internal. If we want people to learn values, values must be internalised. Appropriate learning situations and "teachable moments" should be provided inside and outside the classroom.

A certain scholar did painstaking research to find out the factors that produced human values of the highest order in the people. He took a random sampling of men and women representing the various professional groups. Investigations showed that all those cases, one of the three elements was invariably present. They are: (1) Personal example of the parent; (2) Sound training received in the school/colleges; (3) Inspiration derived from the classic and biographies of great persons. Of all these three, the teacher's role in the school is regarded as the most significant, especially in the formative years of the child.

The teacher's influence should provide ample compensation for the total absence or negative aspects of the father's example and the mother's training outside the school. This being so, schools and colleges should not merely mirror the society they serve. They should be islands of purity in a sea of corruption. Eventually, their wholesome influence will transform the society itself.

It is not enough to set apart one or two periods earmarked for value-oriented education when we seek to achieve total development of the student's personality. Moral education should be conducted as a total school experience, from primary level through secondary grade to college level. Further, this should be integrated with classroom work, extra-curricular programmes and outside interactions. Where possible, there can be separate classes or courses of the whole school. Value-oriented education should include participation by students in decisions about discipline and rules of conduct which should lead to a voluntarily accepted system of public morality. In the opinion of Freud, the great psychologist, every child is a bundle of instincts and drives which must be subordinated to societal objectives and requirements. This socialisation constitutes the ethical developmental process. Sublimation of instincts is the resultant process of socialisation. The teacher has a role as socialising agent.

We get glimpses of India's culture and value system in scriptures and epics like the Ramayana and Mahabharata. The Upanishads and the Puranas tell us about the right conduct. Students should be introduced to such books and literature. Lives of heroes in the epics and the achievement of great men should inspire the young to lead a higher life. In educational psychology, there are three ways of achieving "internalisation" of these moral and spiritual values:

(a) Emulation of the role models, following the example of good people of the past and the present.

(b) The reward system, which reinforces good conduct.

(c) Critical assessment of the norms leading to the acceptance of the standards on the basis of one's validation.

The first and the second method are applicable to school level. The last one is specially suited the tertiary level. We have to design an appropriate curriculum and devise suitable strategies and methods for this purpose.

He should have committed to a society based on justice and should, therefore, strive for the inculcation of these values and extension of knowledge and skills to the society at large. In effect, the teacher should become an effective instrument in the processes of development and social change. He should be a key factor in the transformation of our value system.

To meet the 'new challenges boldly and to play his role meaningfully, the teacher, besides imparting knowledge, has to help the students understand the components of their conscious and unconscious personalities, the meaning of their dreams and aspirations and the nature of their relations with one another and with the community at large. In short, he has to teach his students not only the art of learning but also the art of living and working in a society which they must create as an embodiment of their cherished ideals and realised goals. Unless the teacher looks upon his job more as a mission or a vocation rather than as a mere means of livelihood, he can never discharge his 'new' responsibilities satisfactorily.

Conclusion

Education is becoming day-by-day more or less materialistic and the value traditions are being slowly given up. The modern India is being educated mainly with the bread and better aim of education and as a result most of our graduates run after money, power, comforts without caring for any values. Moral, religious and spiritual education is being deliberately neglected in our educational system. The teacher is the principal agency for implementing educational programmes at various levels. The role of the teacher in this context is not going to be easy and smooth. The teacher has to perform two functions. First, has to play an important role in the transformation of knowledge based on the syllabus and secondly, he should be a key factor in the transformation of our value system.

25

Value Education

Role of Teachers

A. Gayatri*

Dr. V. Dayakara Reddy**

"The end of all education, all training is man-making."

The problem of value oriented education of the young has assumed increasing prominence in educational discussions during recent times. Parents, teachers and society at large are concerned about values and value oriented education.

Teachers in fact are the designers of the future of the students. Teachers are the dynamic forces to inculcate education in students. Directly or indirectly they influence their students, hence teachers should present themselves as ideals.

Introduction

Education is supposed to be a powerful instrument of change and has a progressive impact on human behaviour, but in actual practice, it is doing very little to cultivate moral, social, cultural and spiritual values in our youth and to promote national consciousness in the country. Education is general and value education in particular occupies a prestigious place in the modern context of the contemporary society. The world-wide resurgence of interest in value education has been explained as the natural

* **Research Scholar, Department of Education, Tirupati.**

** **Principal IASE & Head, Department of Education, Tirupati.**

response of the modern societies to the serious erosion of moral values in all aspects of life and the crisis of values experienced in modern times. The factors like personal greed, meanness, selfishness, indifference to others interests and laziness are caused due to value crisis and erosion of values. The problem of value education of the young has assumed increasing prominence in educational discussions. Parents, teachers and society at large are concerned about values and value education of children.

Our children represent 20 per cent of the population but they are 100 per cent of our future, greatest investment and we must help them understand the importance of investing in themselves which is possible through value education. Today education is something to be treasured in both earning and learning potential, which is possible through ideal and dynamic teachers. The parent, the teacher, the planner, the student and the society cannot be segregated. Teachers, parents, social workers, educationalists, administrators should know the importance of value based education and should given grounding to the children and the youth in values as simplicity, obedience, respect for elders, responsibility, discipline and honesty.

Modernity, rapid growth of science and technology and subsequent industrialisation have caused a great threat and danger to our old morals and values. To day not only India but the whole world is facing a crisis of moral, ethical and social values. Deliberations on value-oriented education must be universally applicable to all humankind and the type of value-oriented education suitable to India in this scientific and technological age also should be enlighted. There is an urgent need for a great effort to revive and reform the values of human life and to rejuvenate the foundation of civilization. There is consensus of opinion among the educationalists that in order to respond to the needs and aspirations of the changing society, spiritual values should be inculcated in the minds of the students of schools and colleges through various subjects of the curriculum and not as a part of curriculum.

The main aim of education is the development of an all-round and well-balanced personality of the students. The main aim of value-oriented education is to make the students good citizens who may share their responsibilities in the changing set up of the society in order to give the desired shape and image to the society and the nation at large. For this the teacher has to play a crucial role in the society. The classroom, should sent messages to the young people, message of love, safety, security, belongingness and warmth messages which say that this is the place where the individual; is respected and trusted. Let us provide opportunities to our young ones "to learn, live and flourish" in our classrooms like perfect human beings.

Values

A value, is a state of human mind a mental disposition an attitude or an emotionalised state of mind towards some idea, thing or tradition carrying positive and negative charges within itself. Its formation involves a deeper layer of personality. It is always a result of one's own experiences. Literally, a value means something that an individual considers important something about which he feels strongly.

Value-Consciousness

To think means to remain with consciousness. Thinking means thinking about some place, some thing or some issue. The thinking process moves first to satisfy itself. When there is satisfaction means there is already some importance attached to the place or thing or issue. Thus, the very concept of consciousness is due to the importance or satisfaction of value. It is nothing but value consciousness.

The importance of this value consciousness cannot be minimised in a democratic country like India. In the democratic country control of people's behaviour with coercive methods is not possible. Hence, the only alternative way left is to teach the masses to be self-controlled which is possible only when they are made to learn certain values as values are the prime movers of human action. Once formed, values begin to control and direct human actions. Hence teaching of desirable values should be major concern of the system of Indian education. Values are foundation stones of national solidarity.

The teaching community today faces an endless and challenging task of imparting value education and value based education. The impact of inculcating values among students by the teachers is in fact colossal and quite lasting. Against many destructive non-values, there is still longing for ushering in and striving for a new society based on justice, equality and common fellowship. As teachers have always claimed a special capacity to influence conduct and to shape moral character, the society expects them to develop not only knowledge but also ethical values among students thus creating an environment that would foster fraternity amongst mankind.

Unlike other subjects which can be taught without much difficulty, it is not easy to teach values to the students. The teacher of medicine need not suffer the diseases which he teaches but the one who talks of values has to necessarily practice them. The values are one where the gap between preaching and practicing should not exist; unless the teacher herself or himself practices the values that she/he preaches, she/he would not carry any conviction with her/his students.

To me the crux of value orientation is the teacher and is an important source of values. Her/his thoughts and actions influence pupils a great deal. Value orientation must therefore begin with the custodian of the young.

What is Value Education?

Value education is education in values and towards the inculcation of values.

Is value education important or academic education?

Of course both are equally important.

Academic education helps:

— To develop 3R's—reading, writing and arithmetic.

— Try to manage simple things in daily life.

— Try to get a good job.

Value education helps in:

— Behavioural development.

— Imparting fruitful education.

— Helps to develop welfare of the self and others.

Above all value education helps in different and happy moments.

Here is an article and some queries:

"The wise man built his house upon the rocks. The foolish man built his house upon the sands. Then came the waves and washed the sands away, but the house upon the rocks did not sway."

Queries on Article

1. What do you think the rocks stand for in life?
2. What do you think the sands stand for in life?
3. How would you choose to build your house on life?

General Questions

1. To what extent you agree/disagree with the above article? Does it apply in Indian context?
2. In India, where academic excellence is the emphasis do you think value education will make its impact?
3. In your opinion what values do you think are lacking in the youngsters today? Why are they lacking in them? What can be done about it?
4. If you were to examine yourself, how much of emphasis have you or your parents place on value education in comparison to academic excellence?
5. What are the values that are lacking in you? Have you done any thing on it?

Teaching Values

When a student is confronted by a problem like confusion or state of indecision which has cropped up as a result of some of his wrong actions such as disobedience or even not completing the given assignment, first of all he needs to identify the real problem and know the causes of looking back at his behaviour or action in relation to the problem. If this process is followed he would not only refrain from doing wrong things but also amends his future actions. Being able to identify, able to analyse and assess are important abilities for all the teachers to possess.

The important way which could help in inculcation of right values would be to define or clarify values to the students not only at the school but also at the college levels. A lucid explanation of values would surely develop understanding of values and at the same time may lead to develop moral reasoning which is another way of implementing values among students. The main responsibility of shaping the behaviour of students is in the hands of teachers. Directly or indirectly they influence their students, hence teachers should present themselves as ideals. They should have a clear and clean image among students. They should be honest, sincere, punctual and should follow the professional ethics. They must devote time for discussion with the students. Discussion should be informal, outside the classrooms also, not only on contents but on social problems, individual problems faced by students and on social values. Teachers should be sensitive, sympathetic and have positive attitude towards student's emotions.

A teacher is an educator too, who not only teaches and plans, for the education of his students but also makes his own decisions about 'what to teach and how to teach and at the same time constantly influencing the students in the information of values.

Teaching Strategies

There are certain techniques suggested by different educationists. These techniques are useful in developing values. These techniques are critical inquiry method, case study, role playing, value clarification technique, value analysis model, etc. The main purpose of these techniques is to develop rationality among the students. In all these techniques some issues are raised and with the help of discussion the students try to judge their values. Community extension work or community based projects are also useful, where students go to the people, discuss with them and see the reality of life. Through this activity institution and community come closer to each other, so that, the exchange of ideas can take place. Students can also take part in it.

Role of Teachers in Promoting Value Oriented Education

1. Persons who take teaching as a profession but not as an occupation, alone should enter into teaching.
2. In training institutes, teacher trainees should be given training in developing value oriented curriculum, co-curriculum, teaching methods, research methods, examination systems and evaluation techniques.
3. Every teacher should view life as a process of valuation and drive the same into the head, heart and hand of every learner.
4. Every teacher should identify value consciousness in his thought word and deed and make the learners to identify the same in them.
5. While teaching, the teacher should never think that his duty is over by simply passing on mere information to the learner. On the other hand, he has to explore and expose the different kinds of values ingrained in each lesson and in each concept.
6. While carrying research, the teacher has to dig deep into the subject and expose the different kinds of values and value frames hidden in it.
7. Through both teaching and research, the teacher should aim at transforming students individuality into personality.
8. Always the teacher should strive to rebuild and strengthen the society and the state.

Teachers, therefore, should be aware of the important role they are called upon to play as professionals and citizens as agents of development and change. They must make an effort to light a candle instead of cursing the darkness and sow the seeds of value education with a fond hope that they would diffuse their fragrance towards the creation of a just and new society as they sprout and blossom.

To conclude, values cannot be developed through teaching alone. Value system is related with the affective domain of a person hence it is necessary that a person should live in the atmosphere of value consciousness. All the educational institutions are responsible to create such atmosphere. Developing value consciousness is the major step towards value development.

REFERENCES

1. Sharma, A.P., *"How to Inculcate Values Among Youth"*, University News, pp. 14-16.

2. Gupta, N.L. (1986), *"Value Education: Theory and Practices"*, Krishna Brothers, Ajmer.

3. Mazumdar, H.B., (1983), "A Quest for Values in Education", *Journal of Indian Education*.

26

Sensitising Teachers Towards Value-based Teaching

Dr. (Mrs.) K. Chellamani*

Dr. S. Mohan**

'Globalisation' envelops almost every subject in the present society. Unlike the past, 'money' is the major concern of people today. This mind setup along with the influence of foreign culture in the globalised world slowly vanishes the concept 'values' among people. It raised the eyebrows of Indian educators and they become obsessed with the word 'values'. It seems as though all other concerns in education in this country have been subordinated to this single requirement. Hence, people in this discipline started thinking 'education' in the name of 'values' that can be identified, prioritised and also ranked.

What are Values?

In this country of diversity, if we go for the meaning for 'values' we get into classifications of manyisms, viz, Buddhism, Jainism, Hinduism, Sikhism, Christianity and Islamism. To quote a few, Lord Krishna in the Gita lists some as "fearlessness, purity of heart, steadfastness of karma yoga, austerity, uprightness, non-injury, truth, absence of anger, compassion, modesty, forgiveness,

* Lecturer, Department of Education, University of Madras, Chennai, (TN).

** Professor & Head, Department of Education, Alagappa University, Karaikudi, (TN).

fortitude, renunciation, tangibility absence of fickleness/Hatred/Pride/Covetousness etc.".

According to Vedas, purity of body and mind, self-restraint, non-attachment, truth and non-violence are proper values. Besides these we have Buddhist values as avoidance of two extremes, i.e. following the theory of golden mean. The jains hold compassion, ahimsa, discipline in thought and action, and pursuit of ten-fold morality and righteousness, asceticism, continence and voluntary purity. Islam, Christianity or Sikhism preaches the same ideology. Ultimately, it is clear that the emphasis on values is on renunciation, and leading a peaceful life of co-existence.

Worldview and Values

In this context world-view is taken to mean the summation of, shared outlook of a society regarding the past, present and future of the human order and its components. It takes into account both the qualitative and quantitative dimensions. It attributes, or assumes quality in the elements of the order and its processes are often tends to translate quantity into quality. Values are quality in action. They go with social norms. They attribute quality to different modes of behaviour along a continuum from the most desired to the least desired (and also the undesired). They may be explicit or implicit and there may be a significant gap between the ultimate and the proximate values. In proximate terms the choices may be situational and pragmatic although they may be at variance from the ultimate desired action, which may continue to be articulated and cherished. They form a part of the cognitive universe encompass within aesthetic and evaluative elements. They provide guides to behaviour without being rigidly prescriptive. Often there is a hierarchy of values and the permissible range allows different levels of choices. Some values may be universal to a society; others may be specific to particular groups and categories. Nonetheless, a social order cannot be conceptualised without a scheme of values. In reference to teachers it may be asserted that while they will share some general societal values they are likely also to have a set of values which are specific to their professional category and its cultural role definition.

Teacher, the Key Personnel of the Society

The educational system has to deal with something of a paradox when on one hand it has to transmit the cultural heritage and tradition, and on the other hand it has to transmit the cultural heritage function as a prime mover of change. Teacher, the key in the operational process takes up the major responsibility in bringing up future citizens.

If teachers are the instruments of the society, it is mandatory that teachers must preserve values. In the grim context of today's India it would be useful to start with an inventory of the elements of world-view and values, which are considered desirable and necessary in those who belong to the teaching profession. For a country of India's cultural heterogeneity, social complexity, economic inequalities and ideological different ions, unanimity in respect of all values is not possible or perhaps even desirable. Yet a consensus is needed at some premises and in respect of some core socio-political as well as academics values. Let us see the list of the desired elements of the world-view of teachers as a category.

1. The prioritised principles over persons.
2. Emergence of creative rationality as a key force.
3. Gaining mastery over the physical universe.
4. Establishing necessity of freedom for all human being.
5. Advocating creative expressions.
6. Persistence of cultural differences.
7. Learn to define his role as an architect of his destiny.

Other than the specifications, people will agree on the values as defined in the Constitution of India. Democracy, secularism, and social justice have been enshrined in the Constitution as the three most important national values. It is difficult to estimate how far they have percolated down to common citizens. Ritualistic acceptance of the values by the teachers will not do; these must inform and inspire their teaching. The concept of the autonomous individual must be expanded in reference to his rights and obligations. The classroom itself should become an example of a participative community. It is possible for one to be secular in profession and non-secular in practice. Such publicity must be exposed and genuine secular habits of thought and action promoted. Faith in social justice would necessitate debunking of all discriminatory practices based on ethnic or caste considerations, religion or sex. An attitude of caring for and sharing with, for the deprived and the underprivileged needs to be inculcated. If one accepts social justice as a value, one should learn to be appalled by the enormity of injustice meted to various sections and categories of the community everyday and protest about it. The acceptance of the core values should be judged not by their formal enunciation, but by their practice in life.

Adding to these three, there are three national values. There should be a shift from past present orientation to present future orientation. For the baffling problems of present, history may have the answer; new maladies require new remedies. These must represent a creative response to the challenges that we face today. We need to examine the problems of today in the present-future perspective.

Next is the rejection of the passivity principle. Servility and compliance have to be ruled out. The autonomous individual is an active individual. His consciousness should be extended to enable him critically examine the goings on in the society and judge the rights and wrongs of it. He should not stop at judging, he must learn to do something about the rectifications of the wrongs.

The third related value has a bearing on the cultivation of what has been called the scientific temper. The overt and covert dimensions of this temper need to be worked out meticulously. Pushing aside the protruding tantricks and astrologers, we must learn to seek our solutions through scientific and technology.

Despite the erosion of his influence, the teacher continues to be an opinion leader of considerable power. His faith in the core values is necessary, for the younger generation is not to start on a shady foundation of beliefs and misbelieves.

At this juncture, it is essential to look into the values particular to the academic profession. The following are acclaimed to be central to the value system of teaching profession.

1. Acquisition, transmission and addition of new knowledge
2. Social relevance
3. Extension—organic links with community
4. Irrelevance of some knowledge and the need for continuous renovation and innovation
5. Decolonisation of the Third World mind
6. Cultivation of excellence
7. Freedom and responsibility
8. Importance of freedom to work together
9. Critical awareness and articulation of tradition
10. A social consciousness and unafraid to undertake social criticism
11. Problem solving approach and emergence of new social order, and
12. Pursuit of excellence, creativity and research

We have analysed the values that have to be inculcated if society has to be held together and if it is to progress towards the goals we cherish. Here teacher is the key person rather a special person because of his mission or his duty or professional responsibility. He cannot afford to get lost in the norms of social behaviour, which happened to prevail—because, who then will show us direction or pull us out of the morass? As a man devoted to learning to the pursuit of truth in his creative endeavours, and hence being in a position to see farther then many others as a social critique, the teacher has to struggle for the propagation of the right values. Therefore, we believe that a teacher should be the first to introspect, and scrutinise their own value system so as to rise it to the highest moral value, and they should not shirk from imposing severe restrains on themselves in order that their word may have effect and their conduct may set an example which others may follow.

In the taxonomy of educational objectives Krathwohl (1964) and his associates analysed the affective domain into five categories. Valuing is one among those. They say, valuing includes the worth of a thing or behaviour. Valuing results not by the desire to obey or comply but by the student's commitment to the underlying value that guides his behaviour. As the student successfully internalises values, he starts building up his own value system. In this conceptualisation process, he organises his value system and synchronizes it into a value complex of higher order. In this context it is high time, this educational objective should have more concern in the curricula of student-teachers.

A report of a study on values, which prevail among teachers, collected data on the following values.

1. Personal integrity and devotion
2. Pursuit of academic excellence
3. Scientific temper
4. Commitment to student welfare
5. Community service
6. Patriotism, love for mankind, peace and international understanding
7. Commitment to social justice
8. Concern for nature and ecosystem

Let's take the above values as a standard and see how these could be incorporated in the psychology curriculum of B.Ed. students. The course, Psychology of development and learning is divided into four blocks into which the values can be incorporated. This is illustrated on page 213.

The course psychology to B.Ed. students is aimed at developing understanding of basic concepts and principles of human development and learning and their implications for the teacher. Teaching psychology to student teachers is an experience. It is essential for the teacher to understand the basic concepts of human development and learning. This course explains various aspects of human development together with the learning processes involved. In addition, the course explains the role of the teacher in the growth and learning pattern of the learner. Along with the theory, anecdotes from learning situations should be given

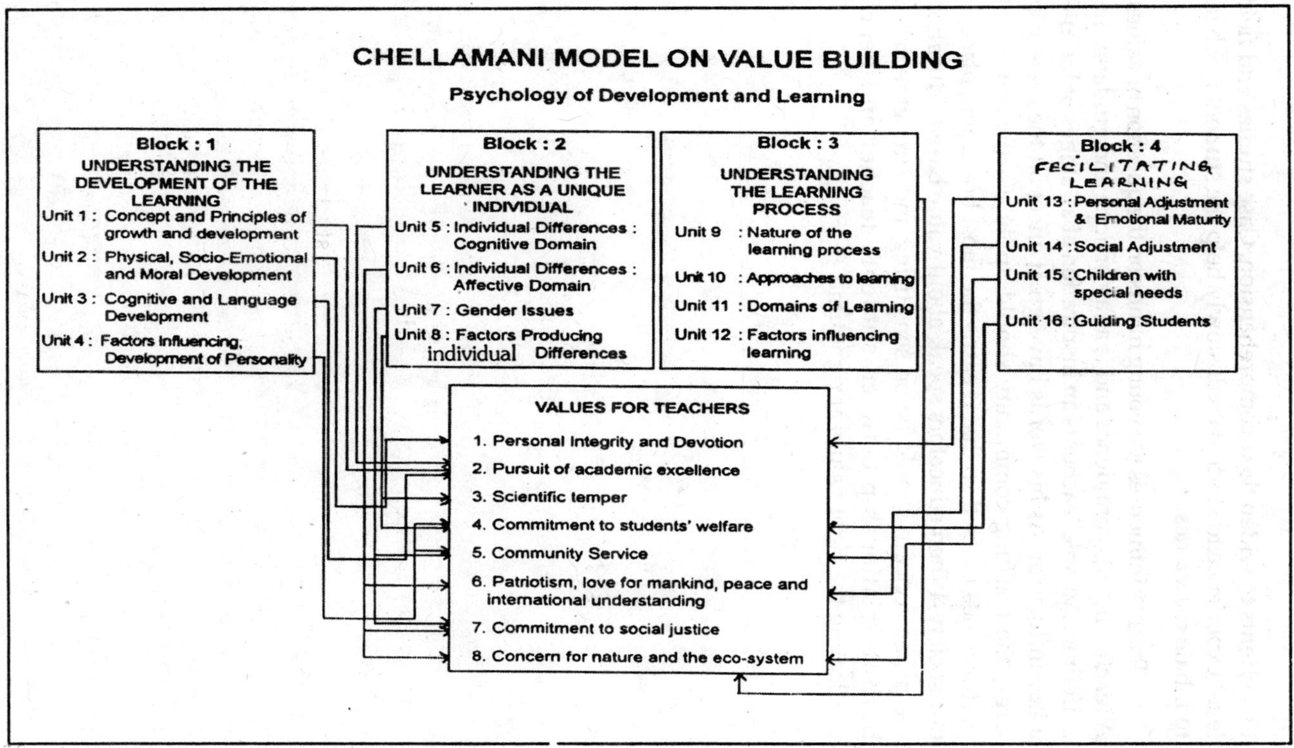
CHELLAMANI MODEL ON VALUE BUILDING
Psychology of Development and Learning
Block : 1
UNDERSTANDING THE DEVELOPMENT OF THE LEARNING
Unit 1 : Concept and Principles of growth and development
Unit 2 : Physical, Socio-Emotional and Moral Development
Unit 3 : Cognitive and Language Development
Unit 4 : Factors Influencing, Development of Personality
Block : 2
UNDERSTANDING THE LEARNER AS A UNIQUE INDIVIDUAL
Unit 5 : Individual Differences : Cognitive Domain
Unit 6 : Individual Differences : Affective Domain
Unit 7 : Gender Issues
Unit 8 : Factors Producing individual Differences
Block : 3
UNDERSTANDING THE LEARNING PROCESS
Unit 9 : Nature of the learning process
Unit 10 : Approaches to learning
Unit 11 : Domains of Learning
Unit 12 : Factors influencing learning
Block : 4
FECILITATING LEARNING
Unit 13 : Personal Adjustment & Emotional Maturity
Unit 14 : Social Adjustment
Unit 15 : Children with special needs
Unit 16 : Guiding Students
VALUES FOR TEACHERS
1. Personal Integrity and Devotion
2. Pursuit of academic excellence
3. Scientific temper
4. Commitment to students' welfare
5. Community Service
6. Patriotism, love for mankind, peace and international understanding
7. Commitment to social justice
8. Concern for nature and the eco-system

to students to widen their comprehension. Case studies and field level experience to students will slowly help the student teachers to inhale the values.

Teacher influences the young minds on the question of values. A teacher instills confidence and is a ray of hope and guidance for a lifetime. An able teacher is an inspiration at all stages of life and a key influencer. As his words have great effect on the society in large, the teaching community should apply worthy criteria of performance to itself so that it earns the most honorable place in our society. When educators speak about value based education the prime concern should be on sensitising and strengthening a healthy relationship between student—teacher and hence inculcating the right values at right time.

27

Prioritisation of School Children's Values by the Teachers

Prof. G. Vijayalakshmi*

Since the values are deteriorating, the value development among the children is the need of the hour. The aim of the present study was the values to be developed among the school children as perceived by their teachers. The variables considered for the study were sex, level of school, medium of instructional and locality. The sample constitutes 80 teachers and the data were collected with the help of a value scale and their bio-data. The method adopted was sample survey. The results revealed that there was significant difference between rural and urban teachers. Moreover there was no significant difference between the mean values of teachers belonging to other categories namely male *Vs* female, Telegu *Vs* English medium schools and primary and secondary level teachers in prioritising the values to be developed among school children.

The values are the salient feature of individual's behaviour in the society. The concept of value is so deeply embedded in all human actions and thoughts, that one should make an effort to implement it. The value governed behaviour is reflected in the external actions of people. But the world at present is passing through value conflict. This is manifested in almost all fields of life. Moreover the values are guiding principles of life whereas the behaviour is outcome of it.

* Professor of Education, S.P. Mahila Visva Vidalayam, Tirupati.

There is no value without education or no education without value. Thus education is a social process of transforming a person from instrinctive behaviour to human behaviour. It enables a person to make a better choice of value based options. Since the society is nothing but the combination of individuals even in the field of education the aims, the curriculum, the methods of teaching, the nature of teacher, discipline, mode of organisation, the evaluative procedures etc. are always conditioned by the value system prevailing in the society. Through values, the social, moral, aesthetic and spiritual concerns of the people can be developed and most often it is undermined as informal phase of education. This value incorporation in education also includes development of proper attitudes, feelings, beliefs, interests and behavioural outcomes across all curricular experiences. That is why the educational thinkers of Indian origin like Yajnavalkya, Sankaracharya, Vivekananda, Gandhiji, Dayananda Saraswathi, Aurobindo Ghosh etc., opined that education is nothing but value development in the individual or education should mould the individuals as ideal persons. In this connection it is quite worthy to see the various Indian Education Commission with regard to their recommendations.

Recommendations of Some Education Commissions on Value Development

Among numerous objectives of education, value development or moral development or ethical concern is one. Accordingly different educational commissions appointed from time to time gave their recommendations. A few were referred here for better understanding of importance of values in education.

Central Advisory Board of Education (1943-46) recommended that spiritual and moral education should be provided to children. The University Education Commission otherwise known as Radhakrishnan Commission (1948-49) also emphasised the need for moral and spiritual instruction at University stage. Sri Prakasa Committee (1959) categorically mentioned that there should be allocation of some periods in the school timetable for conscious and intentional teaching of moral education. The committee on emotional integration (1961) insisted on studying the Indian cultural values on compulsory basis. Kothari Commission (1964-66) stressed the instruction in moral, social and spiritual values at all levels of study. UNESCO (1972) suggested that educational system should encourage the promotion of values of world peace, international understanding and unity of mankind. The National Moral Education Conference (1981) in its first session resolved to inculcate moral and human values among students as a core subject and the content should include the common ethical teachings to highest the unity. National Policy on Education (1986) also stated that value education should be content based on heritage, national goals and cultivation of social and moral values. Union Ministry of Human Resource Development urged the educational institutions in 1988-89 to strengthen culture and values. The ministry also decided to review this in 1990 to strengthen the cultural and value education inputs in school education system. Acharya Ramamurthy Committee (1990) set up by Ministry of Human Resource Development to review the New Education Policy 1986 also stressed that review the child needs to be initiated not only with the world of knowledge and skills but also with values. The Parliamentary Standing Committee on Human Resource Development (1999) observed that it was quite disappointing in the last few decades failed to achieve the results for making education as value-oriented one. But the reports of the above committees and commissions are obvious that there had been consensus of opinion regarding the inclusion of values in education system as a whole. In spite of these, values could not be introduced directly in our educational institutions. Thus it is high time to safeguard the present setup of values from further deterioration and degradation of the society.

A Brief Review of Related Literature

Beveral (1967) studied the economic status and other determinants of values and found significant interaction between economic status and education for religious and aesthetic values. Bhargava (1986) analysed the development of values in the concrete and formal operational periods. Calra (1976) outlined the value based curriculum for India. Chaudari (1974) studied the values in textbooks. Dixit, R.C. and Sharma, D.D. (1971) conducted a study on differential values of high school and University students. Floresca Cawagan (1988) dealt with the issue of evaluating value education programmes, concepts and principles. Gandhi, K.L. (1993) collected public opinion on value education using two questionnaires separately for school and college students. Carg (1983) reported that personal attitude had significant influence on value development. Hardlung L.W. (1944) investigated changes in values during the college days. Harry (1952) investigated the difference in values among engineering students. Lewis (1984) studied the academic and cultural influence on development of values in college students. Patel, K.M. (1981) studied the impact of Sri Sathya Saibaba's preachings on development of value system among college students. Raj Kumar Yadav (1980) examined the relationship between values and preferences of 300 intermediate students. Roy, D.K. (1980) found family and friends as influencing factors of development of values among youth. Seetha Ram, A.R. (1990) studied 3 dimensions of value education and their development in children and young people. Ushasree (1995 and 1996) studied the process of value judgement and value education among secondary school children and found that the factors influenced the values development were the economic system, age, education, family, friends etc. She also suggested that even the teachers should inculcate values either through subjects of co-curricular activities. Vijayalakshmi, G and Padmasree, Y had studied the effect of sex, medium and level of education on children's values and found that there was significant difference among these teachers in perceiving values. Accordingly the teachers should realise that it is not away from the day to day professional responsibilities.

Need for the Study

A serious defect in the present school curriculum is the absence of provision for education in social, moral, and spiritual values. Therefore conscious and organised attempts are to be made for imparting these values through curricular transaction wherever possible. Prioritisation of values differs from persons to person. So, it is necessary to study the values to be developed among children is of great concern.

Statement of the Problem

The problem "Prioritisation of school children's values by the teachers" is selected for the study.

Objectives of the Study

The study was carried out with the following objectives:

1. To see the significance of the difference in the perception of values to be developed among the children between primary and secondary teachers.
2. To see the significance of the difference in the perception of values to be developed among children between teachers working in English and Telugu medium schools.
3. To see the significance of the difference in perception of values to be developed among children between male and female teachers.
4. To see the significance of the difference in perception of values to be developed among children between teachers working in rural and urban schools.

Sample Selected for the Study

A sample of 80 teachers working in primary and secondary schools out of whom 40 working in Telugu medium and 40 working in English medium schools constituted the sample. This sample also included 40 male and 40 female teachers. The method of stratified random sampling procedure was adopted as the sampling technique to select these teachers.

Tools and Collections of Data

The investigator used 2 tools to gather information from the respondents. The first one is value scale consisted of 80 items. For each item 3 alternatives namely 0, 1 and 2 were given against them. Ten teachers were consulted at the time of construction of this tool for item clarity, meaning and its expression. The teachers were asked to mark against each value to prioritise them in order i.e. first or second or third preference. Like that the values were given priority on its importance to the child by the teachers. The second tool along with this is a bio-data sheet in which the information regarding the medium of instruction, locality, sex and level of the school i.e. the variables considered for the study. These two tools were supplied to teachers to collect the data. The information collected in the above manner was codified and a few statistics like mean, standard deviation, t-values were calculated and presented below.

Variable wise Sample Size, Mean, Standard Deviation and t-values

Variable	*Category*	*N*	*Mean value*	*S.D.*	*t-value*
Sex	Female	35	126.31	16.30	0.2652
	Male	45	125.24	21.83	
Level	Primary	40	125.02	25.83	0.8300
	Secondary	40	129.15	17.87	
Medium	Telegu	40	125.42	25.66	0.1404
	English	40	128.75	17.04	
Locality	Rural	54	123.11	21.70	2.4827
	Urban	26	132.65	12.56	
Total		80	127.08	18.66	

From the above table, it can be understood that only at the t-value obtained between the mean scores of teachers from rural and urban localities differed significantly. This indicated that rural and urban teachers differ significantly with regard to prioritisation of the values to be inculcated among school children. Besides this, the above table also reveals that the urban teachers scored more (mean 132.65) followed by the teachers working in secondary (mean 129.15) and English medium school teachers (mean 128.75) whereas the teachers of rural areas was the least among all (mean 123.11) followed by primary teachers (mean 125.02) and male teachers (mean 125.24) in order. When these values are compared with total mean value, the mean values of both female and male teachers, teachers working in primary level in Telegu medium in rural areas scored less when compared to their other counterparts. More values were given preference by the urban teachers than the other categories of teachers. When the values of standard deviations were taken into considerations, there is more homogeneity among female teachers than the other groups of teachers. From the values given in the above table, it can be understood that rural teachers gave first preference for more values than the urban teachers i.e urban teachers ranked them in second and third places. But it was not the case with other category of teachers.

From the analysis of individual values, primary teachers gave more preferences to honesty and manners whereas secondary teachers gave much importance to personal development and environmental protection. Urban teachers emphasised the individual values whereas rural teachers gave emphasis for social values. Among all the values listed in the value scale the value the first three were 'truthfulness'stood in the first place followed by 'trustworthiness' and 'promptness. The three values identified as least important where 'behaving in proper manner at public places', following directions' 'accepting consequences'. Thus differences was witnessed among different categories of teachers in prioritising the values of primary and secondary school children.

REFERENCES

Beveral, 1967, "Economic Status and other Determinants of Values", Unpublished M.A. Dissertation, Andhra University, Waltair, 92-101.

Bhargava, 1986, "New Values and Education Quoted in Human Values and Education, Unpublished Ph.D. Thesis in Education, Punjab University, Chandigarh, 133-144.

Calra, R.M., 1976. *Curriculum Based on Values in a Developing Country with Reference to India*. Indian Publication Bureau, Ambala Cantt, 27-31.

Carg, 1983, "Children's Perception of Parental Disciplinary Practice and its Relation to the Development of Personality Needs". Unpublished Ph.D Thesis in Psychology, Agra University, Agra, 97-110.

Chaudari, U.S., 1974. "A Comparative Study of Values Reflected in National and State Level Hindi TextBooks", Unpublished M.Ed., Dissertation, University of Indore, Indore, 71-82.

Dixit, R.C. and Sharma, D.D. 1971. "Differential Values of High School and University Students and Teachers", *Journal of Psychological Research*, 15 (1), 11-17.

Floresca Cawagan., 1988. *The Issue of Evaluating Value Education Programme—its Concepts and Principles*, Mc Graw Hill and Company, New York.

Gandhi, K.L., 1993. "A Study of Public Opinion on Values in Education", *Value Education*, Gyan Publishing House, New Delhi.

Hardlung, L.W., 1944. "A Value Type Generation Test", *Journal of Social Psychology*, 19, 53-79.

Harry, 1952, "Investigation into the Differences in Values Among Engineering Students", *British Journal of Educational Psychology*, 39, 371-374.

Kothari, D.S. (Ed.,) 1966. Report of the Education Commission, Ministry of Education, Government of India, New Delhi.

Lewis., 1984. "Academic and Socio Cultural Influence on Development of Values Among Students in Two Year Colleges", George Peabody College for Teachers, Unpublished Ph.D. Thesis in Education, Vanderbit University, United Kingdom, 64-69.

National Policy on Education, 1986. Ministry of Human Resource Development, Government of India, New Delhi.

Patel, K.M., 1981, "A Study of the Orientation in the Educational Institutions" Run by Sathya Sai Organisation. Third Survey of Research, M.B. Buch. (Ed.) National Council of Education Research and Training, New Delhi 1978-83, Philosophy of Education (Ph.D) Education, 44-45.

Raj Kumar Yadav., 1980. "A Study of Relationship Between Values and Vocational Preferences of Adolescents", *Quest in Education* 17 (2), 165-172.

Roy, D.R., 1980. "A Study of Some Factors and Process Involved in the Development of Values". Third Survey of Educational Research, M.B. Buch, (Ed) National Council of Education Research and Training, New Delhi, 47.

Seetha Ram, A.R., 1990. "An Evaluative Study of the Objectives, Content and Methodology of Direct Moral Education" Followed in the Secondary Schools of Karnataka State, Unpublished Ph.D. Thesis in Education, Mysore University.

Usha Sree V., 1995, "Preparing the B.Ed. Trainees for Value Education". *The Progress of Education* 19, 84-86.

Usha Sree, V., 1996. "The Process of Value Development and Internalisation of Values by Individuals", Unpublished Article at S.V. University, Tirupati.

Vijayalakshmi, G., and Padmasree, Y., 2003, "Values to be Developed Among School Children" *Edutracks*, 2 (4), 22-25.

28

Dynamic Parenting

Role in Strengthening Value Education

Dr. A. Indira Prasuna*

Sri K. Pencholaiah**

The role of parents in strengthening value education is very vital in the present context. They are primarily responsible for the erosion of values in our country, in fact it is so even globally. If the nation has to proper right guidance and training is needed. Sathya Sai Education in Human Values (SSEHV) programme, (Pal Dhall and Tehseen Dhall of Institute of Sathya Sai Education, Canberra, Australia) introduced several value oriented concepts to children and their parents. "If the nation has to proper improvements must start with the Home and parents. Without peace and harmony at home there can be no peace in the Nation. Parents do not remain passive witnesses of their children's value education, since parents are the first teachers of their children. Their responsibility is multifold. Parents toil to leave their children a pile of riches; but they do not teach them, the proper sense of values by which they can know, how little the riches are worth, and how best to utilise the riches for their advancement. Unfortunately parents fail to foster the very best qualities in our children if our parenting goals are not clear. That is why to day, ninety per cent of the children are spoilt by the parents themselves. Major aspect of parenting

* Assistant Professor, I.A.S.E.

** Lab Technician, I.A.S.E., S.V. University, Tirupati (A.P.)

dilemma is that they tend to adopt the parenting style, which they have themselves experienced, while society needs change from time to time. We need to reevaluate our parenting and make effort to connect ourselves with our spirit and need to focus on their spirituality also. The task of parenting becomes rewarding only when we are able to establish a relationship with our children from our heart to theirs, love with one hand and discipline with the other. We have to be relaxed so as not to convey anger, anxiety, guiltiness and tension to children and yet instill in them skills of problem solving and of meeting with their targets and commitments. The parents are required to give their children a sense of inner peace, contentment and achievement so that they can look at external indicators of success as not only the measure of wealth. If the home is filled with clear fragrance of contentment and peace, all its occupants will be happy and healthy. The elders have therefore a great responsibility towards the generation that is coming up. Along with changing values one serious concern is the 'destruction' of childhood. Our children are becoming more distracted, sensual undisciplined and self centred. This trend has to be changed. Mother plays a key role in up-bringing children more than a father, since she is the first teacher to a child after birth.

Dynamic Parenting

The main function of education is to produce citizens with sound character and a healthy personality. True education humanises persons. Dynamic parents are those who are aware of the current social and cultural trends and their family issues and their origin. They have to equip with certain factors such as:

(a) Awareness of truth

(b) A sense of responsibility

(c) Emotional maternity

(d) Communication skills

Parents can establish themselves in the practice of human values in their family life since parents are the fundamental unit of society. Home and family form the microcosm for the cultivation of character, which is the sum total of attitude, feelings, beliefs and action arising from the thoughts. Home is a place of interaction with people we trust and love. We can be natural and spontaneous at home. Parents strive to create wholeness and well being in their children. Parents are their child's role models, mentors, friends counselling, guiding teachers, as well as care-takers in early and middle childhood. Home is the training ground for addressing the ills of our society. It is the fundamental political, economic and social unit of the society. A society's well being and stability rests on the foundation of good practice of values at home. The family supports the establishment of a stable social system based on tolerance, love equality respect empassion and justice.

"If there is righteousness in the heart
There will be beauty in character
If there is beauty in character
There will be harmony in the home
When there is harmony in the home
There will be order in the nation
When there is order in the nation
There will be peace in the world"

A happy home provide opportunities for meeting with both secular and spiritual needs of the child which leads to advancement in life. Truth, right, conduct, love, peace and non-violence are the true basic values inculcated by parents. As parents gain insight and mastery over self skills they become more effective in changing the family dynamics.

Truth: Parents model a life of truthfulness. As a contrast non-dynamic parents they will be at the mercy of forces operating in the popular culture. They allow their children to be influenced by bad groups by not checking their behaviour periodically. Children are not in birth with their own relatives kith and kin and thereby not in truth with their community also.

Right Conduct

Parents empower themselves and their children through right conduct. Parents teach the children the life of restraint, self discipline, purity simplicity and dedication. Dharmic life gives self confidential. Parents create peaceful atmosphere. They promote learning at home and through personal interaction with their child. Non-violence follow non-violence i.e. see no evil, hear no evil, done no evil.

Love: Parents provide a model of mature love and service to each other. They promote their own and their child's self-regard. They teach the sacred nature of love. Love of man is love of god.

Peace: The parents teach by example strategies of self-management, emotional and self control, anger and frustration management and ceiling on desires. They teach by example proper management of time, energy, money and food. The parents promote devotional singing and silent sitting. They spend time together with the adolescents in some family activities of the adolescents' choice.

Non-violence: The parents teach skills of negotiating, conflict management and resolution, communications skills and human relationship skills. They undertake joint community projects. They develop adolescents' awareness of the environment and of unity of faiths.

What Do We Want of Our Children

Children have unselfish love, they are innocent onlookers, they observe the action of the elders and they learn their lessons from the home much earlier than from schools. So parents have to be very careful in their behaviour with the children and between themselves.

Are Parents Confused?

We love our children and want to fine them the very fast, but we do not always know how? Mortality fathers are confused about their role in the home both with respect to their spouse and to the children many changes have occurred in the family form and function. Both parents are aware that their children are under a variety of influences. The mother often has a job earning money necessary to run the house that needs a dual income, yet she carries a lot of burden of domestic duties.

Sometimes parents are confused because they feel inadequate for the task. All parents want their children to grow up free of stress, anxiety and fear with no inner barriers. They want their children to become educationally and socially competent to have good skills of problem solving, to be loving, gentle, kind and compassionate and to be aware of the true purpose and goal of life. While the parents are clear about their objectives few parents only know clearly how to achieve them. It would be true to say that some parents have never seriously thought about their parenting practice and believe that what they are doing is correct. A few parents are aware that academic education does not necessarily give value education. Parents are the people who determine the destiny of the nation. All the qualities that the parents want their children to have are virtues based on the five fundamental human values. They are truth, right conduct, peace, love and non-violence. Much of the training in human values are essential aspects of good dynamic parenting. The educational system to which the parents look anxiously for direction is not directly concerned with value education. The current educational system plays a great emphasis on equipping children with mental and physical skills because it is geared to the economic needs of the country. It neglects the emotional, social and spiritual aspects of the child's personality. This has disastrous consequences for the children who go through the system. This is the reason that highly tactically trained and skilled doctors, scientists, technocrats, lawyers and professionals may not even know how to handle problems of their inner life. They may be crippled with stress, self doubt and shyness. None of these have any training in handling their emotional or social life and have poor relations with their family and friends. Clever academics may commit crime if they are not in-touch with their spirituality. The challenge for the parents is to give the children mastery over their lives and destiny. Hence, parents need to equip themselves with the best possible means of teaching the children human values.

There are different styles of parenting like authoritative, permissive/authoritarian. Ideal parenthood is neither authoritarian not permissive but it is authoritative and firm without being harsh. Non-dynamic parents will be at the mercy of forces operating in the popular culture right now. They allow their children to be influenced by bad peer groups, by not checking their behaviour from time to time. The flowchart explains the differences between dynamic/undynamic parenting. As earlier mentioned dynamic parents possess certain resources like awareness of truth, sense of responsibility, hoping skills and communication skills. They know that our human goal is not merely to secure an income, a comfortable home, happy relationships but also realisation of God. Let us hope that dynamic parenting helps to strengthen values among children.

Authoritative Parenting	Authoritarian/Permissive Parenting
Enables by promoting	*Disables by promoting*
• Uniqueness	• Unclear self direction
• Creativity	• Conformity
• High self esteem	• Low self esteem
• Responsibility for action	• Irresponsibility
• Problem solving approach	• Dependent on outer controls
• Good goal setting	• Poor goal setting
• High control over emotions	• Low control over emotions
• Resistance to peer pressure	• Closeness with the peers
• Good decision making	• Weak decision making
• Good learning activities	• Poor learning activities
• Acceptance of parental values	• Resistance to parental values
• Warm relationships with family	• Weak relationships with family
• Strong motivation	• Weak motivation
• Good social conscience	• Poor social conscience

DYNAMIC PARENTING
LIFE IS A CHALLENGE - MEET IT!
Problem solving approach
Creativity
LIFE IS A DREAM - REALISE IT!
High self esteem
Uniqueness
Good learning activities
High control over emotions
Resistance to peer pressure
Acceptance of Parental values
LIFE IS A GAME - PLAY IT!
Strong motivation
Warm relationship with family
Good social conscience
Responsibility for action
Good goal setting
Good decision making
FEAR SIN - LOVE GOD
CONSUMERISM
VIDEO
JUNK FOOD
TV
INTERNET
PEER PRESSURE
DRUGS
ALCOHOL
SEX
CIGARETTES
MAGAZINES
FASHION FADS

Human Value	Qualities in Children the Parents Wish the Child to Have
TRUTH	The child is self-aware, in touch with his feeling, thoughts and values. He is truthful, honest, possesses integrity, and a sense of fair play and justice. He is connected to his family and with a network of friends and relatives. He is aware of his cultural traditions and religious heritage. *The child knows his own truth, is self-aware and capable of meaning his mental life.*
RIGHT-CONDUCT	The child is competent, striving, committed and hard working. He is capable and responsible for himself and for his choices. He is disciplined in all his undertakings. *The child is capable of managing all his actions in accordance with Dharma.*
PEACE	The child is happy, peaceful, free of anxiety, tension, stress and fear. He possesses skills of negotiation and problem solving. He is capable of generating and maintaining peace within the family and a circle of friends. *The child is capable of managing his emotional life.*
LOVE	The child is loving, kind, considerate, gentle, compassionate, generous, understanding and dedicated. He knows how to generate and multiply his inner well-being of love, joy and harmony. *The child is capable of managing his personal and social life.*
NON-VIOLENCE	The child is self-restrained, balanced, does not violate himself or others through thought, speech or action. He is aware of himself and of the environment and the need to relate to the whole of creation. He has an appreciation of arts, aesthetics and beauty. He is clear about his purpose in life. He views the world as an expression of God. *The child is capable of managing his spiritual life.*

NON DYNAMIC PARENTING

GOOD PARENTAL RELATIONSHIP

Enables by promoting -

Concentration and Learning
Growth of Trust
High Self esteem
Feel valued
Loyalty to both parents
Confidence
Spontaneity
Stable personality
A good parental model

POOR PARENTAL RELATIONSHIP

Disables by promoting -

Poor concentration and learning
Distrust
Low self esteem
Do not feel valued
Divided loyalty
Diffidence (lack of Confidence)
Guilt, anger and hostility
Unstable personality
A poor parental model

29

Value Education

Role of the School

Dr. Mahender Reddy Sarsani*

Dr. L. Venkat Ram Reddy**

Value is "a conception, explicit or implicit, distinctive of an individual or characteristic of a group, of the desirable which influences the selection from available, means and ends of action.

Value is "something which pervades everything. It determines the meaning of the world as a whole, as well as the meaning of every person, every event, and every action... It can be said of every thing that is either good or bad; it can be said whether it must or must not be, or that it ought not to exist, that its existence is right or wrong (not in the judicial sense)" (Lossky and Marshall, 1935).

Values are the desirable ends, goals or modes of action which makes human behaviour selective. Value not only orients but also determines human behaviour.

Classification of Value

Many thinkers have classified values based on their perception and ideology. They were: Theoretical, Economic, Social, Political, Aesthetic and Religious (Allport and Vernon, 1931), National Integration, Dignity of labour, Freedom, Equality,

* Head and Principal, IASE, Kakatiya University, Warangal, (A.P.)

** Assistant Professor, IASE, Kakatiya University, Warangal, (A.P.)

Character, Intellectual and Health value (Kulshrestha, 1969); Domestic, Scholastic, Economic, Political, Religious, Philanthropic, Hygienic, Recreational, Artistic, Scientific, Linguistic and Military (Dodd, 1951), Values of Heart and Values of Mind (Berelson); Self respect, Duty, Honesty and Recognition (Bansal, 1972); Physical, Recreational, Economic, Social, Democratic, Intellectual, Family value (Dixit, 1972); Personal and Community Value (Mathew, 1972), (Kulshrestha, 1979), Values in general, could be classified broadly under five headings; personal, social, moral, spiritual and behavioural (Venkataiah, 1998).

The above values are important to mould the personality of the students and to make them value-based citizens and all-round development can be achieved in the process of education.

Value Crisis in India

There is a great degeneration with respect to values of people in general. There is also devaluation of values in various aspects of life relating to political, social, philosophical, economic, commercial, educational, cultural and administrative and so many other fields. No conscious efforts are made by the educational authorities, to bring about value-orientation to the educational system as such. Values are only being referred incidentally in courses contained in the textbooks and in the discourses given by the teachers casually during their teaching activities. This is not sufficient enough to inspire the students' population to imbibe in themselves all the desirable moral and social values. Carefully planned and consciously prepared programmes should be organised in order to achieve the desired goals.

The Need of Values

- to guide the human beings in the right path and to inculcate the concept of 'universal brotherhood' and to achieve the absolute values of 'Truth, Goodness and Beauty;
- to guide or give direction and firmness to life and bring joy, satisfaction and peace of life, to preserve our culture and heritage and to develop morality and character;

— to bring the behavioural changes towards positivism;
— to develop the peace and harmony in the individuals and in the society;
— to bring quality of life and sustainable development in the society.

Value Education

Prior to National Policy on Education (NPE)—1986 the terms as religious education, moral education and character education were used but NPE (1986) for the first time coined it as "value education". Its scope is vast in comparison with moral and character education; therefore it was further fixed with specific meaning. Moral education or character education in fact is a part of value education.

Value education means inculcating in the children a sense of humanism, a deep concern for the well-being of others and the nation. This can be accomplished only when we instill in the children a deep feeling of commitment to values that would build this country and bring back to the people pride in work that bring order, security, and assured progress.

Value education has a capacity to transform a diseased mind into a very young, fresh, innocent, healthy, natural and attentive mind. The transformed mind is capable of higher sensitivity and a heightened level of perception (Venkataiah, 1998).

Ancient Indian education—Vedic, Buddhist and Islamic education laid stress on values. But with the arrival of the British and even after independence, value education has taken a back seat in educational institutions. The hope remains, however, the new outlook on education contained in the national policy, implementation strategies will be found, matter will improve and the country will benefit accordingly.

Mahatma Gandhi advocated the values of truth, non-violence and self-reliance which are unique in their relevance to everyday situations in the modern world. The University Education Commission (1948-49) has stressed that the comparative study of religions enables to inculcate the values of faith, courage, discipline and sacrifice.

The Indian Education Commission (1964-66) stressed on the balance development of human values that would come from the skills, morality and religion through the enhancement of science and technology. Democracy value, concept of welfare state, socialism and comprehensiveness of religions had given due importance in inculcation of values. It has stressed moral and spiritual values in order to provide civilised and cultured citizens. To educate in this direction the implemented of proper curriculum, school enterprises and atmosphere is a necessary as a part of education.

Role of School

Education being a social function has to discharge manifold social obligations. In fact, education is a social necessity and the school agency. In the recent times role of the school as an agency of education has been well appreciated. Home is the original social institution and it is the most significant informal agency of education. Hence, education is the joint responsibility of home, school and society.

Today, school stands for specialised and formal agency set-up by the society for imparting education to the rising generations. School extends the enrichment of home experiences. The experiences that are difficult to be assimilated in home atmosphere, are collected through medias of curricular, co-curricular and extra-curricular activities. The effect of school activities has a long-standing and becomes the part of personality.

Education conserves and perpetuates social life. School provides minimum general culture to all the pupils, trains in a manner that they enrich and modify the cultural heritage, to train in democratic methods so essential in democratic society, to prepare the children for post school adjustments. Thus, school helps in this establishment of a better and happier society, the child not only acquires knowledge but also develops the required habits, skills and attitudes. The school is a place where moral and democratic values are aimed at to be fostered among peoples.

The school has to provide total education, i.e., education for knowledge, for skills, for understanding, for culture, for making a contribution, for a sense of belonging, for attitudes and for a proper orientation to the modern world. The school is required to discharge very important functions of modern society. The UNESCO (1998) states that "schools serve at the very core in the efforts to provide the common basis of learning skills, knowledge, culture, respect for constructive achievement and adherence to common codes of behaviour which are essential to economic, social and cultural progress in society. When a society fails to recognise that this role must be played by organised education in the schools and under-values its educational system, the status accorded those responsible for the direct day-to-day performance of the educational function is necessarily reduced" (UNESCO, 1998).

Schools of every type fulfill their purpose in so far as they foster the free growth of individuality, helping every boy and girl to achieve the highest degree of individual development of which he is capable in and through the life of a society.

A search for truth, peace, good conduct, love and non-violence and the spirit of inquiry are the values realised through an open learning climate. Questioning and investigation are encouraged. Ideas, information and perspectives are shared. Austere living and inward discipline are prevalent in value-charged school environment. Functional autonomy to teachers and learning autonomy to students are ensured. The teacher is a facilitator promoting interactive learning experiences.

A teacher too must know that the ideal school is a second home, and that it is his duty to guide the growing child to unfold properly, so that later, he can take his place as an honored citizen in society. Improper behaviour on the part of students can be the result of 'soft discipline', 'heavy discipline', mal-adjustment to a rigid course of studies, harshness and lack of understanding, by over intellectual curricula or by failure to teach 'whole' child, by lack of personal guidance and lack of individual attention.

Finally, while selecting the values to be used in a school, it is important to see:

- that the student has been taught the process how to apply values in life, i.e. that their treatment is sufficiently debated to iron out the inhibitions and inconsistencies that might otherwise overtake a thoughtful person, and

- that in their application and object they find motives worth motivating. They have thus been helped to bring these values into accord with modern scientific view of the world and man, in this way completing the evolutionary profile and reducing the conflict situations that could otherwise arise.

Inculcation of Values among the Teachers and Students through the School Curricular, Co-curricular and Extra-curricular Activities

Value education can be achieved directly, indirectly or incidentally. Direct value inculcation refers to deliberate, systematic instruction given during the time of formation. Indirectly, value orientation can be imparted through the regular subjects of curriculum and co-curricular activities. Incidental value inculcation can be given through events and incidents related to good values occurring around us thus relating value inculcation to concrete situations.

1. The bad habits of the students of disoganised families can be corrected through teaching, learning and organising co-curricular activities, lectures from eminent personalities and creating healthy atmosphere at schools.

2. Value education should have a place of special subject in a school curriculum and integration system should be introduced which also related to social and economic conditions.

3. Problems especially of younger generation should be properly solved and the practical behaviour of the students must be evaluated according to age groups and problem solving method should become an integral part of school curriculum.

4. Value education will not be treated as an independent subject in curriculum but it should lead to integrated development through effective value based curriculum which would give justice to various learning

experiences through the media of subject units. Thus, the components of value education should be moral education, environmental education, population education, human rights and duties, Indian Culture, Art Education, Yoga, Health and Physical Education and History of India freedom movement.

5. Curriculum should be so arranged, that should lead to social, physical, emotional, intellectual and moral development of students.
6. The syllabus of primary, secondary and collegiate education should be so arranged that would bring out the objectives of national faith and unity, and human welfare.
7. Scouts and Guides, NCC and Physical Education should be provided to all the children at primary, secondary and collegiate level.
8. Consciousness about individual progress and progress of society should be created. Values in respect of democracy and culture should be inculcated. Political consciousness and international understanding should be created.
9. Meditation (Yoga) or prayer, occasional reading books and extracts of saints, great persons and philosophers can be arranged before and after the commencement of the routine academic programmes for greater inspiration for the students in the class or at school.
10. Stress should be given on the programmes of emotional integration. Self confidence while removing inferiority complexes and the inherent capacity should be developed.
11. Proper responsibility among students in respect of moral, spiritual, cultural and aesthetic sense should be developed.
12. Consciousness among students in respect of democracy, equality towards all religions, social equality and scientific outlook through value-oriented life based curriculum should be developed.

13. The values should not be inculcated among the learners by authoritarian instruction, exhortation or didactic approaches.
14. Freedom of thinking critically, feel responsibility and concern with courage and conviction should be developed among the students.
15. Majority of the teachers' goal is to promote passive conformity and blind obedience to their instructions. Thus this kind of practice should be avoided.

Activities to be Organised in the Schools to Impart Value Education

The following activities and programmes should be organised in the schools to impart value education among the students.

1. Literary activities to foster the reading habits, knowing the life histories and biographies of eminent role models should be given prior importance in the schools. The essay writing, elocution, poetry, debates competitions, lectures, seminars, work shops, symposia, book exhibitions etc. should be organised.
2. Cultural programmes should be organised while integrating the various cultural themes including drama, songs, music, mimicry, dance, theatre art, film shows, folklore at schools. The inter-school and inter-collegiate competitions, religious festivals, celebrating birth/death anniversaries of the priests and prophets, youth exchange programmes, fields trips and excursions to the historical places etc.
3. Science fares and technological exhibitions, science work shops, seminars and extension lectures, awareness programmes on health and environment, population education, observing important days on science and scientists, scientific achievements and science contribution to human welfare should be organised in the schools.
4. The physical and health education should be given due importance. The inter-school and inter-collegiate, inter-

region, sports, games, tournaments, camps, training/orientation should be conducted. Yoga, meditation also be given importance.

5. The school organisation climate should be properly maintained so that the desirable learning environment fosters the value inculcation among the students. The inter-personal relationships among the students, teachers and the administrators also help in the proper development of human and social relationships.
6. The parent-teachers associations and the school and village education committees and the involvement of the community participation also create a congenial atmosphere in the inculcation of positive and right values among the teachers, parents and the students.
7. The proper maintenance of the school environment, keeping the camps clean and green, proper utilisation of the resources enables the students to feel responsible in their schools.
8. The work experience and SUPW activities develop a positive value towards the work culture, dignity of labour and the proper utilisation of the leisure time. The group and team work develops the spirit of unity among the students.
9. Proper socialisation activities should be conducted in the school campus to enhance their social responsibility and positive behaviour towards the society.
10. Proper guidance and counselling should be arranged to the students to solve the problems of adjustment give a right direction.
11. The alumni of successful students of the school should be invited to inspire the younger generations.
12. The teacher day celebrations, the self-government day and the national festivals should be conducted to foster respect towards the teaching community and to develop patriotism.

13. All the teachers and the headmasters of the schools should act as the role models to the students in preaching and practicing the values.
14. The community and social issues should be brought to the notice of all the students to develop awareness among the students. The community participation and the social service activities should be emphasised in the school programmes.
15. All teachers are teachers of value education whether they are formally involved or not in the programme.
16. The school atmosphere, the personality and behaviour of teachers, the facilities provided in the school have a large say in developing a sense of values.
17. The school itself should act as the centre of the resource and excellence in inculcating the values while bridging the gap between the home, school and the community.

Finally, an 'Ideal School' is a 'Second home' and the teachers are parents in absentia and should give the same education to other children as they would like to give to their own children. In this regard the teachers, principles and other staff should take formal Oath of allegiance to the ethics of their profession like other professions.

REFERENCES

Bhatia. K.K. (1983), *Principles and Practice of Education*, Kalyani, New Delhi.

Chaube and Chaube (1999), *Education in Ancient and Medieval India*, Vikas, New Delhi.

Chilana, M.R., Dewan, M.L. (1998), *The Human Values—A Task for All*, Concept Publishing, New Delhi.

Gawande, E.N. (2002), *Value Oriented Education (Vision for Better Living)*, Sarup & Sons, New Delhi.

Kulshrestha, S.P. (1979), *Emerging Value-Pattern of Teachers and New Trends of Education in India*, Light & Life, New Delhi, pp. 28-33.

Mascranahas. M, Justa. H.R. (1989), *Value Education in Schools and Other Essays*, Konark, New Delhi.

Narayana Karan Reddy, V. (1979), *Man, Education and Values*, B.R. Publishing, New Delhi.

Satya Pal Ruhela, (1990), *Human Values and Education*, Sterling, New Delhi.

Sharma, S.R. (1999), *Education and Democratic Values*, Cosmo, New Delhi.

UNESCO (1998), *World Education Report*, UNESCO Publishing, Paris.

Venkataiah, N. (1998), *Value Education*, APH Publishing Corporation, New Delhi, p. 3.

30

Values and Teacher Education System

Dr. B. Ramachandra Reddy*

What are Values?

Values are the guiding principles, decisive in day to day behaviours as also is critical life situations. Values are a set bring of principles or standards of behaviour. Values are regarded desirable, important and held in high esteem by a particular society in which a person lives. Thus values give meaning and strength to a person is character by occupying a central place in his life. Values reflect one's personal attitudes and judgements, decisions and choices, behaviour and relationships, dreams and vision. They influence our thoughts, feelings and actions. They guide us to do the right things.

Values are the guiding principles of life which are conductive to all-round development. They give direction and firmness to life and bring joy, satisfaction and peace of life. Values are like the rails that keep a train on the track and help it move smoothly, quickly and with direction. The qualities to life.

What is Value Education?

Value education means inculcating in the children a sense humanism, a deep concern for the well being of others and the

* Dr. B. Ramachandra Reddy, Professor and Dean, Faculty of Education, Department of Education, S.V. University, Tirupati–517 502, Andhra Pradesh, (India).

nation. This can be accomplished only when we instill in the children a deep feeling of commitment to values that would build this country and bring back to the people pride in work that brings order, security and assured progress.

Through value education, we like to develop the social, moral, aesthetic and spiritual sides of a person which are often undermined in formal education. Value education teaches us to preserve whatever is good and worthwhile in what we have inherited from our culture. It helps us to respect the attitude and behaviour of those who differ from us. Value education does not mean value imposition or indoctrination.

Value education has the capacity to transform a diseased mind into a very young, fresh, healthy, natural and attentive mind. The transformed mind is capable of higher sensitivity and a heightened level of perception. This leads to fulfillment of the evolutionary role in man and in life. Values in general, could be classified broadly under five headings—personal, social, moral, spiritual and behavioural.

Education in general and value education in particular occupies a prestigious place in the modern context of the contemporary society. The problem of value education of the young has assumed increasing prominence in educational discussions during recent times. Parents, teachers, administrators and society at large are concerned about values and value education of children.

"The destiny of India is now being shaped in her classroom", this is the opening sentence of the Kothari Education Commission report (1964-66). What kind of destiny has been actually shaped during the last forty years?

Nature of Values

The number of values is unlimited. The NCERT listed 83 values. It is unmanageable to deal with so many values in schools. Under the Satya Sai Organisation, these 83 values are classified and grouped under the five well known prime values. These five are: Sathya (Truth), Dharma (Righteousness), Prema (Love in its broadest sense), Shanti (Peace) and Ahimsa (Non-violence) in various forms and actions, thoughts, feelings etc.

We have the Constitution of India which we are bound to follow: Major values embedded therein are: (1) Justice, Equality, and Fraternity; and (2) Democracy, Secularism, and Social Justice.

Next we have individual and personal values: Cleanliness, Neatness, Punctuality, Regularity, Industriousness, Healthcare, Honesty, Self-respect, Self-reliance etc.

We must add values necessary for peace and harmony. These are concern and compassion for others, co-operation, self-sacrifice, national integrity and unity and world/universal brotherhoods. For all values, the approach has to be through a spirit of enquiry, pursuit of truth, logical thinking, open mindedness, sharing and a scientific bent of mind. Again, the list has become too big. So the core principle is:

1. The enjoy life; and
2. Helps others to enjoy it, without harming anybody.

Here in lies the morality of all religious.

Values in Indian Society

There has been a rapid Erosion of Ethical and Moral Values (EEMV) in Indian society after independence. Before independence we were economically poor, our health conditions were deplorable and child morality rates were very high. We had very few universities and almost no heavy industry. Our agricultural production was very low and very often we faced famines. After independence, we have made rapid process in agriculture and industry, in education and in almost every sector of our life. Our progress may not have been as spectacular as that of Korea of Japan. But it is certainty of a level of which we can be proud.

However, we had one thing before independence which we have lost now in a big measure and that was our character and our sense of ethical and moral values. We were then fighting the mighty British Empire with truth and non-violence. We had a noble goal and we were using only noble means. We held our heads high and could give sermons on character and moral values to all nations and we commanded a great deal of respect. Everybody here had a sense of national pride and patriotism and a full faith that once we win our freedom, we shall be able to perform miracles due to our moral and spiritual strengths.

After independence, we made rapid strides in all fields, but we lost our character and pride in our values. It is said that if an individual loses his wealth, he losses nothing; if he losses his health, he loses something; but if he loses his character, he loses everything. What is true of individuals is also true of nations.

What is the situation today? Corruption, nepotism, favoritism are dominating features of our national life. It is true that there is also corruption in other countries of the world like USA and Japan, but there corruption is confined to highest levels only and when corruption is proved, the punishment is very heavy. Corruption there does not affect the daily lives of the people. Here we meet corruption at every point. There, 5 per cent persons may be affected by it, here 95 per cent are affected by it. There a person requires courage to the dishonest, here a person requires courage to be honest.

A child gets his/her first lesson in corruption, when his/her parents going to different quarters for getting recommendation for his/her admission to good schools or when he/she finds parents paying large "donations" for this purpose. In the school he/she finds the teachers not caring for teaching, but caring for building up influence with powerful persons, otherwise they can be transferred at short notice. A student finds that his/her father has to pay heavily for his/her private tuitions and if he cannot pay, the student suffers. The level of corruption gets magnified at the college level, and there the student learn from experience that the jobs are not available on merit, but on the basis of recommendations and even on the basis of money. The students finds all the attendance records are being forged by the teachers and he/she gets a big lesson in forgery. By the time he/she leave his/her college, he/she is convinced that honesty is the worst policy and having high ethical and moral values can be a big obstacle to progress in life.

Under these conditions everybody in society is miserable and everybody has a guilty conscience. How can a society be happy under the unhealthy conditions when it is infected throughout by deadly germs of EEMV?

EEMV is deadly a disease as AIDS. In fact EEMV appears to have killed our will power to fight it, in spite of knowing that due to EEMV our hard-earned freedom is itself in danger. When people want to get money by any means, the means may include selling the interests of the country to others. This is already happening and the manifestations of it are large scale smuggling. Criminalisation of politics, and poor quality of our industrial products. Even our armaments are below world standards because of corruption and the low morale of our scientists and engineers because of EEMV.

Teacher Education System

"Values are to be brought and not taught," is a very old saying. It was perhaps true in days goneby when parents at home and leaders in community in various walks of life were all value-based people. Therefore younger children and growing adolescents could catch values of elderly people are either by imitation or by special efforts developed appropriate values accepted and respected in society. Much water has flowed under the bridge since then and there is a grave deterioration both among parents and community leaders in terms of their being value models for the younger generation. We cannot therefore expect values to be caught from undesirable situations and persons in society. In today's world, therefore values have got to be *taught in addition to being caught* from selected situations and personalities.

Teachers: In today's schools and colleges, we see a large number of teachers who are more often making money by fair means or foul. Such teachers are unscrupulous and stoop to unfair means for making a fast buck through indifference in teaching and conducting private tuition classes for extra income. This has led to malpractices in examinations by students and in some cases by teachers also. Besides this, we see teachers and lecturers, at least a considerable number, addicted to smoking, drinking and even gambling. Therefore, how can such teachers be entrusted with teaching of values to children? This however is a valid objection or doubt; but the answer does not lie in giving up value education altogether. We are in a vicious circle unless we inculcate values in school life, we cannot hope to get value oriented teachers in future.

On the other hand so long as teachers with bad habits are working in schools and colleges, value education cannot be effectively carried out.

Let we observe the teacher education system in the state of Andhra Pradesh, India. There are 305 B.Ed colleges for the academic year 2003-2004 which are running one year behind (April, 2004 to March, 2005). Among these, there are 7 Government colleges, 6 University colleges, 5 aided private colleges, 2 aided Christian minority college and 213 unaided non-minority private colleges, 44 unaided Christian Minority Colleges and and 28 unaided Muslim Minority colleges. There are 34003 B.Ed. students in these colleges. Four universities are running distance education B.Ed. course with 2000 students.

There 25 Hindi Pandit colleges. Out of which 3 are government and 22 are unaided colleges with 1600 students. There are 23 Telegu Pandit colleges. Out of which 5 are government and 18 are unaided colleges with 1150 students. There are 7 unaided Hindi Shikshak colleges with 420 students. There are 8 unaided Hindi Pracharak colleges with 480 students. There are 2 unaided Urdu Pandit colleges with 100 students. There are 3 government and aided and one unaided B.P.Ed. colleges with 285 students.

There are 24 government district institutes of education and training (DIETs) with 2157 students. There are 9 government and aided M.Ed. colleges and 5 unaided M.Ed colleges with 312 students.

Through all these teacher training colleges and institutes in the state of Andhra Pradesh, 42507 student are trained per year. Out of which 36003 are the B.Ed. students.

Let us discuss the system of B.Ed. colleges in the state of Andhra Pradesh. The admissions are done through state-wide Education Common Entrance Test (Ed.CET). All the seats in Government, Universities and Private aided colleges are filled by the Convener, Ed.CET on the basis of merit and rule of reservation.

In unaided non-minority private colleges, 85 per cent of the seats are filled by the convener and 15 per cent of the seats by the concerned managements. In unaided minority collages all the 100 per cent seats are filled by the concerned managements. From 1996 every year on an average about 15000 teachers posts in Government schools are filled through state-wide recruitment test and district Selection Committees. Hence there is a tremendous demand for admissions in B.Ed. Colleges. B.Eds are also eligible fcr secondary grade teacher/primary school teacher posts. Because of this the unaided minority colleges and unaided non-minority private colleges are minting money through management seats. The government fixed Rs. 10,000 as tuition fee and Rs. 800 as special fee per student for the entire B.Ed. course for students admitted through convener in unaided non-minority B.Ed. colleges. But the managements of the colleges are collecting from each student huge amounts unauthorisedly in the name of B.Ed. records fee, practical examination fee, computer lab fee etc.

According to NCTE and government of Andhra Pradesh qualified full-time teaching staff have to be recruited by the managements as per norms and standards. Out of 305 B.Ed colleges only 20 are the aided and 285 are unaided. Especially these private unaided colleges produce the required qualified teaching staff for NCTE teams and affiliation commissions. But most of those staff members are working as full-time employees in government and private schools, Junior Colleges, degree colleges and other institutions. In some B.Ed. colleges hardly there are two or three full-time teaching staff members. The student strength in each B.Ed. college is 100 or more. For a student strength of 100, the required full-time teaching staff is 8. In most of the colleges a lecturer is paid less than Rs. 7500 p.m. In some colleges even less than Rs. 5000 p.m. Most of the private managements try to trap the NCTE teams and university affiliation commissions to get their favour in getting things to be done.

In the name of some function or the other, religious institution/mutt, similar, conference etc. the university officials are collecting money/donations from the unaided private managements. There are no surprise visits either by the universities or Government Officials or NCTE officials during the working days for students. The staff working in the unaided colleges are at the good looks of the managements. Some of the lectures are resorting to unethical means during valuation of practical work and theory papers.

Unless the above things are set righted, we cannot expect values from the trainees and teacher educators and hence from the school education and teacher education system.

Role of Universities

The universities have to play strategic role in set righting the system of education. The following roles are suggested:

1. If we adopt the educational system with its complete openness, with almost no secrecy, with complete democratic functioning, with no arbitrary powers, with every group being accountable to others, with decentralisation of authority and so on, the politicians and bureaucrats will not be able to interfere in the system. The critical areas are admissions, examinations and appointments and once these are fair and appear to be fair and once a student has lived for 4 or 5 years in an environment of fairness and impartiality, he will exert his influence in all sectors of life on coming out of the university. Once we can demonstrate that Erosion of Ethical and Moral Values (EEMV) can be removed in one sector of our life, we would have taken the first major step in restoring the moral health of the nation.
2. The intellectuals in the universities have the responsibility to design political, social, economic and other systems in such a way that they become corruption free. The systems should be open, transparent and decentralised. With our knowledge of political science, economics and social systems and of psychology of human beings, the university academics should be able to design such systems based on mutual accountability. Of course the vested interests will resist such systems and for this reason we have not only to design the systems, but we have to lobby for them.
3. After examining our educational system in depth, it is convinced that given the will and faith, we in the universities can help our nation by designing such systems and working for them. Let us pool all our resources and help in building up such corruption proof systems for our society.

Conclusion

Value crisis is growing at a faster speed than the galloping strides of science. Hence despite man's process and material prosperity, peace and happiness will elude him because of the inward turmoil of feelings and attitudes. In more than 90 per cent of homes, desirable value inculcation becomes impossible due to various reasons. Politics, economics, industry and even cultural activities are becoming more and more barren of values. Even religious heads have slipped into the traps of materialistic temptations. Spiritual favour has become an insignificant appendage at the periphery of Mutts, monasteries and mosques. Schools are only hope of sustaining ethics in life.

It is, however obvious that success in value education/ inculcation depends upon the enthusiasm and commitment of teachers and managements/Government. Let us emphasise that, *"value education/inculcation is not an additional subject. It should permeate all work and activities in educational institutions like a Guardian angel"*.

Values therefore have to be inculcated through deliberate effort and not left to chance. Values have to be both *caught* and *taught*.

REFERENCES

1. Prof. S.R. Rohi Dekar, *Inculcation of Values How?* Sri Rukma Prakashana, 66, Ist Cross, 5th Main, Padmanabha Nagar, Bangalore—70, 2nd Edition, 2003.
2. Dr. N. Venkataiah, *Value Education*, Editor, APH Publishing Corporation, 5, Ansari Road, Daryaganj, New Delhi—110 002, First Edition, 1998.
3. Usha Rani Negi, *Value Education in India*, Editor, Published by Association of Indian Universities, AIU House, 16 Kotla Marg, New Delhi, 2000.

31

Promoting Values in Professional Teacher Education

R.H. Naik*

Introduction

It is always to understand the changes taking place in a particular society and accordingly to prepare the teachers for that society. The stresses these are creating on the established traditional values also need to be understood continuously through the institutional activities and programmes. From this emerges the need for a regular programme of development and action research in the institution. Every institution and each teacher could think of utilising the 'thought for the day'; morning assembly; meditation, story telling, prayers, community singing, festivals, days of national importance; social activities etc., for ensuring a loving environment that would be conducive to the education for and internalisation of human values. While organising activities in institutions, it has to be ensured that in all programmes, celebrations, gatherings and significant occasions, no religious or cultural group is neglected or isolated. The institutional response to emerging situations like floods, fire, droughts also make learners realise the need for cooperative action and combined efforts in life. It is also established that young students and student leaders if tackled carefully by the teachers, they would certainly show the best within them.

* **Lecturer, University College of Education, Karnataka University, Dharwad-580 001 (Karnataka).**

Value

Values are regarded desirable, important and held in high esteem by a particular society in which a person lives. Thus values give meaning and strength to a person's character by occupying a central place in his life. Values reflect one's personal attitudes and judgements, decisions and choices, behaviour and relationships, dreams and vision. They influence our thoughts, feelings and actions. They guide us to do the right things.

Values are the guiding principles of life which are conducive to all-round development. They give direction and firmness to life and bring joy, satisfaction and peace to life. Values are like the rails that keep a train on the track and help it moves smoothly, quickly and with direction. They bring quality to life.

Finally we can say that, any human activity, thought or idea, feeling, sentiment or emotion, which could promote self-development of the individual in all its dimensions could be said to constitute a value. The other complementary function of a value is it should also contribute to the welfare of the larger social unit such as the family, the community and the nation of which the individual is a member.

Value Education

Value education means inculcating in the children a sense of humanism, a deep concern for the well being of others and the nation. This can be accomplished only when we instill in the children a deep feeling of commitment to values that would build this country and bring back to the people pride in work that brings order, security and assured progress.

Through value education we like to develop the social, moral, aesthetic and spiritual sides of a person which are often undetermined in formal education. Value education teaches us to preserve whatever is good and worthwhile in what we have inherited from our culture. It helps us to accept respect, the attitude and behaviour of those who differ from us. Value education does not mean value imposition or indoctrination.

Value education has the capacity to transform a diseased mind into a very young, fresh, innocent, healthy, and attentive mind. The transformed mind is capable of higher sensitivity and a heightened level of perception. This leads fulfillment of the evolutionary role in man and in life.

All-round development of the child—its head, heart and hand, is emphasised in basic education proposed by Gandhiji. He identified certain values as the bases for the establishment of a new social order in India. They are truth, non-violence, democracy, sarvadharma, equality self-realisation, self-discipline and cleanliness.

Objectives

The main aim of value-oriented education is to make the students good citizens who may share their responsibility in the changing set-up of the society in order to give the desired shape and image to the society and the country at large. The following can be enumerated as the general objectives:

- To promote in student-teacher such basis and fundamental qualities as truthfulness, co-operation, love and compassion, peace and non-violence, courage, equality, justice, dignity of labour, common brotherhood of man, scientific temper;
- To train student teachers to become responsible citizens in their personal and social lives;
- To enable them to understand and appreciate the national goals of socialism and democracy and to contribute to their realisation;
- To create in them an awareness of the socio-economic condition, and to motivate them to improve the same;
- To enable them to become open-minded and considerate in their thought and behaviour and rise above prejudices based on religion, language, caste or sex;
- To help them understand and appreciate themselves and continually strive for their inner-development and

becoming thus moving towards the goal of self-actualisation; and

- To develop in them proper attitudes:
  - (a) Towards one self and fellow beings;
  - (b) Towards one's own country;
  - (c) Towards people of other countries, leading to international understanding;
  - (d) Towards life and environment; and
  - (e) Towards all religions.

Educational institutions are the places to prepare the future citizens. A proper value system must be inculcated by educational institutions through educational process based on rationality, scientific and moral approach to life, and hence a need of value-oriented teachers. It was recommended in the report of Education Commission (1964-66). "The destiny of India is now being shaped in her classrooms". Our educational institutions can play a vital role in this regard. Educational institutions can impart values to influence human life along with imparting general instructions.

Teacher education at the pre-service level should focus on preparing teachers with adequate skills to develop proper value system among children. The values are inherent in the school subjects, for example, Science aims to develop values like neatness, cleanliness, the systematic approach, the rational approach etc. social studies aims at developing socialism, secularism, nationalism, equality, social justice, etc. The teachers should understand the values inherent in the subjects and try to highlight those values while teaching. So during teacher training, the values should be integrated with the methodology of teaching and practice teaching.

As teachers are supposed to look after the total development of children and their performance is the most crucial input in the field of education (POA, 1992), their training should be adequate to stimulate the socio-cultural and moral development of the child. Hence, an immediate breakthrough is necessary in our teacher education programme, so that it can meet the challenge of value crisis among our younger generation.

There are different approaches for value inculcation. But it is very difficult to select a specific approach for value inculcation. It is always situation specific. Any approach of value inculcation would be useful if the teachers are motivated and willing to do it with real spirit. Generally, the approaches adopted to inculcate values are from amongst the following:

(i) A specific subject in the curriculum like value education.

(ii) No specific subject but integrated across subjects such as social studies, languages, sciences, SUPW etc.

(iii) Both specific subject in the curriculum and integration across subjects.

(iv) Infuse through the non-formal school programmes such as extra curricular activities and school projects, school assemblies, campaigns, school discipline and reward systems etc.

(v) Parent-teacher and parent-school interaction; and

(vi) Traditional system of imparting religious based education.

The role of teachers is quiet significant in the development of society. Teacher are the real nation builders. It is the teacher community who moulds the future society. Teachers are the section of society who can influence the future generation towards a positive attitude with a healthy value base. The extent of influence which a teacher castes upon the children is well known and understood. The teacher is the role model for the child and what they imbibe gets multiplied subsequently in the society.

A teacher easily inculcate values if he has professionalism and love towards his profession and children. Love is the eternal value through which a real teacher can inculcate other values of life among children. There is no need of prescribing any method to teach values for a devoted teacher who loves his pupils.

The pragmatic, skill oriented and responsive teacher education programmes will help to prepare skilled teachers through in-service and pre-service programmes. The products of these programmes should necessarily have the following traits in the context of value education.

(i) Capacity to observe learners and analyse their needs to provide the necessary inputs, through deep insight and understanding and concern;

(ii) Involvement, tact in dealing with individual as well as group behaviour of learners and capacity to understand and utilise the same;

(iii) Develop through well cultivated interest, capability to motivate and encourage learners in the art of self learning. Furthermore, the teacher has to become a partner in this processes as well;

(iv) Ability to guide and counsel, more by suggesting and by practical examples than by preaching;

(v) Interesting in identifying and utilising more formal and informal situations through different techniques;

(vi) Conceptual understanding of the art and science of developing human personality in all its aspects with emphasis on integration, harmony, truth, beauty and excellence;

(vii) Pleasing, cheerful disposition, capable of inspiring students to pursue values, morals, ethics and excellence with sincerity and devotion; and

(viii) Willingness to establish close rapport with the community, parents and others working on voluntary basis on social and educational aspects.

To develop these qualities among teachers, the major role would be played by the teacher training institutions. Those institutions should work in a pragmatic way to enrich teachers with adequate attitude, interest and skills. Here the task is tedious. But it can be achieved, may be in a long run if proper planning and implementation would be done by individual teacher training organisations and the apex bodies like NCTE and UGC.

Suggestions

Following may be taken as specific suggestions for promoting value in teacher education programme to prepare teachers with adequate, skills, interests and attitude for developing values among children.

(i) *An Alternative:* An integrated teacher education programme like B.Sc. B.Ed., B.A. B.Ed., having four years of duration suggested by the National Commission on Teachers, the National Policy on Education and the National Council of Teacher Education which is also experimented as effectively in Kurukshetra University, Regional Institutes of Education and Gandhigram Rural Institute, should be adopted.

(ii) *Residential:* Residential teacher education progammes should be encouraged, which would maximise human relations. Ample scope to work with community should be given to teacher trainees.

(iii) *Face to Face Programme:* Legal steps should be taken to stop pre-service teacher education through distance modes, which has less practicability. Steps taken by NCTE was quite encouraging which was in the form of press notes through newspapers and magazines, like "considering the knowledge, skills, attitudes and values that need to be developed in the teacher at the school for effective discharge of his function, the NCTE has decided that, pre-service teacher education for the first degree/diploma should be only through face-to-face institutional courses of teacher education of a minimum of one academic year duration". Further NCTE advised candidates aspiring to join teacher training course, not to join any course other than face-to-face full time course.

(iv) *In Service Programme:* Adequate provision should be there to orient in-service teachers through different modes with enriched materials/packages on value education. Compulsory in-service training programmes of at least face-to-face one month duration for teachers should be organised by teacher training institutes. It should be at least once in every years of service.

(v) *Curriculum:* Need-based and value-based curriculum relevant to Indian society should be there in teacher education, which has been clearly visualised by NCTE.

It should be integrated and interdisciplinary in approach. It should be task-oriented and practical. It would promote productivity and community services. The components of spiritual and moral teachings should not be ignored. It should be imparted carefully. The CABE (1945) recommended the same thing that spiritual and moral teachings, common to all religions, should be an integral part of the curriculum.

(vi) *Competencies:* In order to achieve the objectives of values oriented education, teacher trainees and teacher educators need to develop following competencies:

— Philosophy of education

— Society, culture and education

— International understanding

— Current problems of Indian education

— Knowledge and understanding of methods, media and approaches useful in teaching school subjects

— Content mastery and modern trends in education

— Accountability, honesty, commitment and love for profession

— Rationality, objectives, integrity, positiveness, critical thinking and inquiry mind

— Sharing, team spirit, participative and open mindedness

— Self-control/self restraint and self confidence

— Good and suspended judgement

— Persuasiveness, assertiveness and adaptability

— Industriousness, service mindedness and dignity of labour

— Forgiveness, sympathy and patience, and

— Non-violence and respect for democracy

(vii) *Objectives:* The objectives of teacher education should be redefined in the light of value-oriented education.

(viii) *Networking:* Proper networking should be established between teacher training institutions like, university teaching departments, CTEs, DIETs, etc. (POA 1992).

(ix) *Present System:*

— The teacher educator should use progressive methods of teaching. He/she should involve trainees in discussions, activities, projects, practicals, independents study and observations.

— At the time of practice teaching, the value components of school subjects should be reflected in general and specific objectives and evaluation. One more specific teaching point in the name of 'value added/included' should be incorporated in the lesson plans.

— Universal values should be practiced in day-to-day life of students, teachers, and teacher educators.

— Co-curricular activities like NCC, NSS, Scout, field trips etc. should occupy a dominant position in the teacher education programme. At least one activity should be compulsory for teacher trainees. It has been the experience of many heads of institutions that group activities and participatory programmes like dances, dramas, sports, national integration campaign become much more effective when staff members also participate and enliven the total learning environment.

— Experts from philosophy, yoga ethics and moral values should be invited to give lectures on values. The teacher educators should demonstrate the human values through their day-to-day dealings with trainees. They should be models of politeness and tolerence, love and kindness, discipline and character.

— There should be orientation courses for all teacher educators of every institution of teacher education for 3-4 days in the beginning of every session to focus their attention on the need, goals and means of value-orientation of teacher education curricula.

— Theory courses at all levels of teachers education should be revised and revitalised incorporating in them value content, new ideas, concepts and progressive outlook.

— In order to change the climate of passivity and culture of mediocrity, the institutions should encourage seminars, discussions in the classes, in the faculty and in the community.

Conclusion

Education without vision is waste; education without value is crime; education without mission is life burden". Education in our life enables us to become comfortable and to look after our family well. But so far as the social progress is concerned, value-based education is an unavoidable necessity. "A nation with atomic power is not a strong nation; but a nation with people with strong character is indeed a strong nation". If a nation is to be strong, then the character of the people of that nation needs to be elevated. For this purpose, value-based education is an indispensable device.

I wish to conclude by saying "Values are not to be taught, but to be caught". Once this is realised by a teacher educator, half the task is done.

REFERENCES

1. Gupta, N.L. (1986) *Value Education: Theory and Practice*. Krishna Brothers, Ajmer.
2. Ministry of Human Resource Development Govt. of India, (1992) *Programme of Action*, New Delhi.
3. NCTE, (1978) *Teacher Education Curriculum: A Frame Work*, New Delhi.
4. Pandurangi, K.T. *et. al.* (1999) *Indian Thoughts on Human Values*. Gandhi Centre of Science and Human Values, Bangalore.
5. Ruhela, S.P. (1986) *Human Values and Education*, Sterling Publishers Private Limited, New Delhi.
6. Venkataiah, N. (1998) *Value Education*. S.B. Nangia for APH Publishing Corporation, New Delhi.

32

Educational Values Fostered Through Distance Education

Dr. S. Thavamani*

Introduction

The vision of developed India 2020 put forward by the President of India which presents a huge challenge before the country. The vision—2020 refers to quality education. Quality improvement in educational sector is the only mantra to develop India by 2020. Therefore, educational sector should strive for the quality on its own. In order to establish quality education the education system itself should possess its standards in the form of educational values. The education system which may reconstruct the society must be capable to mould the mode of thinking, behaviour and promotes mental excellencies. Man becomes 'man' through education. He is what education makes him.

Education for Today and Tomorrow

We can say that an education for today and tomorrow must be an education which prefers for social changes, seen and as yet unforeseen, prepares them not only in terms of skills, but in terms of character, perspective and a personality capable of adopting wholesomely to new situations.

* **Assistant Director-Cum-Lecturer, Directorate of Distance Education, S.V. University, Tirupati–517 502 (A.P.)**

Educational Values

Educational values are enduring preferences for certain modes of conduct (e.g. honest) or life situations (e.g. inner peace). They usually cluster to born a value system in which particular values are ordered according to a certain priority of importance. According to social scientists, these values are learned—they do not come "Pre-package" in the newborn baby, education has been significantly contributes for the development of these values in man in the form of personal development. Value education has the capacity to transform a diseased mind into a very young, fresh, innocent, healthy, natural and attentive mind. The transformed mind is capable of higher sensitivity and a heightened level of perception. This leads to fulfillment of the evolutionary role in man and in life.

Value Crisis Today

Advancements in science and technology have minimised the distance and made whole world a global village. No doubt science made man more sophisticated and also mad. Man physically so comfortable but mentally frustrated. What made him frustrated? Erosion of values in the human life is the sole cause for these frustrations. In olden days life was said to be relatively, peaceful, free from tensions, anxieties and depressions from which the present man is suffering. Modern life has brought forward several types of challenges to man—climatic, inflectional physical emotional. Emotional challenges relatively produce a much more powerful strain on the human system, in spite of the compensatory automatic process in the body itself.

Place of Values in the Modern Education System

Old values are fast disappearing and the pity is that so far, we have not established new ones. The increasing gap between spiritual and material values is responsible for the present world-wide unrest, incidents of indiscipline and moral degeneration. Therefore the present generation is confused and led astray.

Distance Education

Distance education is a new trend and new innovation in the field of education, which has an immediate socio-economic relevance as well as philosophical basis. In India the system has grown into a dynamic and vibrant system of teaching and learning that boasts of 11 open universities and more than so distance education institutes attached to the regular Universities (Mishra, 2003). Masses of educated people have been produced every year through this system. As a social service education is catering to the requirements of the individuals in society. The inculcation of such qualities as courage and endurance, honesty and integrity, selfless devotion and patriotism, passion for truth and clarity as against emotionalism and hide-bound ideas appear to be the primary task of education in India.

One of the reasons for shifting from conventional to non-conventional mode of education called distance education in the complementary society is the challenge posed by a larger percentage of the youth in the society. The youth stage in the life of an individual is an important and crucial stage which tends to bring several changes—physical, emotional and intellectual—in his life, and may cause damage to his personality unless proper care is taken.

Today's experience shows that in the world youth are falling as easy preys in the hands of deviant elements, turning them to be anti-social elements. Keeping in mind these negative consequences, society needs to take up vigorous action in providing proper education and training to the youth. This will not only enrich self-confidence, self-control and feeling of sense of belongingness, division of labour and dignity of labour in the youth but also encourages them to be active participants in the developmental activities of the society. As formal type of education can not provide this type of facility to the people distance education provides an answer to these challenges.

It is because distance education is known for providing cost-effective education with wider accessibility, higher productivity and greater flexibility. Distance education system serves the youth, who can not get seat in the formal education system and it also serves the dropouts, deprived ones, working adults, retired people and house wives.

Is if Possible to Develop Values in Distance Learners?

The "Distance" aspect of distance learning takes away much of the social interactions that would be present in traditional learning environment. Geographical isolation has been identified as one of the major problems for distance students. In addition to the practical problems of contacting academic and administrative staff, obtaining study materials and borrowing library books, distance education suffer from the disadvantage of being unable to interact with other students and are often denied the perception that they belong to the scholarly community. This may lead to feelings of inadequacy and insecurity, and a lack of confidence in their own abilities.

Distance students are also at the risk of dropping out unless they develop study survival skills as rapidly as possible. Another problem encountered by distance students is the lack of student training, particularly in reference to technical issues. Many adult students are not well versed in the uses of technology such as computers and the Internet. Using electronic medium in distance learning can inadvertently exclude students who lack computer and writing skills. (Monika Mahajan—2004). Though the system is facing number of problems with respect to quality, the dramatic growth of the adult learner population is making distance learning an increasingly popular choice of learning techniques. The system today accepted, assimilated and absorbed the fast growing and emerging area of information and communication technology ensuring-cost effective, flexible education, with global access. Now, the system is emerged as new, pragmatic and more dynamic in providing high quality course material with multimedia and ICT (Information Communication Technology) inputs to support and strengthen the learning process.

The use of ICT allows us to address the issues of quantity, quality access and success. Therefore, here also the educational values can be developed using the improved technology systematically and in a proper path.

How Can Distance Education Meets the Challenge of Today

Distance education system also can impart value education as follows:

- Providing value incorporated high quality study material.
- Regular and periodical on line touch with the students.
- Arranging debates, discussions on leaders of national and international importance and scientists.
- Arranging guest lectures on social awareness programmes.
- Value based education in the form of assignments.
- Introducing the project work on national leaders, religious, morals, work of community importance—taken into consideration for internal assessment.

These sort of work should be planned, developed and implemented for the development of value education in distance learners.

Educational Values Developed in Distance Education

The educational values developed in distance learners are:

1. Co-operation

Distance learners associate for some time during their contact classes and exams. They develop a sort of mutual co-operation in learning, taking notes, making notes, discussions and also they maintain correspondence with the co-learners and teachers.

2. Learning while Earning

Here majority of the learners are earning members, it may be government or private employment, because they are adults. As a part time job they are coming to learn. They keep learning as a life-long process once they entered into the distance education, join one course after the other. In the changing economies of society life-long education really caters to the needs of people to develop either new skills or to improve their already existing skills or qualifications to face the competition posed by the new system of economies. Today life-long education has brought several changes in the attitudes of the people. It gives tension-free education.

3. Self-reliant

Self study in distance education makes the learner self responsible, self confident and self development.

4. Hard Work

Because they feel nobody is there to give spoon feeding to them. They themselves have to do the hard work to go through the exam and other formalities. They take their own risk.

5. Independent Study

In traditional system of education some one cares for the student. Here learners are adults they themselves have to take care of them. This kind of independent study develops self-responsibility in the learner.

6. Oneness

In this system of education there is no discrimination on age, sex, caste, region and religion. Anybody can join in any course. They meet at least during contact classes and during the final exams. Therefore, unity in diversity developed.

7. Equality

In Distance Education System educational opportunities are equal. Courses are varied. They can choose their course on their own interest. All are equal here. All are treated equal. By involving in this system 'equality' concept will be developed in the learners.

8. Social Awareness

Some people due to ragging, or fear to go to college will be dropped from the traditional system of education such people join here. While coming and going from distance places to the study centres, internet centres, social awareness will be created in the learner.

9. Dignity of the Labour

Distance learners take their own risk in learning, it develops dignity of labour in the learners.

10. Fearlessness

Learners in the distance education system attend the contact classes, exams at the every centres or nodal centres. For this purpose they have to go far places/distant places, fear of travelling alone will be decreased especially in women students.

All these values are developed apart from the intellectual values.

Conclusion

Truth, beauty and goodness were the supreme values of ancient India and they served as the guiding lights for men in their lives. In the present materialistic era, there is evidently an urgent need for developing a better sense of values and qualities of character among the youth. Whatever may be education system, parents and teacher too, require a proper sense of values and religious education. Work environment and culture in the non-conventional mode i.e. Distance mode of education is more demanding. To make 'Vision of Developed India—2020', a practical reality, our policy planners, distance educations requires to design suitable modalities to infuse relevance and quality in distance learning adopting innovative research oriented approach.

REFERENCES

1. Amitabh Mattoo, 2004, *Journal of Distance Education*.
2. Bhatia and Narang—1988, *'Principles of Education'* Published by Prakash Brothers.
3. Gadgil, 1978, *Value Oriented Education, Strategy it for Action in Maharashtra*.
4. Mishra, S (2003): Human Resource Planning and Development for Distance Education in India, University News, 41 (46), pp. 8-13.
5. Monika Mahajan, 2004. "Distance Education; Problems of Quality". J. of *Dis. Education*, Vol. XI, No. 1.
6. Siddhasharma *et al.*, 2003, Problems and Perspectives of Social Philosophy *ICSP*.
7. Venkataiah, N. *Value Education An Overview*.

33

Value Education

Contribution of Home Science in the Promotion of Values

Dr. R.K. Anuradha*

Introduction

Value education means a positive effort for bringing about a synthesis of physical, intellectual, emotional, moral and spiritual values in a human being.

The importance of value education cannot be minimised in a democratic country like India. In a democratic country control of people's behaviour with coercive methods is not possible. Hence, the only alternative way left is to teach the masses to be self controlled, which is possible only when they are made to learn certain values as values are the prime movers of human action. Once formed, values begin to control and direct human actions. Hence, teaching of desirable value should be the major concern of the system of education. Values are foundation stones of national solidarity. So let us have a discussion about some aspects of values. Value education and contribution of home science in promoting values.

* **Lecturer, Institute of Advanced Studies in Education, Sri Padmavathi Mahila, Visvavidyalayam, Tirupati—517 505**

Concept of Value

Value literally means something that has a price, precious, dear and worthwhile; hence something one is ready to suffer and sacrifice for. In other words value are a set of principles of standards of behaviour.

Value is what is desired, liked or preferred. Values refer to those things that man desire, like prefer, and men do in fact desire many things like money, power, food, clothing shelter wealth and adventure. Men do not desire certain other things, e.g. suffering pain, hunger, poverty and ignorance. The desires of men extend from highly concrete, mundane, petty and immediate desires to lofty, general, ultimate and abstract ideas; from marriage, job, house, promotion to social justice, peace, secularism, equality, judgement about good and bad exist only because people value some things over others value pre-suppose conscious beings with likes, dislikes, preferences and prejudices.

Whenever we choose to perform an act, we do so because we have decided that it is the right thing to do, it is what we ought to do. Of all available alternatives, it is the best thing to do and it will lead to more satisfactory consequences. So values are outcomes of human choices among competing human interests. The taste for A becomes a value after it has been chosen over taste of B. Values can also be defined as standards or principles for judging worth. They are the criteria by which we judge things to be good, worthwhile and desirable.

Place of Values in the Present Education System

Social and educational needs are changed due to modernisation, westernisation and industrialisation. Since the drawn of independence, India adhere to socialist, secular and democratic principles to accomplish justice, liberty, equality and fraternity. Hence modern educational thought, in free India, depicts the values of democracy, secularism, socialism and dignity of work on one hand, and justice, liberty, equality and fraternity on the other. Further, scientific and technological development poses a challenge to educational practices to inculcate scientific temper, scientific insight and inquisitiveness among younger generations besides preparing them for democratic citizenship. To inculcate these values among younger generations, modern classroom practices have become more sophisticated and technologically oriented and this is the context where exactly the ancient system of education is believed to be inadequate.

It is apt to identify or prioritise the values that are relevant to modern context. Physical, social, economic, aesthetic, ethical and spiritual values are some values that may be suitable to educate our younger generations. Physical values relate to good health; social values arise out of satisfactory inter-personal relationship; economic values insist on providing food, clothing and shelter; aesthetic values envisages the appreciation for the truth, beauty and goodness; ethical values are concerned with the criteria of making the right choice or decision; and spiritual values reflect the comprehensive way of life. All these values even though they are distinct, there is an interdependence and interrelationship between them.

Society has developed the ideal of individualism due to modernisation. The concept of 'self recognition', also has undergone change. Now it means the realisation of potentialities of the individual self to its maximum possibility. Individualisation education is done on the basis of proper selection of the persons. Guidance is a technique for the selection of a person's motivational powers as well as cognitive, effective and behavioural components.

Value Education

Value education implies inculcating in the children a sense of humanism, a deep concern for the well-being of others and the nation. This can be accomplished only when we instill in the children a deep feeling of commitment to values that would build this country and bring back to the people pride in work that brings order, security and assured progress.

The social, moral, aesthetic and spiritual sides of a person which are very often undermined in formal education are developed through value education. It teaches us to preserve whatever is good and worthwhile in what we have inherited from our culture. Also it helps us to accept respect the attitude and behaviour of those who suffer from us. Value education does not mean value imposition or indoctrination. It has the power to transform a diseased mind into a very young, fresh, innocent, healthy, natural and attentive mind. The transformed mind is capable of higher sensitivity and a heightened level of perception. This leads to fulfillment of the evolutionary role in man and in life.

We should know that it is not always end (ista) aimed at which is termed a 'value'; the means to it (istasadhana) also are often described so. But, as subserving ends other than themselves, they can only be instrumental and not intrinsic values like them. That is to say, though the term value is primarily applied to the ends that are sought, often the means to their attainment are also secondarily called so. Water is an instrumental value and the quenching of thirst by means of it is an intrinsic value.

Value may be defined as a conception of standards, cultural or merely personal, by which things are compared and approved or disapproved related to one another. A child is not born with a set of values. Values have to acquired through the process of education.

Role of Values

Values are multifaceted standards that guide our conduct. They lead persons to take particular positions; they predispose humans to favour on particular political/religious ideology. They are the standards to evaluate and judge to praise and blame persons. They have a strong considering value realisation by modern society. Education preserves the old worthwhile values to transmit to the new generation in proportion of their acceptability in the modern society and implement the new values which suit to the needs of the society.

The Aim of Values in Education

Education aims to impart knowledge, to inculcate skills to fit people for work in adult life and above all to help young people develop as full human beings, to lead the good life. In this task, values play a major role as value aim at humanisation, realising the higher reaches of man's potential that pre-supposes freedom and imply a vision of good life. However, values in education mean, value oriented education and not education of values. Value education is meant for excellence and ascent of man.

Objectives of Value Education

The main aim of value education is to make the students good citizens who in turn may share their responsibility in the changing setup of the society in order to give the desired shape and image to the society, and the country at large.

The following are enumerate as the major objectives of value education.

They are:

1. To promote in children basis and fundamental qualities like truthfulness. Co-operation, love and compassion, peace and non-violence, courage, equality, justice of labour, common brotherhood of man and scientific temper;
2. To train children to become responsible citizens in their personal and social lives;
3. To enable children to become responsible citizens in their personal and social lives;
4. To enable children to understand and appreciate the national goals of socialism and democracy and to contribute to their realisation;
5. To create in children an awareness of the socio-economic conditions and to motivate them to improve the same;
6. To enable children to become open and considerate in their thought and behaviour and rise above prejudices based on religion, language, caste or sex;
7. To help them understand and appreciate themselves and continually strive for their inner development and becoming, thus moving towards the goal of self-actualisation; and
8. To develop in them proper attitudes towards (a) oneself and fellow beings, (b) one's own country, (c) people of other countries, leading to international understanding, (d) life and environment and all religions.

Inculcation of Values through Home Science

"Home science is concerned with the attainment of the well-being of individuals and families, the improvement of homes and the preservation of values significant in home life".

—Ellen Richards

Generally there is a misunderstanding the Home Science constitutes just cooking, knitting, tailoring and these skills can be learned at home. But Home Science comprises all those factors and fields which cater to the physical, psychological and emotional needs of the pupils and influence their development and life in the family and community.

During the few decades, society has undergone marked changes due to unprecedented progress in scientific, social, economic and occupational fields and in communications. Women are coming out in increasing numbers, to take up employment outside their homes. The time available for physical tasks within the home has been reduced considerably. Consequently, the concept of home science, which had been traditionally known as a discipline for women, when her place was conceived to be exclusively within the homes, also changed. As a result, its earlier focus on home-making skill, hospitality and child rearing practices are becoming enlarged, to embrace all other aspects of living in the home and community. Home Science today means preparation for careers also.

With vast technological and economic changes sweeping the country, families and individuals have become consumers of a large array of mass produced goods, such as processed food, clothing, prefabricated houses, toys, and labour-saving devices. Home Science is concerned with examining these facts from the consumer's and national view.

The trend towards urbanisation is growing. Urbanisation has been accompanied by an increasing proportion of women combining homemaking with work outside the family. This trend calls for numerous adjustments in the official, personal, familial, social, economic and management aspects within the home.

The occupational prospects of women have become spectacular. No longer are their choices limited to a few occupations. A considerable percentage of married women pursue permanent work outside the home on a par with men. The proportion of women workers in the social services is also rising. In tune with these developments. Home Science has undergone a major reorientations towards the social sciences along with its earlier foundations of basic and applied sciences. These profound changes indicate clearly that Home Science courses cannot any longer be confined to preparing pupils solely for life within the home.

With a fast-changing society, men need to share some of the responsibilities of home-making where women go out for work and the increasing need for raising happy families. Home Science can no longer be said to be a discipline earmarked for girls alone. Inculcation for spiritual values, personal hygiene, good grooming, graceful living, nutrition, bringing up children and community services are important aspects of home science, which boys also need to learn.

With the changing value in society, migration to cities, influence of advertisements and other mass media and education of women, the joint family system has become obsolete. In its place, there is a rapid emergence of 'nuclear' or 'extended' families. In this changed context, the study of human relationships and population education at all levels, particularly at the formative secondary school stage, has become indispensable.

The effects of the physical environment upon the quality of life are far-reaching. Industrialisation and modern ways of life have led to an unprecedented pollution of the environment and these are being discussed in national and international conferences. Home Science should reflect these concerns in its housing, design and architectural aspects.

The mistaken notions can be expelled by the realisation that Home Science consists of a combination of the understanding of sciences, humanities and the fine arts and their applications. The sciences that are applied in the home and outside are physical, biological, and behavioural sciences which are necessary because we live in a scientific world. We think, talk and breathe science in this era. Therefore, Physics, Chemistry, Botany, Zoology, Physiology, Microbiology and other related subjects are parts of Home Science. The Humanities; Psychology, Sociology, Civics and Economics are also related to Home Science as they help in understanding human nature and conduct. The applications constitute the components of Home Science, which are spiritual values based on the best in our cultural background; child-care and development; Human relations; Nutrition; Household management; Housing (furnishing); Related Art; Textiles and clothing; Health; Home nursing and Sanitation and First Aid.

The study of Home Science offers general education and opportunity to achieve their three most cherished goals; all-round development of their personalities, preparation for a career and the ability to manage their homes. Successful home and family life and home making are challenges that demand the best in education. No other educational programme offers opportunities to achieve all these goals at the same time.

Spiritual values are most important in family living. Home Science being built on the solid foundation of the noblest traditions of the past, helps in the discernment and preservation of the best in our precious heritage. Home Science caters not only to the physical aspects but also to the moral and spiritual needs of the pupils. It helps them to flower as integrated personalities and assume responsibilities and leadership in the society. Because of these values, Home Science makes a worthy contribution to society by:

1. Fulfilling the objectives of general education, namely education for living, personality development and national service.
2. Preparing pupils for a large number of careers such as teaching in pre-schools, housing, nutrition, dietetics, food service and interior decoration.
3. Helping towards relation of national aspirations for development, family planning, applied, nutrition, child welfare, savings and national integration.

The contributions of the different components of Home Science are:

In the Area of Spiritual Values

Spiritual values which are necessary for promoting intellectual, social and emotional development must radiate from the home. Satisfaction of the physical needs of shelter, food and clothing will become futile if they are not accompanied by spiritual values such as affection and appreciation. Love cannot be purchased with money and the affectionate Tender Loving Care (TLC) of the mother can't be substituted with paid service.

Pupils studying Home Science will highlight spiritual values in all the aspects by:

1. Offering prayers daily.
2. Fostering patriotism and pride in National Solidarity among the members of the family.
3. Giving their utmost willingly and happily for national progress.
4. Following Gandhian Principles of Ahimsa in thought, word and deed.
5. Living in harmony will all people.
6. Developing community spirit and eagerness to do social services, avoiding gossip and rumours.
7. Leading an orderly and disciplined life as a good example to others.

In the Area of Child Care and Development

Home Science alerts pupils to the importance of keeping children healthy, happy and secure by:

1. Taking care of younger children in the home when their mother are away.
2. Helping children develop self-reliance.
3. Keeping children constructively occupied when their parents are busy.

4. Helping in crèches established for working women.
5. Helping in Balwadis.

In the Area of Food and Nutrition

Home Science education can help pupils to produce more food and utilise food effectively by:

1. Understanding the principles of nutrition and good eating habits so that optimum health is achieved.
2. Selection and use of protective foods which are rich in nutrients and at the same time low cost, such as leafy green vegetables, high lysine maize, ragi and many others. This will ensure good health with no additional expenditure on tonics and drugs.
3. Use of inexpensive food supplements which are now produced in the country such as the Indian Multi-purpose, Miltone and Malt in the place of costly chocolate milks, infant foods, canned foods and imported foodstuffs.
4. Use of proper methods of cooking, which conserve nutrients.
5. Recognising the need to avoid extravagance, conspicuous consumption and display of affluence in festivals and entertaining guests.
6. Sensitivity to over eating and thus promote better health, and saving of food and money.
7. Preservation of surplus foods to make them available in places and times of scarcity.
8. Using every centimeter of space available, for raising kitchen gardens to help increase food production.
9. Spreading of the principles of good nutrition in the community.
10. Evaluation of food habits born out of social prestige, position, caste and traditional practices in the sensible light of sound nutrition.

In the Area of Home Management

Home Science helps pupils recognise how good management in the home making full use of their resources and abilities can save for the nation by:

1. Spending every paisa wisely so that maximum money could be saved for national growth.
2. Teaching that saving is investment for future spending and therefore should be willing and spontaneous.
3. Maintaining Hundis in which saving can be kept and turned over to development efforts through deposits in post offices and Banks.
4. Spending time fruitfully so that maximum work can be accomplished in minimum time.
5. Spending time productivity in simple and creative wealth producing activities such as gardening, spinning, knitting and garment making.
6. Using time efficiently to release adults from their household responsibilities for more urgent tasks.
7. Spending energy profitably so that energy is conserved for noble causes.
8. Taking care of personal property as well as school's property to save costs of repair and replacements.
9. Contributing labour for social service activities.
10. Consuming less to keep the price down and combat adulteration.
11. Practicing economy in the use of electricity and other fuels, water and utilities.
12. Avoiding locking up money in jewels and gold.

In the Area of Housing

Home Science impresses upon pupils the relation of adequate housing to good health and comfort by:

1. Understanding the requirements of good housing.
2. Maintaining cleanliness in the house and surroundings.

3. Avoiding accumulating unnecessary articles in the house and surroundings.
4. Contributing all the unnecessary articles for social service.
5. Avoiding or eliminating unnecessary furnishings.
6. Avoiding extravagance in the use of space.

In the Area of Clothing

Home Science helps pupil understand the principles and practices important in the selection, care and repair of textiles and clothing by:

1. Having the minimum amount of comfortable essential clothing, regardless of fashions and notions.
2. Washing clothes properly.
3. Making clothes attractively.
4. Storing clothes so that they give full service.
5. Mending clothes promptly to extend their usefulness.

Outcomes of Studying Home Science

If the idea of Home Science education is to develop balanced personalities, will trained Home Science pupils will radiate health and joy; be affectionate and attractive; poised and practical; honest and upright; sound in thinking and making decisions; resourceful and adaptable; tactful and thoughtful; chaste in tasks and skillful in dealing with people. They will be careful in their use of the God-given gifts, time, money, effort and human resources. They will be mindful of other's difficulties and needs, appreciative of their achievements and considerate to their feelings. They will respect dignity of labour. Their attitude, ideals, appreciation and habits will be directed towards abundant living.

Thus the outcomes of Home Science education help pupil to:

- Cultivate deep faith in spiritual values;
- Preserve the best in our culture, discarding the useless practices in the traditions of the past;

- Prepare towards a vocation;
- Make decisions wisely; and
- Copy with changing situations in life.

Therefore, the study of Home Science has a wide appeal to pupil who are the future parents, citizens and leaders. It is necessary to include Home Science as one of the core subjects in schools for both boys and girls.

34

Value-Oriented Education

Methods and Strategies

Dr. Vanaja, M*

Dr. M.V. Ram Kumar Ratnam**

India is passing through a period of value crisis. Massive industrial infrastructure is being built with an increasing insistence on efficiency needed for an industrial society, leaving no room for the growth of humane and spiritual consciousness. Our social life is full of corruption, violence, cynicism, hypocrisy, exploitation, disparity and disruption. The National Policy on Education (1986) made the following observations about the value system prevalent in our society. "The erosion of values is now a national phenomenon, so complex and gigantic that a more balanced school curriculum, new learning materials and competent teachers, alone can correct this phenomenon.

The picture is dismal and dreadful everywhere in schools, at homes, in offices, in the assemblies and in parliament also. Hope cannot sustain for too long and mere promises will not sustain life. The school, the home, the community and the government are all blaming one another and it appears that introspection is nobody's concern. The many ills that our society is facing is traced to the crisis of value. Values in public life seem to be at cross roads. The people are losing ground in cherished values that this nation

* **Lecturer, St. Joseph's College of Education for Women, Guntur.**

** **Associate Professor, Acharya Nagarjuna University, Nagarjuna Nagar.**

stood for in ancient past. There is erosion of social, moral, social, cultural, economic and political values at all lends. The erosion of values has led to the spread of callous, selfishness, unlimited greed, bribery, corruption, narrowism, rowdyism, hooliganism, violence, destruction, abuse of human rights, gross injustice, frustration and crisis of character.

Much of the blame, for this sorry state of affairs is being put on the present system of education that is divorced from the realities of life, cultural heritage, and human values. The growing concern over the erosion of essential values and an increasing cynicism has brought to focus the need for readjustment in the curriculum in order to make education a forceful tool for the cultivation of social and moral values. The main function of education is the development of an all-round and well balanced personality of the students. Today's education lays more emphasis on knowledge and is information oriented. As a result, aspects of their personality like physical, emotional, social and spiritual area not properly developed by providing for the growth of attitudes, habits, values, skills and interests among the pupils.

We, teacher educators as moulders of the future generation of Indian-world citizens cannot remain silent spectators. It is time of us to appropriate and realise the needs of the hour.

What then is the solution?

Inculcation of desired values-ethical, moral and spiritual,

which is the Indian way of life appears to be the only way out.

We have three main alternatives in dealing with value development:

(i) To do nothing about value development

(ii) To transmit a pre-existing set of values to student

(iii) To help and guide students to find out their own values and develop their own system—Value Clarification.

Value Education

Value education is essentially 'Man Making' and 'Character Building'. Value education, as it is generally used, refers to a wide gamut of learning and activities ranging from training in physical health, mental hygiene, etiquette and manners, appropriate social behaviour, civic rights and duties to aesthetic and even religious training.

To some, value education is simply a matter of developing appropriate behaviour and habits involving inculcation of certain virtues and habits. In opposition to such a conception, it is pointed out that value education has an essentially cognitive component in it and that this should not be ignored. Actually, the ability to make moral judgement based on sound reasoning is a very important aim of value education and has to be deliberately cultivated.

Moral development of a child, according to some results automatically from the social life of the school. The child as a member of the group imbibes the attitudes, values and general behaviour of the group and continually tries to mould himself according to the group norm. Such adjustment to life constitutes his moral development. Value education is a process of aiding the child in such adjustment. Such a view is contested on the ground that although children learn the rules of group living from the social life of the school, such learning does not constitute value education. For mortality, it is pointed out, is not concerned so much with *'what is'* as with *'what ought to be'* and *'what ought to be done'*.

Value education, according to one more view, is essentially matter of educating the feelings and emotions. It is the 'training of the heart' and consists in developing the right feelings and emotions. It does not involve any cognitive abilities that can be trained. Like poetry, it is 'caught' rather than taught. It is essentially a matter of creating the right atmosphere, imitation and learning by example communication with nature or modelling one self after an ideal. Such a view is countered by saying that mere imitation of a 'good' person and modelling oneself after an ideal does not confer any morality on an individual. Morality is not a thing that simply *'radiates'* from one person to another. Moral development includes both thinking morally and behaving morally. Moral thinking is a distinct type of thinking characterised by the exercise of rational choice. A moral person is not only a person who does the *'right'* thing but also one who does not the *'right'* thing for the *'right'* reason.

Objectives of Value Education

- To kindle the aesthetic sensibility of children through exposure to appropriate objects events and experiences.
- To enhance the awareness and sensitivity to moral aspects of major issues and concerns of modern life like poverty, illiteracy, human rights environment, population, peace etc.
- To develop an ability to reflect with an open mind on the moral dimensions of contemporary social events and incidents of every day occurrence.
- To help students understand and appreciate the value of democracy, secularism, social justice, scientific temper and other values supportive of social cohesion and national unity.
- To enable students to develop a concern for and commitment of these values.
- To provide appropriate opportunities for students to practice and line by these values.
- To develop a dedication to uphold the integrity and honour and foster the development of the country.

Inculcation of basic human values of love, truth, non-violence, co-existence, co-operation, critical thinking and scientific temper must be emphasised as pointed out in the New Education Policy (1986).

The ultimate aim of value education is to enable a student to be:

(a) Really Indian;

(b) Truly modern; and

(c) Deeply human

APPROACHES TO VALUE EDUCATION IN SCHOOLS

1. Direct Approach

This is the approach, which is usually followed in the schools. In the timetable there is a period allotted called moral science/

moral education. In this class, which is seldom utilised for the purpose it is meant for, there is lot of sermonising that children generally fail to appreciate and many a time the effort is a waste.

2. Critical Enquiry Approach

Value education should ideally begin with critical inquiry and clarification of values. This approach believes that the child has to be allowed to discover what is right through constant inquiry and this enabled to harness their inherent energies for the pursuit of sound values. The child with the help of the teacher undertakes value inquiry and while doing so, the child perceives the right and valuable and it is automatically accepted and followed, since it constitutes the solution to a problem that the child seeks to solve. Thus, this approach tries to bridge the gap between discovery and action. Value discussion and value clarification methods can be used in this approach.

3. Total Atmospheric Approach

Another view on values is that knowledge of right and wrong and reasoning in value is not difficult to attain, the problem of value-oriented education is rather one of character or will, of having the moral fibre to do what is right and not to do what is wrong. This approach works on the premise that "Values are not taught but caught" and hence aims to influence the values of children in school through organisation and maintenance of conducive atmosphere. The Indian Education Commission recommended that, "the school atmosphere, the personality and behaviour of the teachers, the facilities provided in the school will have a large say in developing a sense of value". All the activities of the school viz. School assembly, curricular activities, co-curricular activities, celebration of religious festivals, work experience, games and sports, subject clubs, social service programme should permeate consciousness of values.

4. The Integrated Approach

Probably this modern method has to be advocated. Here there is no specific time allotment. As a teacher teaches her/his lessons, he is supposed to incorporate his value orientation. The process is a dynamic one where the initiative of the teacher is of utmost importance.

Ex: (1) Science and Honesty:

While teaching about colours the following could be used as an example by the science teacher.

In the vegetable market, I went to a carrot stall and picked up very appealing Orange coloured carrots. I went on to pick up fresh green peas and beans. As, I left the market, I found the carrots paler and greens not so green. I went back and was dumbstruck at the lighting arrangement.

The questions that may follow are:

(i) Could you guess how the lights were arranged?

(ii) What coloured lights could have been used?

(iii) Should we support the action of vegetable seller?

Ex: (2) Mathematics and Dishonesty

Discussing about discounts the teacher cold think of this example.

A person bought an article of Rs. 1000 from a shop where the discount board reads: 20% + 20% = 40%

Calculate:

(a) The discount given at the rate of 20% + 20%

(b) The discount at 40%

(c) What is the difference in discount given?

(d) Is the shopkeeper justified?

5. Evocation Approach

The students are encouraged to make spontaneously free, non-rational choices, without thought or hesitation. It provides an environment which allows maximum freedom for students, and provides a provocative situation for which spontaneous reactions are elicited, e.g. The reaction to a picture of starving children.

6. Inculcation Approach

Students are forced to act according to specific desired values. A positive and negative reinforcement by the teacher helps value inculcation. This can be done by a teacher's natural actions and responses.

7. Evocation Approach

Students are encouraged to make spontaneously free, non-rational choices without thought or hesitation. It provides an environment, which allows maximum freedom for students, and provides a provocative situation for which spontaneous reactions are elicited e.g. the reaction to a picture of starving children.

8. Inculcation Approach

Students are forced to act according to specific desired values. A positive and negative reinforcement by the teacher helps values inculcation. This can be done by a teacher's natural actions and responses. This time-honoured method has been notably unsuccessfully.

9. Awareness Approach

This approach helps students to become aware and identify their own values. The students are encouraged to share their experiences. The teacher presents value-laden situations or dilemmas through readings, films, role playing, small group discussions and simulation. Students thus engage themselves in the process of making inferences about values from the thoughts, feelings, beliefs or behaviour of themselves and others.

10. Moral Reasoning Approach

Kohlberg's theory of six stages of moral development is the framework most frequently used in this approach. The teachers setup learning experiences, which will facilitate moral development. These experiences fall under the general category of what Kohlberg calls role taking. The critical factor in role taking is empathy. Through placing themselves in a role and experiencing the process of deciding, students can begin to see moral decisions in a larger framework than their single point of view. It consists of the students discussing a dilemma and by reasoning; they attain higher level of knowledge. In this way by discussion and reflection students are encouraged to express a value position rather than compromise on a consensus.

11. Analysis Approach

The group or individuals are encouraged to study social value problems. They are asked to clarify value questions, and identify values in conflict. They are encouraged to determine the truth and evidence of purported facts, and arrive at value decision, applying analogous cases, inferring and testing value principles underlying the decision.

12. Value Clarification Approach

It helps students to use both rational thinking and emotional awareness to examine personal behaviour patterns, classify, and actualise values. This approach has been detailed by Raths et. al. (1966) and Simon et. al. (1972) where the child is made to jot down a self analysis reaction work sheet, consisting of drawings, questions and activities.

13. Commitment Approach

It enables the students to perceive themselves not merely as passive reactors or as free individuals but as inner-relative members of a social group and system. The Action Project helps to clarify and restructure one's value system and to ascertain the depth of commitment of one's values.

14. The Union Approach

The purpose is to help students to perceive themselves and act not as separate egos but as part of a larger inter-related whole- the human race, the world, the cosmos.

15. Awareness Approach

This approach helps students to become aware and identify their own values. The students are encouraged to share their experiences. The teacher present value-laden situations or dilemmas through readings, films, role playing, small group discussions and simulation. Students thus engage themselves in the process of making inferences about value from the thoughts, feelings, beliefs or behaviour of themselves and others.

16. Moral Reasoning Approach

Kohlberg's theory of six stages of moral development is the framework most frequently used in this approach. The teachers setup learning experiences, which will facilitate moral development. These experiences fall under the general category of what Kohlberg calls role taking. The critical factor in role taking is empathy. Through placing themselves in a role and experiencing the process of deciding, students can begin to see moral decisions in a larger framework than their single point of view. It consists of the students discussing a dilemma and by reasoning, they attain a higher level of knowledge. In this way by discussion and reflection students are encouraged to express a value position rather than compromise on a consensus.

17. Analysis Approach

The group or individuals are encouraged to study social value problems. They are asked to clarify value questions, and identify values in conflict. They are encouraged to determine the truth and evidence of purported facts, and arrive at value decision, applying analogous cases, inferring and testing value principles underlying the decision.

18. Value Clarification Approach

It helps students to use both rational thinking and emotional awareness to examine personal behaviour patterns, classify, and actualise values. This approach has been detailed by Raths et al. (1966) and Simon et al. (1972) where the child is made to jot down a self analysis reaction work sheet, consisting of drawings, questions and activities.

19. Commitment Approach

It enables the students to perceive themselves not merely as passive reactors or as free individuals but as inner-relative members of a social group and system. The action project helps to clarify and restructure. One's value system and to ascertain the depth of commitment of one's values.

20. The Union Approach

The purpose is to help students to perceive themselves and act not as separate egos but as part of a larger inter-related whole—the human race, the world, the cosmos.

The report of the UNESCO, APIED on Education for Affective Development has identified the following methods/strategies that can be used for teaching values in character building activities:

1. *Telling:* A process for developing values that enables a pupil to have a clear picture of a value-laden situation by means of his own narration of the situation.
2. *Inculcating:* An approach geared towards instilling and internalising norms into person's own value systems.
3. *Persuading:* The process of convincing the learner to accept certain values and behave in accordance with what is acceptable.
4. *Modelling:* A strategy in which a certain individual perceived as epitomising desirable/ideal values is presented to the learners as a model.
5. *Role Playing:* Acting out of the true feelings of the actor(s) by taking the role of another person but without the risk of reprisals.
6. *Simulating:* A strategy in which the learners are asked to pretend to be in a certain situation called for by the lesson and then to portray the events and also by imitating the character's personality.
7. *Problem Solving:* An approach wherein a dilemma is presented to the learners asking them what decisions they are going to take.
8. *Discussing Situations, Stories, Pictures, etc.:* This technique asks the learners to deliberate on and explain the details in the lesson.
9. *Studying Biographies of Great Men:* This is an approach that makes use of the lives of great as the subject matter for trying to elicit their good needs and thoughts worthy for emulation.
10. *Moralising:* The process of working out a sense of morality through active structuring and restructuring of one's social experiences (e.g. moral reasoning and analysis).
11. *Values Clarification:* Value clarification as a strategy for values development may be considered as learner-centred. It relies heavily on the pupils ability to process his belief, behave according to his beliefs and to make a decision whenever confronted with a value dilemma.

Models of Value Education

In case of value education a model of teaching is a way of thinking and doing for the development of moral caring, judging and acting. In an educational setting model of value education includes a theory or a point of view about how people develop morally and a set of strategies or principles for fostering moral development. Thus, a model of teaching for value education helps teachers to understand and practice value education effectively. The value education of a person is the integrated structure of caring, judging and acting. The models of value education provide a broad based pedagogy to mobilise feeling to guide thinking and to sustain action. The models of teaching which could be utilised in developing the various aspects of human values are:

- Rationale Building Model
- Consideration Model-Value Clarification Model
- Value Analysis Model
- Cognitive Model Development Model
- Social Action Model
- Value Discussion Model
- Jurisprudential Inquiry Model
- Role Playing Model

1. Rationale Building Model

James Shaver, the developer of this model views moral education primarily from the perspective of a pluralistic society. The rationale building approach emphasises the role of critical reflection on the part of the teachers and students alike in value education. He focuses on the need to teach the specific analytic skills essential to democratic citizenship.

2. Consideration Model

McPhail the developer of this model emphasises the importance of caring as distinct from judging. The task of moral education is to build on the fundamental core of consideration that all people naturally possess. The consideration model assumes that moral behaviour is self-reinforcing.

3. Value Clarification Model

Louis Raths, Merrill Harming and Sidney Simon (1978) developed this model is an attempt to help people to decrease value confusion and promote a consistent set of values through valuing process. The value clarification process is designed to promote intelligent value choices through a process of choosing, prizing and behaving. The value clarification has four key elements: *(i)* a focus of life; *(ii)* acceptance of what is; *(iii)* an invitation to reflect further; and *(iv)* nourishment of personal powers.

4. Value Analysis Model

Coombs (1971) developed this model helps students to learn a highly systematic, step-by-step process for making moral decisions. It trains peoples to deal rationally with ethical problems having social issues, in other words it deals with gathering and weighting facts in a value judgement.

5. Cognitive Moral Development Model

The Cognitive Moral Development Model was developed by Lowrence Kohlberg and introduces emphasis on moral reasoning. Kohlberg's theory of moral development and moral education consider moral judgement as representing a naturally autonomous thought process.

6. Social Action Plan

Fred Newman (1975) developed Social Action Model, which aims to teach students how to influence public policy. Newman is concerned with developing students' moral reasoning, but he gives more attention to the environmental competencies that sustain moral action.

7. Value Discussion Model

Based on Kohlberg's Cognitive of Moral Development, Value Discussion Model aims to enhance the stage of moral reasoning of students. The model is useful in improving the listening skills, self-esteem, attitude towards school and knowledge of key concepts.

8. Jurisprudential Inquiry Model

Donald Oliver and James P. Shaver (1974) developed Jurisprudential Inquiry Model, to help students to learn to think systematically about contemporary issue. This model aims to develop the capacity for analysing issues, to assume the role of others and social dialogue.

9. Role Playing Model

Fannie Shaftel and George Shaftel (1967) developed this model, which aims to involve students in a real problem situation and provides a live sample of human behaviour that serve as a vehicle *for* students to: explore their feelings, gain insight into their attitudes, values and perceptions, develop their problem-solving skills and attitudes, and explore subject matter in varied ways.

Conclusion

Education in the 21st century has to strive for a cohesive society in which people learn to live together. This would be feasible only when schools, apart from imparting general education, perform the function of value inculcation among young persons who would become the citizens of the 21st century. Value inculcation takes place only in those institutions, which function on value based norms and are staffed by a faculty that leads a value-based life. This is itself defines the shape of a teacher training institution and its functioning. It also provides the guidelines for teacher education programmes. If this is accepted, a total transformation of teacher education system may become feasible and may lead to a system that is responsive to the emerging needs.

REFERENCES

1. Aggarwal, J.C. (1995), *Teacher and Education in a Developing Society*, Vikas Publishing House, New Delhi.
2. Gupta, N.L. (1986), *Value Education: Theory and Practice*, Krishna Brothers, Ajmer.
3. Gupta, N.L. (2000), *Human Values in Education*, Concept Publishing Company, New Delhi.
4. Kapani, Madhu (2000), *Education in Human Values*, Sterling Publishers Pvt. Ltd., New Delhi.

5. Kaul, G.N. (1988), *Values and Education in Independent India*, The Associated Publishers, Ambala Cantt, India.

6. Kishore, Lalit (1990), *Value Oriented Education: Foundations and Frontiers—World Overview*, Doaba House, New Delhi.

7. Ruhela, S.P. (1986), *Human Values and Education*, Sterling Publishers (Pvt.) Ltd. New Delhi.

8. Saraf, Sommath, (2002), Vikas Publishing House, Mumbai.

9. Sinha, H.S. (1968), *The Value Crisis in Education*, The Progress of Education, Vol. XLII, No. 8, pp. 291-295.

10. Tilak Raj Bharadwaj (2001), *Education of Human Values*, Mittal Publications, New Delhi.

35

Promoting Values in Professional and Higher Education

Teaching Strategies

B. Yella Reddy[*]
Dr. V. Dayakara Reddy[**]

The erosion of values in society is a matter of great concern to every right thinking citizen in a bid to arrest this erosion and down scaling of values. So in this context values are determinants of human behaviour. Today 'being' is subordinate to 'having' wide spread affluence in our country, which co-exists with harsh poverty, aggravates the situation and the impact has been felt on the young who want to succeed at any cost. The purpose of promoting values in professional and higher education is to fight obscurantism, religious fanatism, violence and to promote and nurture critical thinking, reasoning and build-up a humane approach to life. In this critical situation what are the teaching strategies to promote values professional and higher education, is dealt in this chapter.

Need for Value Education

The erosion of values in society is a matter of great concern to every right thinking citizen. In a bid to arrest this erosion and down scaling of values.

* **Lecturer in Mathematics, Sri Rama College of Education, Tirupati.**

** **Principal IASE & Head, Department of Education, S.V. University, Tirupati.**

Values are determinants of human behaviour. They play vital role in the lives of every individual. Values are enduring and they facilitate standards that guide the conduct of human beings.

One of the most celebrated thinkers on education Mahatma Gandhi considers values as an inseparable competent in the full flowering and development of personality. For him every value component is a typical way of life that distinguishes one human is being from another. This the personality of a person that characterises his individuality finds an appropriate avenue of self development.

The NEP 1986 too highlights the need for inculcation of values. "The growing concern over the erosion of values and an increasing cynicism in society has brought to focus the need for readjustment in the curriculum in order to make education of forceful took for the cultivation of social and moral values".

What is Value Education?

Statement and judgement lead to values value is an end belief that a specific node of conduct or state of existence is personality or socially preferable to an opposite or converse node of conduct. Mohan Rakesh is one of his novels states that the real problem in this world is not that there is a fight between right and wrong.

The purpose of value education is for the development of body and mind to develop integrated and balanced personality.

The Truth, Good and Beauty—these three intrinsic values are directly linked with intellect, will and feeling respectively i.e., Jnana, Karma and Bhakti "valuing is the tendency of a person to show preference".

—Carl Regers

What we believe—Professional values

What we practice—Operational values

What we learn—Experience in order to adopt and renew traditions received from the past traditional values.

—Dr. Prem Kirpal

To state one's aim of education is at once restate his educational values.

Gandhi's Classification

Truth	Equality
Non-violence	Self realisation
Freedom	Purity of ends and means
Democracy	Self discipline
Sarvo dharma Samabhana	Suddhi

Education means an all round drawing out of the best in child and man—body, mind and spirit.

—Mahatma Gandhi

Importance

Education plays a vital role in giving human beings proper equipment to lead a gracious and harmonious life. Education is a fundamental means to bring any desired change in society which is an accepted fact throughout the world.

Education in general and value-oriented education in particular occupies a prestigious place in the modern context of the contemporary society.

Every human is witnessing tremendous value crisis throughout the world today lacking vigour and determinant attitude towards value and its institutions is pervasive in the world today. As the vitality of human belief in values is dying in our vary land, the younger generation has started to pool—pool the unique religious epics and religious institutions giving room for erosion of spiritual and moral values of mind. As a result, the mind of mean has been caciniated into small fractions and fragments which make the value content of human life a diminishing factor in modern times.

The purpose of value-oriented education is to fight obscurantism, religious fanaticism and violence and promote and nurture critical thinking, reflection reasoning and build-up a human approach or life.

Professional Colleges

I will not grudge the darkness, but I am not the sun either! What is the harm if I be a glow-worm, and do my humble bin in dispelling darkness.

—**Prof. P.L. Dhar**

Prof. P.L. Dhar has pioneered a systematic study of how best one can integrated human values in technical education, particularly in the IIT system.

Anupam Sengupta and Devasun Ghosh guidance of Prof. cadre point out their generating the sustained interest in the scientific discipline, will need continuity in provision of employment.

Higher Education

Srivastava 1981 measured the moral ideal and values of PUC, BA class students.

- For every increase in the educational leader there is a corresponding decrease in moral values.
- After high school education a decrease in the magnitude of moral values.
- Education is inseparable from value oriented education, it is a man making and character building programme, it is the training of mind, body and soul. This the hunt for the goal, which liberates from fear, ignorance and superstitution.

Read education should combine ethics and science. It should excite a passionate hunger for truth. It should aim at perfection and excellence. It should become an instrument of social change and National development. It should be more towards humanism, liberalism and universalism. It should help man reach his destiny, which is an aristocracy of intellect and sublimity of soul.

In existing conditions, in India a revolutionary change in the field of values due to western culture, industrialisation urbanisation and other international transition. It is necessary for us to preserve our traditional values.

Education has become a form of pre-professional training without disciplinary perspectives to bind the norms of intellect to the demands of conscience.

—**Richard L. Morrill**

Today 'being is subordinate to having widespread affluence in our country, which co-exists with harsh poverty, aggravates the situation and the impact has been felt on the young who want to succeed at any cost.

Teacher Role in Higher and Professional Education

Teacher will have

A. 1. Celebrate life

2. Be a model

3. Organise mock birthday parties

4. Behave with family members as if behaving with guest

B. Switch off the T.V. at home and talk communicate with each other.

C. Encourage use of social lubricants.

D. Emphasis on values through reaching scholastic subjects. Finishing school for senior students.

Sources and Approaches of Value Oriented Education

Source

1. School curriculum
2. Co-curriculum activities
3. Atmosphere of the school
4. Healthy environmental climate

Approaches

Critical enquiry approach	—	Direct teach
Total atmospheric approach	—	with examples
Integrated concurrent approach	—	combining both the approaches

Our education system must prepare our young people to be more responsible and resourceful. It must take note to the problem, needs and aspirations of youth as well as the challenges of a changing world. It should reach our young people to see regional problems in the international perspective. It should inculcate moral and social values, attitudes of non violence and tolerance.

—Indira Gandhi

"A teacher can never truly teach, unless he is still learning himself. A lamp can never light another lamp unless it continues to burn its own flame".

—Tagore

Anything that yields as satisfaction is designated as value.

—Allport

Strategies for Voluntary Actions to Promote Values

1 Voluntary actions from religious institutions—compassions, charity, help, duty, love, peace.

2. Voluntary actions from social and charitable organisations—task of explaining and practicing values.

3. Voluntary actions from students—dignity of labour, honesty, sincerity.

4. From elderly persons.

5. Voluntary actions from Panchayat.

Co-curricular Activities

- Arranging excursions, field trips and service camps and making the students to participate actively in them.
- Organising service agencies like JRC, Scouting, NSS, Clubs, Association, etc.
- Arranging debates, discussions, easy writing competitions etc. on topics like national integration, literacy campaign.
- Celebrating birthdays of national leaders, important persons and events.

- Arranging inter-collegiate an inter-university sports, athletics, games, etc.
- Dramatization and role play;
- Making the students responsible in various school managements and college activities—student perception.
- Organisation of science clubs, literary, associations, music centres, recreational centres, adult education programmes etc.
- Organising morning prayers, celebrating certain social-cultural festivals, anniversaries, school day, teachers' day, parent-teacher association meetings etc.
- Encouraging values in the students by giving the talented and devoted persons awards, gifts, titles, rolling shields etc.

Educational Implications

Avoiding pedigrees and deliberately condensing the substance of the presentation. New education needs to perform the following functions as it readies students to relate to the problems of today world. The education implications of value oriented education can be described as follows:

— By inculcation of physical education, health, strength, ability and beauty can be laid.

— Sports centred value-oriented education develops energetic action, rapid decision and action sportsmanship and leadership qualities.

— Work experience in value-oriented education helps on perfecting skills, utilising materials, tools and process of works.

— With the degree of realism in value-oriented education pupils are encouraged to live in the harmony with nature of art, music and build good nation.

— Value-oriented education based teacher training programmes made nation builders in the form of teachers.

— Inculcating examples of national leaders in value-oriented education, values can be included with in human ease and natural setting.

— Value-oriented education at university stage inculcate moral and human values in students to make them better and more useful members of society.

— The moral and value-oriented education with the inclusion of common ethical teaching of all great religious highlights the nation unity.

— Value-oriented education with a course in comparative religion promote social harmony a liberal attitude and less fanatical approach to religion.

— Stories, illustrations and events mainly from Indian nation and its literature from various religions that included in value-oriented education leads to nation integration.

— Value-oriented education will only eliminate obscurantism, religious, phanatism, violence, superstitions and fatalism.

— Only value-based education system cultivate the basic values of humanism, democracy socialism and secularism.

— Only value-oriented education inculcate a love for motherland and proper praise in our cultural heritage and achievement.

— Value-oriented education strengthen national integration by accelerating the process of modernisation and development of scientific temper and outlook.

Conclusion

Due to liberalisation, industrialisation and globalisation repaid changes are occurring in almost all social sciences. The value possessed and their attitudes according to the changes should be known upto date vast changes are occurring in the education. So-called philosophical foundations of India are declining day to day. With the country in a state of social turbulence, the goals and functions of formal education need to be reassessed and updated.

REFERENCES

Buch, M.B., 1955. *Education in Human Resource Value*, A Bouquet of 70 Stories, Jaipur.

Dayakara Reddy, V. and B. Yella Reddy, 2004. *A Study of the Attitudes of Engineering Students Towards Value Oriented Education in Kadapa district*.

Dayakara Reddy, V. and Sridhar Babu, 2002. *Experiments in Education, A Study of the Attitudes of Intermediate Students Towards Value Oriented Education*.

Gupta, N.L. 1986, *Value Education; Theory and Practices*, Krishna Brothers, Ajmer.

Gupta, N.L., 2000. *Human Values in Education;* Concept Publishing Company, New Delhi.

Mangal, S.K., 1981. *Philosophical Foundations of Education*, Prakash Brothers (Educational Publishers), Ludhiana.

Report of New Education Policy, 1986, Government of India, Ministry of Education India.

36

The Developmental Values of Environmental Education

Dr. Gara Latchanna*

The objective of this chapter is to initiate educational officials, experts and teachers to re-examine the educational programmes regarding environmental education. Environmental issues are global concerns, from perspectives of ecological, economic and moral considerations. However, in this decade school curriculum in most cases criticized for being inadequate, outdated and not properly designed to meet the growing needs of modern world. Therefore there is a need to put emphasis on how environmental issues are reinforced through the school curriculum, and how the existing discipline used to accomplish objectives of environmental education.

Thus to direct environmental education programmes towards the development of attitudes, values and behavioural skills in the areas of emotional decision-making and problem-solving, it is recommended that to adopt a holistic perspectives aiming at building up a sense of values centering on practical problems and integrating environmental education into the curriculum of school education to provide opportunity for students to explore their environment sensorial, physically, intellectually and to obtain both the motivating concern as well as the factual knowledge necessary

* **Associate Professor, Department of Education, Andhra University, A.P. Waltair–530 003, Visakhapatnam.**

to become an environmentally literate citizens. Furthermore classroom teachers should be well trained and be knowledgeable about the aspects of environment to integrate it into instructional strategies and be able to convey the information to the students effectively.

Introduction

It is relevant to discuss the relationship between the behaviour of man and his environment. Until the last few centuries, man and his environment worked well together. Environment was allowed to function without much interference from man. The increasing population, the development of culture and technology might improve the living standards of the people but it has resulted more pressure on environment. The perception of man today is that environment is utilised to the maximum extent so as to make human life more and more comfortable.

Maslow's theory of human behaviour based upon the notion that humans seek to acquire happiness and meaning from life through striving to satisfy their needs. Further these can be identified and ordered in a hierarchy according to their immediate importance for survival. His hierarchy begins with the most basic and immediate needs, physiological that must be satisfied for people to exist.

Now-a-days the basic needs of man, food, water, clothing and shelter, psychological and social security of life can be granted through better education, better health, and better environment. Search for prosperity and the exception of poverty with other factors have resulted environmental pollution degradation. On top of these, increasing population explosion and resource depletion or environment crisis are becoming the challenges of this century. So that environmental education is a means that provides foundation for a new international order, which will guaranty the conservation and improvements of the environment.

The peaceful co-existence of man with environment will be possible if the school curriculum is properly designed to modify the behaviour of the people towards environment.

Conceptual Framework

The concept environment refers to the circumstances of life of a person or society. The environment can be classified as Environmental Studies. Environmental Science and Environmental Engineering of Physical and Social Environment and can be studied in these aspects.

Education refers to the process of training and developing of skills, knowledge, attitude and values. According to John Dewey, education is the development of all those capacities in the individuals that will enable them to control the environment and fulfill those possibilities. Therefore physical and social environment can be improved through gearing education to individual social needs and solving the problem by utilising the existing facilities.

The NPE (1986) inter alia, states that protection of the environment is a value, which along with certain other values must form an integral part of curriculum at all stages. Further, paragraph 8.15 of the policy states:

> There is a paramount need to create of consciousness of the environment. It must permeate all ages and all sections of society, beginning with the child. Environmental consciousness should inform teaching in schools and colleges. This aspect will be integrate in the entire educational process.

Environmental education is concerned with the biophysical environment and its associated problems. These aspects of human behaviour are directly related to mans' interaction with biophysical environment and ability to resolve them. Thus environmental education can be conceived as a process of recognising values and clarifying concepts in order to develop skills and attitudes to understand and appreciate the interrelatedness among man, culture and his biographical surroundings. Moreover environmental education entails practice in decision-making and self-formation of a code of behaviour about issues concerning environment qualities.

Environmental education is aimed at producing a citizenry that is knowledgeable concerning the total environment and its associated problems, conscious and skilled in how to become involved in helping to solve these problems and motivated to work toward their solution. Environment provides various resources to mankind to live happy, whereas education improves the capabilities of the individuals and enables to make optimum use of environment. These fundamentals should be kept in mind and the following goals while in designing and selection of content and methodology for school subjects.

According to UNESCO's Tbilisi conference, the goals and objectives of environmental education are:

Goals

— To foster a clear awareness regarding economic, social, political and ecological interdependence in urban and rural areas.

— To provide opportunity to every individual to acquire knowledge, values, attitudes. Commitment and skills needed to protect and improve the environment.

— To create new patterns of behaviour among all the individuals on the society towards environment.

Objectives

Awareness

— To help social groups and individuals for acquiring awareness and sensitivity to the entire environment.

Knowledge

— To make the people to gain variety of experiences to obtain a basic understanding of environment.

Attitudes

— To make the people to acquire set of values and feelings for environment and motivate them actively in participating in solving the problems of environment.

Skills

— To make to acquire the skills for identification and finding remedies for environmental problems.

A model of an attitude-behaviour of an individual can be illustrated as follows:

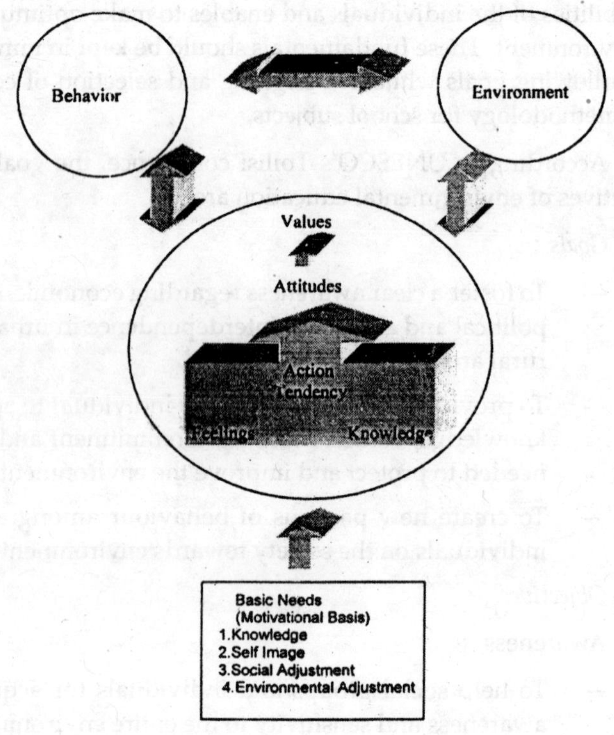

In order to satisfy the basic psychological needs of the every individual, motivation is necessary. In attempting to fulfil the needs an individual is motivated to develop attitudes, which helps to meet the needs. In this respect attitudes are necessary for satisfying different basic needs of the individual. Needs motivate an individual to adopt certain attitudes, which is turn satisfy those basic needs. Attitudes consist of feelings (affective), knowledge (cognitive) and tendency to act (psycho-motor) which helps together to form values. Values motivate and guide the actions of the individuals. Thinking consists of mental process, which interplays between the components of attitudes and values and direct behaviour. It is believed that behaviour occurs because of attitudes and values, which have adopted to fulfill needs and also behaviour helps to fulfill these needs. This implies a two-way relationships between attitudes and behaviour, attitudes cause behaviour and behaviour can influence attitudes.

The other aspect of this model is environment. The behaviour of the individual brings changes in the environment and in turn the changing conditions in the environment may change the behaviour of the individual in certain ways. Feelings and knowledge may affect attitudes of the individual. In both cases there is a two-way relationships.

In this model, values hold a certain place both in the fulfillment of basic human needs and the motivation of the behaviour of the individual. The implication is that values indicate ethical and moral responsibilities for the protection of environment. Thus environmental education should provide opportunities for value development in school education system.

Approaches to Environmental Education

There is a growing effort on educational front in addressing environmental issues in school systems. In order to direct environmental education programmes towards the development of attitudes, values, and behavioural skills in the areas of emotional decision-making and problem-solving, environmental education should be integrated in to the whole system of education, and its interdisciplinary nature enables to adopt a holistic perspectives aiming at building up a sense of values centering on practical problems. Couples of experiences around the world have shown that environmental education is not a separate branch of science but carried out according to the principles of the life long integral education. Thus widely used varieties of strategies include the integration of environmental issues in the existing educational programme. In cognizant of the fact in Indian context environmental issues should be seen from macro and micro level perspectives. Therefore education for the environment, education about the environment and education through environment will be meaningful.

Issues for Consideration

The objectives of environmental education are to provide facility to the students to have basic understanding of the environment in general and of the process of environmental education in particular at various levels of education. The programmes of environmental education should enable students to acquire a synthetic and holistic understanding of the content of environmental studies, examine the process of education from the environmental perspectives and also what ideas and methods are central to the process and what specific techniques are available to facilitate the process and make to learn the content and techniques essential to the functions in the professional role which he/she wished to play.

However, the central point is how education is applied to protect environment. How the existing discipline used to accomplish objectives of environmental education, and how should environmental issues be reinforced through the curriculum, by infusion or integration?

There are two alternatives in the development of curriculum of environmental education; single subject approach and integrating environmental issues in the existing programmes like science and social studies subjects. Nevertheless, mostly school curriculum is criticized for being in adequate and outmoded and not properly designed to meet the needs of modern times. Therefore, how the curriculum of environmental education shall be taught? Is instruction given in or outside the classroom? Is environment used as teaching aid? Is environment used as a medium to learning? How effective are in-service/pre-service teacher training programmes in motivating teachers, imparting skills, updating their knowledge and changing their behaviour in relation to environment? Parents/family, peer group, school, community and mass media would influence students value system and mode of behaviour towards environment. Which agency's influence would be more in moulding the behaviour and value system of the students towards environment? These are pertinent issues that need to be highlighted.

Environmental education programmes should be integrated into the curriculum of school education to provide opportunity for students to explore their environment sensorial, physically, intellectually in order to obtain both the motivating concern and the factual knowledge necessary to become an environmentally literate citizen. Our curriculum should consider in assisting students to become more sensitive to the environment, more informed about environment, and more inclined and skilled in coping with environmental problems.

Classroom teachers should be well trained in the integration of environmental education into instructional strategies. The teacher first should be a knowledgeable about the aspects of environment. Then they are able to convey the information to the students effectively. They help students to acquire beliefs, attitudes, values, and skills conducive to the development of an environmentally literate citizenary.

REFERENCES

Kochhar, S.K. (1991), *The Teaching of Social Studies*, New Delhi: Sterling Publishers.

Swan, A.J. and W.B. Stapp (1974), *Environmental Education Strategies Toward Amore Livable Future*, New York: Sage Publication.

Sharma, R.C. (1986), *Environmental Education*, New Delhi: Metropolitan.

NCERT (1986), *School Education in India*, Present Status and Future Needs.

GOI (1988). *Scheme of Environmental Orientation to School Education*, New Delhi: MHRD, Department of Education.

"Survey of the Environment" (1993), Published by *Hindu*.

—(1994), Published by *Hindu*.

—(1995), Published by *Hindu*.

37

Women Empowerment as a Tool for Enhancement of Values in Education

An Hypothetical Analysis

Dr. D. Pulla Rao*

Introduction

Everybody speaks about values. But no two persons agree upon a single set of value parameters. Value parameters differ from person to person, society to society, culture to culture and nation to nation. They also differ in time. Coming to the field of education there are a set of parameters, which is suggested for the enhancement of value education in the country. Education is expected to be a powerful tool for moulding the social, economic, political, ethical, cultural and spiritual values. Thus the value education is expected to influence the value systems in other fields of human life. Therefore, the value education which is supposed to be the basic weapon, shall be itself a strong, powerful and highly effective one.

In order to make value education as a powerful tool, education shall be made more open, more reflective and more vocal with greater participation of teachers, students, parents and the society in deciding all major aspects of education.

* Associate Professor, Department of Cooperation & Applied Economics, Andhra University, Visakhapatnam.

So far the education system in India is a very closed one without dated teacher training programmes and syllabi, heavy and mind bogging exercises with more paper work. There is little that a student can look into the society and learn and much less the relevance of his learning to the society. Most of the time the parents look at their children like scape goats, since they cannot participate in their education. Thus, in our country education itself has become a blunt and invalid tool. Therefore, education lost its relevance to the social, economic, political, ethical, cultural and spiritual values of our country. Under such circumstances one cannot except the education to play the role of a most effective powerful tool that can influence the human life.

It is under this context we will examine the role of women in education particularly school education and the need for greater involvement of women in education in order to make it highly value based one.

Historical Perspectives on Women Education

The history of India as well as the history of Andhra Pradesh records that women enjoyed a higher status in the society. They were provided educational opportunities comparable to men. The social evils like purdah, sati, enforced widowhood and child-marriages etc., crept into the society in the later period resulted in the degradation of women status. There were no institutions for education of girls during Muslim periods, but girls did receive religious èducation in the recitation of the Quran in their homes.

Under the British rule, the East India Company was reluctant to take up the responsibility of girl's education for a long time, due to the doctrine of religious neutrality, which was adopted by the Government so as not to offend the natives even on social customs that had nothing to do with religion. The Indian Education Commission (1882) took a serious notes of the status and education of women and rated it to be extremely backward, and recommended measures for improvement. But because of certain socio-political reasons, not noticeable progress could be made.

After independence, the University Education Commission (1948-49), set up by the government of India, laid special emphasis on the education of women and recommended that in view of the similar fields of activity for men and women, and some specific requirements of women, maximum facilities should be given for education in Home Economics and Home Management.

During the post-independence period, the main strategy adopted to achieve equalisation of educational opportunities has been to make school accessible to every child. It was thought that expansion of educational facilities, as a part of providing universal elementary education for all would make education available to the weaker sections of the society including women.

As per the National Policy on Education (NPE)—1986, the government of India launched several programmes. One such programme was the Mahila Samakhya, whose main emphasis was empowerment of women. The programme endeavours to create a learning environment where women can collectively affirm their potential, gain the strength to demand information and knowledge and move forward to change and take charge of their lives. Due to the existing programmes, and some initiatives on the part of the government, the girl's education has developed faster than that of boys in Andhra Pradesh after the formation of the state.

Objectives

The paper addresses itself to the qualification of advances made by girls in respect of basic education in Andhra Pradesh.

The specific objectives are:

1. To estimate the growth of enrolment of girls vis-à-vis boys in primary, upper primary and secondary education;
2. To examine the increase in the number of women teachers employed in primary, upper primary and high schools; and
3. To estimate disparity index between male and female literacy rates.

The Data

The secondary data relating to the enrolment of students by sex in primary, upper primary and secondary stage and the number of teachers by sex working in primary, upper primary and high schools for the period 1959-1960 to 1999-2000 in Andha Pradesh are obtained from the offices of the Bureau of Economics and Statistics, Hyderabad and the Commissioner and Director of School Education, Hyderabad, Andhra Pradesh.

Progress of Female Literacy Rate in Andhra Pradesh

As per the figures based on 2001 census, women constitute about 49.44 per cent of the total population of Andhra Pradesh. In fact this percentage should have been 50. The sex ratio is adverse. In the field of education these disparities between males and females are still larger. Table—37.1 shows the gap between the literacy rates of male and females. It shows how the gap has been persisting since 1961. In 1961 the female literacy rate was 12.03 per cent as against 30.19 per cent among males. The disparity index (ratio of male literacy rate to female literacy rate) in 1961 was 2.51. The literacy rate of female rose to 51.17 per cent in 2001 even as the rate for males increased to 70.85 per cent. As shown in Table—37.1, the literacy rate among females has increased at a faster rate than among males. This is evident from the successively decreasing trend of disparity index from 2.51 in 1961 to 1.38 in 2001. In Andhra Pradesh females responded far more enthusiastically than males to the Total Literacy Campaigns launched by the government with the help of non-governmental organisations and the cooperation of NGOs.

Table—37.1 Gender-wise literacy rates in Andhra Pradesh (1961 to 2001)

Year	*Male Literacy Rates*	*Females Literacy Rates*	*Disparity Index*
1961	30.19	12.03	2.51
1971	33.18	15.75	2.11
1981	39.26	20.39	1.92
1991	55.13	32.72	1.68
2001	70.85	51.17	1.38

Source: Handbook of Statistics, Bureau of Economics and Statistics of the Respective Years, Hyderabad, Andhra Pradesh.

Progress of Girl's Education in Andhra Pradesh

Table—37.2 shows the progress of girls' enrolment in primary, upper primary and secondary stages. In 1959-60, the enrolment of girls was 37.88 per cent (10.63 lakhs out of 28.06 lakhs) at primary stage, 22.94 per cent (61,752 out of 2.69 lakhs) at upper primary stage, and 17.88 per cent (39,594 out of 2.21 lakhs) at secondary stage. By 1999-2000, the situation had considerably improved with girls' enrolment reaching 48.39 per cent (44.09 lakhs out of 91.12 lakhs) at primary level, 44.21 per cent (8.67 lakhs out of 19.62 lakhs) at upper primary stage and 42.45 per cent (39,594 out of 2.21 lakhs) in secondary stage.

Table—37.2 Percentage of girls enrolment to total enrolment by stages 1959-60 to 1999-2000

Year	*Primary (I-V)*		*Upper primary (VI-VII)*		*Secondary (VIII-X)*	
	Boys	*Girls*	*Boys*	*Girls*	*Boys*	*Girls*
1959-60	62.12	37.88	77.06	22.94	82.12	17.88
1969-70	59.72	40.28	70.49	29.51	75.91	24.09
1979-80	58.67	41.33	66.38	33.62	69.91	30.09
1989-90	57.45	42.55	63.37	36.63	66.18	33.82
1999-2000	51.61	48.39	55.79	44.21	57.55	42.45

Source: 1. Commissioner and Director of School Education, Hyderabad, Andhra Pradesh.

2. Statistical Abstracts of Andhra Pradesh, Hyderabad, for various years.

The enrollment of girls has increased at a faster rate than that of boys at primary, upper primary and also necessary stage. During out study period (1959-60 to 1999-2000) the Annual Compound Growth Rate or enrolment of girls was 3.62 per cent as against 2.51 per cent of boys in primary stage. The corresponding figures were 6.83 and 4.24 in upper primary stage and 7.82 and 4.58 in secondary stage respectively. The foregoing analysis shows that during the whole period of 40 years after formation of the state of Andhra Pradesh, the growth rate of enrollment of girls has been higher than that of boys. It shows clearly in Table—37.3.

Table—37.3 Annual compound growth rate of enrollment by stages 1959-2000

Stage	*Annual compound growth rate during 1959-60 to 1999-2000*	
	Boys (%)	*Girls (%)*
Primary	2.51	3.62
Upper primary	4.24	6.83
Secondary	4.58	7.82

* Compound on the basis of enrollment of boys and girls in different stages.

Progress of Female Teachers in Different Stages of School Education of Andhra Pradesh

Table—37.4 shows the percentage of female teachers to total teachers in primary, upper primary and high schools. The female teachers constitute only 18.20 per cent in primary schools, 22.49 per cent in upper primary schools and 16.10 per cent in high schools compared with the corresponding percentage of 81.80, 77.51 and 83.90 among male teachers in 1959-60. These figures increased to 35.12 per cent in primary schools, 43.22 per cent in upper primary schools and 42.08 per cent in high schools as against 64.88 per cent in primary schools, 56.78 per cent in upper primary schools and 57.92 per cent in high schools among male teachers in 1999-2000. One should consider that increase in the number of women teachers is a healthy sign for the reasons (1) that it contributes to gender equality, and (2) the women teachers exhibit care and patience, their general traits, in teaching in primary, upper primary and secondary levels.

Table—37.4 Percentage of female teachers to total teachers by type of schools

Year	*Primary schools*		*Upper primary schools*		*High schools*	
	Males	*Females*	*Males*	*Females*	*Males*	*Females*
1	2	3	4	5	6	7
1959-60	81.80	18.20	77.51	22.49	83.90	16.10
1969-70	78.56	21.44	74.91	25.09	80.73	19.27

(Contd...)

1	2	3	4	5	6	7
1979-80	73.81	26.19	70.52	29.48	75.18	24.82
1989-90	72.15	27.85	67.86	32.14	69.89	30.11
1999-2000	64.88	35.12	56.78	43.22	57.52	42.08

Sources: 1. Commissioner and Direct of School Education, Hyderabad, Andhra Pradesh.

2. Statistical Abstracts of Andhra Pradesh, Hyderabad, for Various Years.

During the period of our study (1959-60 to 1999-2000) the Annual Compound Growth Rate of female teachers was 3.12 per cent as against 0.85 per cent of male teachers in primary schools. The corresponding figures were 7.37 per cent and 4.81 per cent in upper primary schools and 6.91 and 3.41 in high schools respectively. These data indicate that the participation of women has been increasing. It shows clearly in Table—37.5.

Table—37.5 Annual compound growth rate of teachers by type of schools 1959-2000

Stage	*Annual compound growth rate during 1959-60 to 1999-2000*	
	Male teachers (%)	*Female teachers (%)*
Primary	0.85	3.12
Upper primary	4.81	7.37
High schools	3.41	6.91

* Computed on the basis of male and female teachers appointed in differ stages of schools.

To repeat, the number of women teachers reached on all time high at primary, upper primary and high schools stage in 1999-2000. The number of both male and female teachers in primary, upper primary and high schools shows an increasing trend over the period of our study. It is particularly noteworthy that the index of female teachers recorded a much higher increase than that of the male teachers. This may be due to implementation of 33.33 per cent of reservation policy in Andhra Pradesh in favour of women.

Problems of Girls' Education

Though, the Government of Andhra Pradesh has made earnest efforts, since formation of the state in 1956, to improve the educational status of females, and met with considerable success, yet there is much to be done to bring them on par with males. There are certain factors, which hamper the progress of girls' education at the school level.

1. A large number of girls of school going age are not enrolled because they have to assist their mothers in domestic work. They have either to participate directly in the cooking work or assist their mothers indirectly by bringing food and fodder for domestic animals, keeping younger siblings and bringing water and fuel.
2. "Child marriage" is another problem. Child marriage, which is still prevalent in some regions/tribes especially in North Talangana districts in the state. Even as child marriage remains a legal offence, it continues to be prevalent in the state. According to the Child Marriage Restraint Act 1978, the minimum age of marriage is 21 years for boys and 18 years for girls. But in violation of these laws, the evil of child marriage still persists. This is a great problem affecting the education of girls adversely.
3. Girls have been taught to believe that domestic work is the only occupation for them. They do not think of any thing other than getting married, going away to in-law's house, and bearing and rearing children. Marriage and motherhood are, practically speaking, the only career options for majority of women, and for which they are groomed from childhood.
4. Illiteracy among mothers is another problem. Jawaharlal Nehru had once said that when we educate a boy we educate a single individual, but when we educate a girl we educate a family. There is a strong linkage between socio-economic factors and family size. This has been proved through numerous research studies conducted in Andhra Pradesh and India.

5. The economic dependence of women on men (husband or fathers) is a great barrier threatening their self-respect. The dominance of male members of the family over female members can also be explained in terms of economic dependence. Attempts have to be made to educate girls in such a way that they become economically independent. This will lead to an overall improvement of their quality of life.

Conclusions and Suggestions

At the time of the formation of the state, females were way behind males in terms of educational attainments, as elsewhere in the country. This is not a surprise given the cultural taboos that come in the way of educating females and given the son preference that is so glaring in our society. However, as time passed by, females made rapid progress especially in school education, the constitutional provisions and special efforts at the state level coming in handy. A process has set in motion where by the gap between males and females in literacy rate is getting reduced, the growth rate of enrollment of girls at the school level is exceeding that of boys, the gender disparity index is fast decreasing and, more importantly, large number of females are taking to teaching in schools. Though women share is about fifty per cent in the total population, their involvement in the education system is quit far far behind. Mother as the first teacher of the child, herself being an illiterate, one cannot expect miracles from her. It is a shame that we have kept Mother India illiterate, ignorant and second grade citizen of the society. Unless, all the ladies are totally educated we cannot expect them to play any effective role in the society.

Therefore, it is time that we concentrate on women education as a first priority. If resources are scarce it is highly advisable that the women educational needs are satisfied first.

REFERENCES

1. Altekar, A.S. (1951): *Education in Ancient India (Fourth Edition)*, Nan Inshore and Bros., Banaras (Variance).
2. Chalam, K.S. (1988): *Education and Weaker Sections*, InterIndia Publications, New Delhi.

3. Chalam, K.S. (1993): *Educational Policy for Human Resources Development*, Rawat Publications, Jaipur.

4. Chickermane, D.V. (1962): *A Study of Wastage in Primary Education*, Education and Psychology Review, Vol. II, January.

5. Gopinathan Nair, P.R., (1981): *Primary Education Population Growth and Socio-economic Change*, Allied Publishers, New Delhi.

6. Government of India (1969): *Education and National Development*, NCERT, New Delhi.

7. Naik, J.P. (1975): *Elementary Education in India—A Promise to Keep*, Allied Publishers, Bombay.

8. Nurullah, S. and Naik, J.P. (1943): *History of Education in India During the British Period*, MacMillan, Bombay.

9. Rajaiah, B. (1987): *Economic of Education*, Mittal Publication, New Delhi.

38

A Study of Moral Judgement of Pre-University Students in Relation to Gender, Socio-economic Status, Course of Study, Religion and Moral Judgement of their Teachers

Dr. M.S. Talawar*

Dr. G. Sheela**

This chapter is an outcome of the research conducted in Karnataka. The moral judgement of pre-university students is studied in relation to their gender, socio-economic status. Course of study, religion and moral judgement of their teachers.

INTRODUCTION

India is a spiritual land with rich culture. It's philosophy is full of values. It's values are reflected in every aspect of its life and practice. Values are the essence of a cultural and civilised society. Our's is one of the oldest civilization and it owes its long survival to its values. The fundamental characteristics of any society are a reflection of its basic values. Indian society is marked by spiritualism, principles of honesty, obedience, non-violence.

* **Professor, Department of Education, Bangalore University, Bangalore–560 056.**

** **Guest Faculty, Department of Education, Bangalore University, Bangalore–560 056.**

Values are surely tinged with a moral flavour. Morals are such human behaviours which are deemed to be right or good in a society. Every society prescribes for its members certain rules of conduct which ought to be observed by them. These rules are imposed for harmonious are peaceful living in society. These rules and principles concerned with good and evil as manifested to us by conscience constitute to the concept of morality. Moral values and standards differ from one society to the other. Morality is therefore the law of humanity in terms of behaviour and the conduct of Universal law of harmony. It is the internalisation of as set of values, ideas and values sanctioned from society.

A child is born into a society. He should follow the rules of conduct prescribed by that society. These rules, morals and values are transferred and inculcated in the child form the very beginning by its elders. The moral behaviour of the child is mainly influenced by the *home,* the *school* through the conduct and behaviour of the teachers and the social community and the *public* of the locality.

If all the elders of the society have an obligation of helping a child in developing appropriate skills and judgement capacity to cope with variety of moral choices, then it is necessary to understand how children develop morally. The child born to this world is neither moral nor immoral; it is "amoral" and a social. A moral sense must come from his society. So, the status of the morality which an individual attains is largely determined by the nature of his society. It is the outcome of one's own awareness, interaction the life view developed due to the interactive process of growth.

Moral development is an integral part of the personality development. It is a comprehensive process whereas individuals learn to considerably adopt the norms or moral conduct and behaviour. The true end of this development is to make the individual morally autonomous, leading to a state where the individual is able to act in accordance with universal moral principles which he accepts in relation to the larger society.

Kohelberg considered conscience or morality to be a set of cultural rules of social action which have been internalised by the individual. Moral development has been conceived as increase in internalisation by basic cultural rules. The process of internalisation of moral values involves three essential components:

1. *The Behavioural Component:* Refers to resistance to temptation or the inhibiting of behaviour which is regarded to be wrong.
2. *The Emotional and Learning Component:* Refers to emotion of guilt. The individual behaves morally in order to avoids the feeling of guilt.
3. *The Judgemental Component:* Refers to the ability to make moral judgements in terms of standards and justify maintaining the standards to oneself and others. The main basis of such judgement is the golden rule that one should take full account of the rights of other people.

There are several attempts being made by developmental psychologists to explore the nature and content of moral development in children and adolescents. Among them the work of Jean Piaget and Kohlberg are discussed here. There view is that moral development, like intellectual development, passes through different stages of development and the behaviour is characteristics of each stage of moral development. These behaviours according to them could be clearly described for each stage. They view moral development as an active, dynamic constructive process leading to a state where the individual is able to act according to moral principles which he either accepts because he understands them and agrees with them or which he has worked out for himself.

Moral judgement is the highest level of moral development wherein an individual considers judgements about moral behaviour. The basic assumption of moral judgement is that human beings not only generate behaviour but also categorise, evaluate and judge them. Moral judgement is a process of defining a happening in terms of moral justifiability. It is the cognitive capacity which helps an individual to evaluate the worthiness or unworthiness of an action.

Moral judgement is defined in five dimensions in this study.

Dimensions of Moral Judgement

1. *Honesty:* is the starting stage of ethical behaviour. It is a social obligation. An individual should be honest to his family, friends, colleagues, people of the state and to the world.
2. *Truthfulness:* Truth is a value by itself. Being truthful is being reliable.
3. *Non-violence:* Ahimsa is the Indian term for non-violence. It does not confine itself to non-injury at the physical level but also extends to the mental level.
4. *Obedience:* It means an individual's submissiveness to a superior's will. It originates out of respect for the person in command.
5. *Justice:* It is the fairness of the individual in and towards a situation/individual. These are the dimensions of moral judgement that are universally accepted in all the civilised societies.

NEED AND IMPORTANCE

A society to be stable, to lead a life of joy, peace and serenity needs a firm foundation of morality. It needs its members to exhibit behaviours and possess conduct of universal law of harmony. But in today's technological world the values and morality of individuals are being swept away to gain the worldly pleasures. Individuals achievement and position is preferred even if a sacrifice of values, ethics and morals is demanded for it. But for the universal harmony of our society it is essential to inculcate values and develop morals in children from their early stages. Schools like the family, is a context for moral development. Teachers are models of moral and ethical behaviour. They have a tremendous impact on their students.

With the advent of computer and information technology in the country and Bangalore city in particular it is seen that the students of pre-university stage are more exposed to immoral behaviour which may not be good for the well being of our society.

Therefore it was felt that there is need to take up a society of moral judgement in relation to some sociological variables.

REVIEW OF THE RELATED LITERATURE

Colby, Anne, Kohlberg, Lawrence, John and Lieberman, Marcus (1983) in their longitudinal study found that moral judgement was positively correlated with age, SES, I.Q. and education. Pieget's (1932) studies concerns the nature of children's moral judgements Schunrer's (1976) study on moral reasoning in young adults revealed difference in favour of males over females in the attained level of moral reasoning.

Warshaw (1978) found that males achieved significantly higher levels of moral reasoning than females. He also indicated that the climate and the environment of the school would be a significant factor of moral judgement. But found that socio-economic factors were relevant in any consideration of moral judgement, and that social-class factors were a significant variable even with the youngest of his sample.

Researches done by Sieffering (1981) Tifis Daniel (1978), Dockstander (1978) Benninga Jaeques (1976) and Johnson (1981) indicated that there was no significant sex difference in moral judgement. Flyn (1984) indicated that age and sex were significantly related to both moral judgement measures. Prahallada (1985 showed that there are social class differences that affect children's moral development. Studies by Sears et al. (1957), Kohn (1958), Kohlberg (1966), Kay (1968) and Bull, to mention but a few, all suggest that children from families of higher social status show greater maturity in moral judgement than those from lower social class backgrounds.

Karla V. (1978), found that socio-economic status was positively related with the level of more judgement. Hilton (1978) revealed a positive correlation between the dependent variable moral judgement and socio-economic status of students. Evans (1980), Gongre (1981) and Johnson (1979) found no relationship regarding socio-economic status and stages of moral development and moral judgement.

OBJECTIVES OF THE STUDY

The following are the objectives of the present study:

1. To find, if there is any significant differences in honesty, truthfulness, non-violence, obedience and justice—

components of moral judgement and total moral judgement of first year pre-university boys and girls.

2. To find, if there is any significant difference in honesty, truthfulness, non-violence obedience, and justice-components of moral judgement and total moral judgements of first year pre-university students belonging to high and low socio-economic status.

3. To find, if there is any significant difference in honesty, truthfulness nonviolence, obedience and justice components of moral judgement and total moral judgement of first year pre-university students of science, arts and commerce.

4. To find, if there is any significant difference in honesty, truthfulness, non-violence, obedience and justice—components of moral judgement and total moral judgement of first year pre-university students of Hindu, Muslim and Christian religions.

5. To find if there is any correlation between moral judgement of students and their teachers.

METHODOLOGY

Variables of the Study

Dependent Variable

In the present investigation, moral judgement was treated as dependent variable.

Independent Variable

Independent variables considered in this study were:

1. Socio-economic status
2. Sex
3. Religion
4. Course of study
5. Moral judgement of teachers

Hypotheses

Based upon the objectives of the study the following hypothesis were formulated:

- There is no significant difference in honesty, truthfulness, non-violence, obedience, and justice components of moral judgement and total moral judgement of first year pre-university boys and girls.
- There is no significant difference in honesty, truthfulness, non-violence, obedience and justice-components of moral judgement and total moral judgement of first year pre-university students belonging to high, moderate and low socio-economic status.
- There is no significant difference in honesty, truthfulness, non-violence, obedience and justice-components of moral judgement and total judgement of students selecting science, arts and commerce as courses of their study.
- There is no significant difference in honesty, truthfulness, non-violence, obedience and justice-- components of moral judgement and total moral judgement of first year pre-university students of Hindu, Muslim and Christian religions.
- There is no significant correlation between moral judgement of status and moral judgement of teachers.

Tools used for the Research

The following tools were used to collect the data:

1. *Moral Judgement Scale:* Moral judgement scale developed by B.G. Sudha and Satyanarayana was used to measure the moral judgement of high school students. If is a self-reporting scale, the items of which are situational. The scale consists of 30 items. The scale measures five dimensions of moral judgement viz., honesty, truthfulness, non-violence, obedience and justice. The scores on all these components add up to form the score of total moral judgement.

2. *Socio-economic Status Scale:* Data relating to socio-economic status was collected by the revised socio-economic status scale (revised 1983). This scale has the three main categories, education, occupation and income.

3. *Personal Proforma:* was used to collect information about sex and types of colleges, course of study and religion.

Sampling Procedure

The population for the present study was the student studying in first year pre-university in government and private aided and private unaided colleges in Bangalore city. First year pre-university students would have just finished their school education and this would show the effect of our total school programme on their moral judgement. Moral education stops from this stage of education. Hence, first year pre-university students were selected. Random sampling method was used. The gender, the course of study and also the religion, to which they belong were kept in view while selecting the sample. 78 boys and 91 girls were selected, totaling to 169 students of first year pre-university in Bangalore city.

Forty teachers from the same colleges from where the students were selected were included in the study.

Statistical Techniques Used

t-test: "t-test" was used to find if significant difference existed between two groups in respect of their moral judgement in total and by components of moral judgement.

Correlation: Pearson Product Moment Correlation technique was used to find if there was any correlation between moral judgement of students and that of their teachers.

MAJOR FINDINGS OF THE STUDY

- There is no significant difference in honesty, truthfulness, non-violence and obedience, components of moral judgements and total moral judgement of boys and girls of pre-university colleges. However, in terms of justice-component of moral judgement female students have scored significantly higher than their male counterparts.

- There is no significant difference in honesty and truthfulness-components of moral judgement and total moral judgement among pre-university students belonging to high and low socio-economic status. But it is seen that students of high socio-economic status differ in non-violence, justice and obedience-components of moral judgement. Students from high socio-economic strata and more non-violent and posses high justice and are less obedient than students of low socio-economic status.
- It is seen that students of Arts and Science courses differ in their moral judgement and four of the components except for obedience whereas students of Arts and Commerce and students of Science and Commerce do not differ in their moral judgement in total and in terms of its components. Students of Science have scored higher in honesty, truthfulness, non-violence, justice-components of moral judgement and total moral judgement.
- It is seen that students of all of the religions do not differ in moral judgement as a whole and in terms of its components except for honesty where Christian students show higher honesty score than their Hindu counterparts.
- The moral judgement of students is highly correlated to that of their teachers.

EDUCATIONAL IMPLICATIONS

- It was found that Hindus, Muslims and Christian students do not differ significantly in their moral judgement. Traditionally religion has been the basis of morality. A glance at the history of mankind reveals that religion has been the chief agent in promoting morality. It is the standard by which the acts and attitudes of the larger whiles are evaluated. In the early stages of society, religion promoted morality by certain commands and prohibitions set-forth by some divine personality. They served as a powerful source to lead to moral conduct. In Vedas Dharma is the name for the code of conduct prescribed for doing what is proper, right and good. According to the Hindu conception, morality is synonymous with Dharma, (The highest moral behaviour) as the greatest virtue and a matter of supreme importance. Prophet Mohammed laid down his code of moral conduct by specifying certain acts which must be done as being good acts. In the holy Quran the moral code taught by the Prophet as the messenger of God to his followers, consisted of recommending aims giving charity, kindness, modesty, honesty in dealings. With the advent of Jesus Christ, the moral code took a more refined shape. In almost all religions one can discover and pick out from their general and universal principles on which development of morals depends and which can serve to raise high moral standards. Religion is thus the main spring of moral values. All religions basically preach the universal values of worldly peace and harmony. Hence it is essential that students should be made to understand these core principles of every religion. This helps in developing secular values and this would contribute to global peace.

- It is found that there is no significant difference in moral judgement of male and female students. This shows that there is less disparity in the way both male and female children are brought up in the present modern society. This appears to be a positive sign for the development of the society. Our education is also overcoming the gender bias in schools through revamping its curriculum and its activities. The moral conduct in schools not show any gender differences.
- It is seen the science students have higher moral judgement than students studying in Arts courses. Science as a subject develops scientific and thinking thus making the child more open minded. These qualities might contribute to right thinking and judgement among the students. Hence it is essential that scientific way of thinking be developed in students of Arts courses.

- It is found that students from low socio-economic status are obedient. This indicates that they may be submissive to authority. This could be used in a positive direction to develop goods morals in them. Students from lower socio-economic status are less non-violent and prefer violent behaviour. Many studies have shown that the strata or class of society to which an individual belongs affects the behaviour of that individual. It is been known popularly that the middle class are most concerned with conformity to generally accepted standards of behaviour in a society. Prestige might be a prime factor here. Since societal approval is highly valued among them, moral values are also highly valued. The expectation from the lower class is not the same. The feelings of lack of opportunity may be a part of the personality pattern of individuals at the lower stage. Holligshead and Redich (1958) noted a deep distrust of authority figures in the lowest strata. Hostility, disobedience and feelings of being exploited by their high ups permeates the behaviour of many of those at the bottom of the social scale. Styles of life, taste, values, and behaviour pattern vary with class placements. Education is one of the potent instrument to reduce this disparity in the society. Hence education should be given to all and should aim to develop moral values among all its clients.
- It is seen that moral judgement of students in highly correlated to that of their teachers. Schools like the family, is the context for moral development. Teachers are models of ethical behaviour. The school community especially the teachers could enable the child to internalise democratic mores and become a contributing citizen of society. The teachers should possess and exhibit moral behaviour. The students tend to imitate and follow the behaviour of their teachers. The basic purpose of education is to produce useful citizens and the understanding of human relationships which ensure the order of good welfare of the community. This should be kept up to by its teachers.

39

Value Orientation Among School Teachers

Dr. Rajendra Prasad, D.*

Introduction

The forty-sixth session of the International conference on education took place from 5th to 8th September 2001 in Geneva on the theme of "learning to live together". It therefore closed three days before the disastrous strikes at World Trade Centre and other places in the United States. The conclusions and proposals for action related to teachers are improving the education of teachers so that they can better develop among pupils' behaviour and values of solidarity and tolerance so as to prepare them to prevent and resolve conflicts peacefully and to respect cultural diversity; changing the relationship between teacher and pupil to respond to the evolution of society. Hence, it shouldered great responsibility on the teacher with a fore vision of protection of the universe, nature and society by way of educating the future generations.

Economic requirements in some countries, ideological goals in others, the struggle for national liberation in many parts of the world and even, in some cases, the fear of social unrest, all contributed to the pressing need to make education more domestic. And there are signs of considerable progress. Both modern and traditional societies have created conditions to enable more people

* Associate Professor, IASE, Kakatiya University.

to attend school. Industrialised countries, whether socialist or capitalist, are continually expanding school education. Philip H. Coombs (1985) stated that increased bureaucratisation and sociological diversity of the greatly enlarged education systems not only altered the atmosphere and human relations within the schools but also eroded their relations with parents and the community.

Crisis in values is discussed all over the world. Pluralism and pragmatism in values are prevailing. Considering this, value education is given much importance right from school to teacher education level. Teachers are value inculcators in the students and in the community at large. Hence, in the process of globalisation and privatisation there is a need to understand prevailing values and value system among teachers.

Today, globalisation of trade, privatisation of education and computerisation of institutions is extending in every field including education. This situation is significantly influencing school environment, teacher-student relations and values. Fifth Survey of Educational Research (2000) reported thirty-one studies in the area of moral, art and aesthetic education and among them only two are related to teachers' values.

Objective of the Study

To study the preferences of values and value system of the teachers with regard to (a) *terminal values*—a comfortable life, an exciting life, a world at peace, equality, family security, freedom, happiness, pleasure, self-respect, social recognition, true friendship and wisdom, (b) *instrumental values*—ambitious, broadminded, capable, courageous, forgiving, helpful, honest, independent, intellectual, obedient, polite and responsible.

Tool

Rokeach Value-Survey (RVS).

Sample

A sample of 300 teachers was selected from 90 schools for the collection of the data. Random sampling method was adopted. The sample included male and female; married and unmarried. It included secondary grade teachers, school assistants and post-graduate teachers. The sample also included teachers of different academic and professional qualifications, teachers experience and place of residence.

Table—39.1 Median ranking and composite rank order of the teachers towards terminal values

N = 300

Sl. No.	*Terminal Value*	*Median Ranking*	*Composite Rank Order*
1.	A comfortable life (A Prosperous life)	21.5	3.5
2.	An existing life (A stimulating, active life)	23	6.5
3.	A world at peace (Free of war and conflict)	19.5	1
4.	Equality (Brotherhood, equal opportunity for all)	21.5	3.5
5.	Family security (Taking care of loved ones)	24.5	10.5
6.	Freedom (Independence, free choice)	21	2
7.	Happiness (Contentedness)	25.5	12
8.	Pleasure (An enjoyable, leisurely life)	23.5	8
9.	Self respect (Self esteem)	24.5	10.5
10.	Social recognition (Respect, admiration)	23	6.5
11.	True friendship (Close companionship)	24	9
12.	Wisdom (A mature understanding of life)	22	5

Note: Lower the median the higher is the relative importance of the value.

Table—39.2 Median ranking and composite rank order of the teachers towards instrumental values

N = 300

Sl. No.	*Instrumental Values*	*Median Ranking*	*Composite Rank Order*
1.	Ambition (Hard working, aspiring)	22	5
2.	Broadminded (Open minded)	24.5	12
3.	Capable (Competent, effective)	22	5
4.	Courageous (Standing up for beliefs)	21.5	3
5.	Forgiving (Willing to pardon others)	23	8
6.	Helpful (Working for the welfare of others)	24	11
7.	Honest (Sincere, truthful)	19.5	1
8.	Independent (Self-reliant, self-sufficient)	21	2
9.	Intellectual (Intelligent, reflective)	22	5
10.	Obedient (Dutiful, respectful)	23	8
11.	Polite (Courteous, well-mannered)	23	8
12.	Responsible (Dependable, reliable)	23.5	10

Note: Lower the median the higher is the relative importance of the value.

Findings and Conclusion

The more preferred terminal values of the teachers are in the order of: (1) A world at peace (free of war and conflict); (2) Freedom (Independence, free choice); (3) A comfortable life (A prosperous life) and equality (Brotherhood, equal opportunity for all); (4) Wisdom (A mature understanding of life).

The less preferred terminal values are in the order of: (1) Happiness (Contentedness); (2) Family security (Taking care of loved ones) and self respect (Self esteem); (3) True Friendship (Close Companionship); (4) Pleasure (An enjoyable, leisurely life).

The value system of the teachers for terminal values is found in the order of: (1) A world at peace (Free of war and conflict); (2) Freedom (Independence, free choice); (3) Equality (Brotherhood, equal opportunity for all) and A comfortable life (A prosperous life); (4) Wisdom (A mature understanding of life); (5) An exiting life (A stimulating active life) and Social recognition (Respect, admiration); (6) Pleasure (An enjoyable, leisure life); (7) True friendship (Close companionship); (8) Family security (Taking care of loved ones) and self respect (Self esteem); (9) Happiness (Contentedness).

Hence, they are found at higher level of social consciousness.

The more preferred instrumental values of the teachers are in the order of: (1) Honest (Sincere, truthful); (2) Independent (Self-reliant, self-sufficient); (3) Courageous (Standing up for beliefs); (4) Ambition (Hardworking, aspiring), capable (Competent, effective) and intellectual (Intelligent, reflective).

The less preferred instrumental values by the teachers are: (1) Broadminded (Open minded); (2) Helpful (Working for the welfare of others); (3) Responsible (Dependable, reliable); (4) Forgiveness (Willing to pardon others), Obedient (Dutiful respectful) and polite (Courteous, well-mannered).

The value system of the teachers for instrumental values is found in the order of: (1) Honest (Sincere, truthful); (2) Independent (Self-reliant, self-sufficient); (3) Courageous (Standing up for beliefs); (4) Ambition (Hard working, aspiring), Capable (Competent, effective) and intellectual (Intelligent, reflective); (5) Forgiving (Willing to pardon others), (Obedient (Dutiful, respectful) and polite (courteous, well-mannered); (6) Responsible (Dependable, reliable); (7) Helpful (Working for the welfare of others); (8) Broadminded (open minded).

Hence, they are honest, independent and courageous but not broadminded and least helpful.

REFERENCES

1. NCERT, *Fifth Survey of Educational Research*, 1988-92, Vol. I, New Delhi, NCERT, 1997, pp. 399-403.
2. NCERT, *Firth Survey of Educational Research* 1988-92. Vol. II, New Delhi: NCERT, 1997, pp. 1333-1356.
3. Sinha, S. "Valuational Generation Gap in the View of Students and their Parents on Student Unrest". Ph.D. Psychology, Agra University, 1981. In Buch, M.B. (ed.), *Third Survey of Research in Education*. 1978-1983, New Delhi: NCERT, 1987, p. 219.
4. Dilip Kumar Ray, Selection of Student Teachers: Predicting their Value Systems. Cited by C.L. Kundu (ed.), *Indian Year Book on Teacher Education*, New Delhi: Sterling Publishers Limited, 1988, pp. 173-174.
5. Feather, Norman T. *Values in Education and Society*. New York: The Free Press, 1975, p. 109.
6. Campbell, E.Q. "Adolescent Socialisation". In D.A. Goslin, (ed.) *Handbook of Socialisation Theory and Research*, Chicago: Rand McNally, 1969, pp. 847-851.
7. Rao, R.B. "A Study of Inter-relationship of Values, Adjustment and Teaching Attitude of Pupil-teachers at Various Levels of Socio-economic Status". Ph.D. Education, Avadh University, 1986. In Buch, M.B. (ed.), *Fourth Survey of Research in Education, 1983-88*, Volume II, New Delhi: NCERT, 1991, pp. 980-981.
8. Sharma, I.C. "Teaching Aptitude, Intellectual Level and Morality of Perspective Teachers, Ph.D. Education". M. Sukh, University, 1984. In Buch, M.B. (ed.), *Fourth Survey of Research in Education, 1983-88*, Volume II, New Delhi: NCERT, 1991, p. 986.
9. Mohan Rao, C.N.S. "An Evaluation of the Factors that Effects the Teacher Morale in School Setting". Ph.D. Education, Andhra University, 1985. In Buch, M.B. (ed.), *Fourth Survey of Research in Education, 1983-88*, Volume II, New Delhi: NCERT, 1991, p. 963.
10. Kaul, S. "Personality Factors, Values and Interests Among the Most Accepted and Least Accepted Secondary School Female Teachers in Mathura District". Ph.D. Psychology, Agra University, 1987. In Buch, M.B. (ed.), *Fourth Survey of Research in Education, 1983-88*, Volume II, New Delhi: NCERT, 1991, p. 950.
11. Bhushan, "A Value Across Sex and Family Vocations". School of Education Himachal Pradesh University, 1979. In Buch, M.B. (ed.) *Third Survey of Research in Education*, 1978-1983, New Delhi: NCERT, 1987, p. 113.
12. Kumari, P., "Personality Needs, Moral Judgement and Value Patterns of Secondary School Teachers—A Critical Analysis". Ph.D. Education, Gorakpur University, 1981. In Buch, M.B. (ed.), *Third Survey of Research in Education, 1978-1983*, New Delhi: NCERT, 1987, p. 371.

13. Raj, G.S. "Attitudes and Values of Teachers in the Context of Socio-cultural Background. A Comparative Study of Expatriate Indian and Native Teachers of Ethiopia". Ph.D. Education, Maharaja Siyajirao University of Baroda, 1981. In Buch, M.B. (ed.), *Third Survey of Research in Education, 1978-1983*, New Delhi: NCERT, 1987, p. 258.

14. Chandra D., "A Study of Perception of Work Values in Teaching and Certain Non-teaching Occupations". Ph.D. Education, Aligarh Muslim University, 1977. In Buch, M.B. (ed.), *Third Survey of Research in Education. 1978-1983*, New Delhi: NCERT, 1987, p. 116.

15. Sharma, D.D. "Differential Values of Students and Teachers—As a Function of Various Social Factors". Ph.D. Psychology Department, Jodhpur University, 1977. In Buch, M.B. (ed.), *Third Survey of Research in Education, 1978-1983*, New Delhi: NCERT, 1987, p. 206.

16. Sharma Meenu. "A Study of Teachers' Socio-economic Status and Values with Reference to their Attitude Towards the Nation". Ph.D. Education, Agra University, 1992. *In the Fifth Survey of Educational Research 1988-1992*, Volume II, New Delhi: NCERT, 2000, p. 1347.

17. Srivastava, Vinodini, "A Study of Change Proneness and Job Satisfaction Among Teachers with Reference to Teacher Values". Ph.D. Education Agra University, 1990. *In the Fifth Survey of Educational Research. 1988-1992*, Volume II, New Delhi: NCERT, 2000, p. 1351.

18. Clemence, S. Mary. "A3 * 3 Anova of Job Satisfaction Among High School Women Teachers by Their Role Conflict and Dimensions of Values". M.Phil, Education, Bangalore University, 1989. *In the Fifth Survey of Educational Research, 1988-1992*, Volume II, New Delhi: NCERT, 2000, p. 1443.

19. Rawat, S., "A Study of the Expectations and Realities of Job, Job Satisfaction and Values; Pattern of Secondary School Teachers in Relation to their Sex". Ph.D. Education, Rohilkhand University, 1992. *In the Fifth Survey of Educational Research. 1988-1992*, Volume II, New Delhi: NCERT, 2000, p. 1471.

20. Kukreti, B.R. "A Study of Some Physical Correlates of Successful Teachers", Ph.D. Education, Rohilkhand University, 1992. *In the Fifth Survey of Educational Research. 1988-1992*, Volume II, New Delhi: NCERT, 2000, p. 1415.

21. S.P. Kulshrestha. *Emerging Value-pattern of Teachers and New Trends of Education in India*. New Delhi: Light and Life Publishers, 1979, p. 243.

22. J.S. Rajput, "School Curriculum in India with Focus on Value Education and Work Experience", *Journal of Indian Education*, Special Issue on Curriculum Development-I, November 1999, Vol. XXV (3), p. 1.

23. A.N. Maheshwari: *Value Orientation in Teacher Education*. Article on the web site in NCTE, 2003. <*http://www.ncte-in.org*>

24. Editor "Moral Decline". *The Wall Street Journal*, March 5, 1998, p. A14.

25. Nussel, E.J. "The American Value System: A Study in Contradictions". *Phi Kappa Phi Journal*, pp. 23-29.

26. Pamela A., *Attitudes and Job Satisfaction*, Braden, Division of Business and Economics, Value, Parkersburg: West Virginia University.

27. Jacqui Lockaby, Matt Baker and Jon A. Hogg. *The Influence of Foundational and Expressed Values on Teacher Behaviour.* 28th Annual National Agricultural Education Research Conference, December 12, 2001, pp. 374-381.

28. Longstreth, L.E. "Values in the Social Studies: Implicit, Explicit and Ignored, Social Education". In S.P. Kulshrestha, *Emerging Value-pattern of Teachers and New Trends of Education in India*. New Delhi: Light and Life Publishers, 1979, p. 39.

29. Janet Powney and Ursula Schlapp, "How do Primary Teachers Foster Values? SCRE Spollights. *The Scottish Council for Research in Education*, No. 56, 1996, Edinburg EH3 6NL. pdf.file.

30. Norman T. Feather, Op. cit. pp. 208-228.

40

Attitude Towards Value-Oriented Education in Primary School Children

Dr. T. Rajasekhar Reddy*

Education is expected to play a major role in promoting national development. At the same time it should bring about harmonious development of all the faculties-towards adequate preparation for life. Every human is witnessing tremendous value crisis throughout the world today. As the validity of human belief in values is dying out in every land, the younger generation has started to pooh-pooh the unique religious epics and religious institutions giving room for erosion of spiritual and moral values of mind.

Unfortunately education is becoming day-by-day more or less materialistic and the value traditions are being slowly given up. Modern Indian is being educated mainly with the bread and butter aim of education as a result most of Indian graduates run after money, power, comforts, without caring for any values.

Values simply stated are the determines in the man that influence his choices in life and that decide his behaviour. Values as indicated are inherent, in individual man but they are additionally inherent although perhaps less definably so, in collective man in a given culture that is or in a combination of cultures. Whatever the exact nature of human society, values exist

* **Research Associate, Department of Education, S.V. University, Tirupati.**

in some form. In primitive society, they reside in the minds of individuals handed down from generation to generation.

In respect to individual and culture values are circular, existing in individuals they flow into and help to shape the culture, existing condition, without categorically dictating the values developed by individuals in those cultures. It is important that all individuals habitually interact certain values from their respective cultures.

Values are described as the socially defined desires and goals that are internalised through the process of condition, learning and socialism.

Values are goals set for achievement and they motivate, define and colour all our activities cognitive, effective and conative. When education builds up true values in the life of our student, it has equipped the ship of students with RADAR and compass to sail clear on the stormy sea of life.

According to Carl Rogers in 'Freedom to Learn' (1969) valuing is the tendency of a person to show preference.

The moral and aesthetics, principles, belief and standards that give coherence and direction to a person's decisions and actions. Where such values are held by or are imposed upon the majority of people in a society they may be known as social values.

Value education we would like to develop the social, moral, aesthetic and spiritual sides of a person which are often underlines within formal education Value education teaches us to preserve whatever is good and worthwhile in what we have inherited from our culture.

Value Education—In Emerging Indian Society

The challenge before our country and all sections of our country is inoculation of ethical, social and spiritual values. The present malady by in our society is the absence of ethical conduct. We have become slaves of material civilization. How to give our society a worthy purpose in life motivated by ethics, social and spiritual values in the main problem facing in nation.

The present situation in India, demands such a system of education which apart from strengthening national unity must strengthen social solidarity through meaningful and purposeful constructive value education by adopting inter-disciplinary approach.

Problem

Primary school teachers attitude towards value-oriented education.

Objectives

— Is there any significant difference between urban and rural teachers on 'value oriented education'.

— Is there any significant difference between Govt. Teachers and Private School Teachers on value oriented education.

Hypotheses

— 'No significant difference between Rural and Urban teachers on value-oriented education.

— No significant difference between Govt. and Private Primary School teachers on 'Value, Oriented Education'.

Tool

A questionnaire of attitude scale was adopted which was developed and standardise and administered for the same purpose.

The instrument is having two items with five alternatives SA, A, D, DA, SDA. In the 70 items 66 items are positive a d four are negative items (4, 11, 25, 67). A range of 5 to 1 points a e given for a positive item in the order of their alternative and 1 to 5 points are given for a negative item in the order of their alternatives. The total score range between 70 to 350.

Sample

The random sampling was made to select a sample of 300 primary school teachers from Chittoor district.

	Urban	-	151	\
Locality				300
	Rural	-	149	/

Management Government – 173 \
300
Private – 127 /

Analysis

The data relating to the scores of Primary school teachers regarding attitude towards value oriented education has been summarised in a data sheet for 300 teachers according to locality, management, appropriate coding was given to facilitate statistical calculation.

Table—40.1 Mean and SD's of rural and urban primary school teachers towards value oriented education and result of 't' test

Variable	*Category*	*Number*	*Mean*	*S.D*	*'t'*
Locality	Rural	151	280.51	32.71	2.125*
	Urban	149	287.83	26.62	

t is significant at 0.05 level.

The rural primary school teachers obtained a mean score of 280.51 and the urban teachers scored 287.83.. It shows that the urban primary school teachers are higher mean scores than the rural primary school teachers.

The difference between the two means was tested for significance. The obtained 't' value was 2.125. The table value for 298 df was found to be 1.96. The obtained t value was found to be more than the table value at 0.05. Hence the difference between rural and urban primary school teachers was significant at 0.05 level. Therefore, the 'Null Hypothesis' has been rejected.

Table—40.2 Means of SD's and government and private primary schools teachers towards value oriented education and results of 't' test

Variable	*Category*	*Number*	*Mean*	*S.D*	*'t'*
Management	Government	173	281.44	32.65	1.86@
	Private	127	287.83	25.68	

@'t' is not significant at 0.05 level.

The government primary school teachers obtained a mean score of 281.44. The private primary school teachers obtain 287.33. The private primary school teachers were showing higher mean score when compare with their counter parts.

The obtained t value is 1.83, which is very less for 298 if at 0.05 level. Hence the difference between government and private primary school teachers was not significant. Therefore the 'Null hypothesis' has been accepted.

'Value can not be saught but caught' as for as the value oriented education is concerned we can say that values are indispensable for those who want to lead virtuous life in this world.

— With the degree of realism in value oriented education pupils are encouraged to live in the harmony with nature are, music and build good nation.

— The moral and value oriented education with the inclusion of common ethical teachings of all great religious highlights the nation unity.

Value oriented education strengthen national integration by accelerating the process of moderanisation and development of scientific temper and outlook.

Value based education system cultivate the basis value of humanism, democracy, socialism and secularism.

REFERENCES

Allport, G.W. 1929. "The Composition of Political Attitudes", *American Journal of Society*, 35 pp. 220-238.

Dayakar Reddy (1984), *Geethamath & Dayakar Reddy Study of Moral Judgement*, S.V. University, Tirupati (1987).

Thurstone. L.L. 1929 Theory of Attitude Measurement Psychology Bull, 36, pp. 222-241.

41

Promoting Values in Teacher Trainees

M. Rajini*

Introduction

Education is the key that opens the door of life. It plays a pivotal role in the social change, by bringing perfection in the human life, besides an upward mobility in social status, a radical transformation in outlook and perfection. Education is widely accepted as the essential tool, for the attainment of developmental goal. It is the principal instrument in awakening the child to cultural values.

Teacher plays very important role in the process of education. In India, most of the classroom teaching is dominated by the teachers. Thus, the new entrants to this field must possess worthy values, which will enable them to inculcate these values among students.

The contents of education still belong to the past. Education suffers basically from what the report describes as the gap between its contents and living experience of its pupils, between the system of values that it preaches and the goal and set-up by society, between its ancient curricula and the modernity of science. Education values are interdependent and inseparable. Education

* **Research Scholar, Department of Education, S.V. University, Tirupati.**

leads to inculcation of values and the cherished values of society provide direction to the education process as the ancient Sanskrit verse says:

"Vidva dadati Vinayam;

Vinaya dadati patratam;

Patratuad dhanam apnoti;

Dhanad dharmanm ta totoh sukham"

Education develops as a disciplined mind, disciplined mind leads to worthiness, worthiness brings prosperity, and prosperity enables a person to lead a dutiful life and ultimately to happiness.

The ultimate purpose of education is to develop humanitarian qualities in man. Education which is a cultural phenomenon, supports, accompanies and leads each individual to become matured, responsible and a successful citizen. While indicating the act of education Jonas (1979) writes "...Education has a particular objectives—the independence of the individual, which essentially comprehend the capacity for responsibility". Education helps in the attainment of so high degree of intellectual and moral maturity that a person can lead his life with independent responsibility for himself and others. In other words education leads individuals towards a value oriented life.

Value education intended for desired modification in the student's behavioural patterns apparently involves four factors:

1. Society environment
2. Individual and school
3. Individuals personality is projected as good or bad as a result of his/her interaction with society
4. Environment and school synchronically environment and school together play a vary significant role in building the personality of the individuals because values grow from individuals purposes, aspirations, beliefs, attitudes, feelings, interests, convictions, etc.

Before we begin our study of ancient Indian values, we should consider the basic education. What is a value? The value of an act or an object may broadly be defined as its worthiness to be chosen. In our dealings in life we desire certain things and prefer to act in certain ways and also avoid certain other things and actions.

Accordingly to an idealist values are the supreme ends foreseen, planned desired and willed by God, the cosmicmind and gradually realised through the world. As saying goes "values are not taught but caught". They are not "existents" but "subsistents" real and unchanging. In the terminology of Indian History the term "value has not yet been well-set, because the term of "value education" was initially acknowledged in the form of "religious education" or "moral education". Infact value education is more wider, practicable and adoptable than the former two.

Values impart significance to life. Edger, S. Brightman (1958) says "In the most elementary sense, values means whatever is actually liked, prized, esteemed, desired approved or enjoyed by the any one at anytime. It is actual experience of enjoying a desirable object or activity". Parker (1957) defined values as, "either a joy giving activity or passivity or else as the management of desire". According to Allport (1950): "Anything that yields a satisfaction (or provides a means for such satisfaction) is designated as value".

As a result of scientific and technological development man has shifted his way of living from spiritual to materialistic approach. This shift has taken gradually consequent to alien cultural influence. Due to Mughal and especially British rule the entire system of Indian education, educational thought and practices have completely changed. Ancient Indian education thought is wrongly conceived to be irrelevant in the modern contest. Ancient values and traditions are being criticised and misinterpreted. Gone were the days of Gurukulas, where education was mostly spiritual and pupil belonged to teacher but not to an institution or school. But in modern days pupil belongs to a school where teacher teaches pupils by classes and not as individual with this uniqueness and differences. In the changing scenario, the aims of education are redefined, they are:

1. To prepare individual for social and economic changes pertinent for national development, scientific and technological advancement.
2. To guide and direct individuals to accept these changes and to receive benefit from such changes.
3. To create a dynamic non-conformist and non-conservative frame of mind in them.

The idea of national unity and the unity of mankind should be introduced in the curriculum with due regard to the children's age and understanding. The Indian education commission (1964-66) recommended instruction on moral, social and spiritual values at all levels of studies. Character building as an object of education was stressed in the curriculum frames by the National Council of Educational Research and Training in 1975. The UNESCO in its report of the international commission in 1972 suggested that the educational system should encourage the promotion of the values of world peace, international understanding and unity of mankind.

Sample

Total of 300 teacher trainee selected from Diet Colleges of Rayalaseema (Dist.) for evaluating this attitudes towards value-oriented education.

Objectives

1. To know the significant difference between males and females students in Diet Colleges in possessing attitudes towards value system in education.
2. To know the significant difference between the Diet students studying in Govt. and Private colleges in possessing attitude towards value system in education.
3. To know the significant difference between the Diet students studying in Rural and Urban localities in possessing attitudes towards value system in education.

Hypotheses

1. There is no significant difference between male and female studying in Diet colleges in possessing attitude towards value system in education.

2. There is no significant difference between the Diet students studying in Govt. and private colleges in possessing attitude towards value system education.
3. There is no significant difference between the student teachers studying in Rural and Urban localities possessing attitude towards values system in education.

Analysis

Table—41.1 Means and S.D.'s of urban men and women attitude scores towards value-oriented education

Category	*N*	*Mean*	*S.D.*	*'t' value*
Urben Men	75	262.8	34.25	3.00*
Urban Women	75	277.7	26.03	

* 't' significant at 0.05 level.

The difference between the two means was tested for significance by *'t'* test. The obtained *'t'* value was 3.00. The tabulated value for 148 *df* was found to be 1.98 at 0.05 level and 2.61 at 0.01 level. The obtained value was found to be greater than the table values at both the levels. Since the difference between the two groups was significant at 0.05 level, the null hypothesis has been rejected.

Table—41.2 Means and S.D.'s of Govt. and Private college students attitude scores towards value oriented education

Category	*N*	*Mean*	*S.D.*	*'t' value*
Govt.	50	275.3	29.32	1.3@
Private	50	267.5	31.89	

@ 't' not significant at 0.05 level.

The difference between the two means was tested for significance *'t'* test. The obtained *'t'* value was 1.3. The tabulated value for 98 *df* was found to be 1.98 at 0.05 level and 2.63 at 0.01 level. The obtained value was found to be less than the value was found to be less than the table value at 0.05 level. Since the difference between the two groups was not significant at 0.05 level the null hypotheses has been accepted.

Table—41.3 Mean and S.D.'s total urban and rural students attitude scores towards value-oriented education and result of 't' test

Category	*N*	*Mean*	*S.D.*	*'t' value*
Urban	150	269.9	27.19	2.91*
Rural	150	279.3	28.8	

* 't' is significant at 0.05 level.

The difference between the two means was tested for significance by *'t'* test. The obtained *'t'* value as 2.91. The tabulated value for 298 *df* was found to be 1.97 at 0.05 level and 2.59 at 0.01 level. The obtained value was found to be greater than the table value of both levels. Hence the difference between the two groups was significant. Therefore the null hypothesis is rejected.

Conclusion

Based on the above tables, we find out and concluded the results:

1. There is a significant difference between male and female students studying in Diet colleges in passing attitude towards value systemised.
2. There is no significant difference between Diet students studying in Govt. and private colleges in possessing attitude towards value system in education.
3. There is significant difference between student teachers studying in rural and urban localities possessing attitude towards values system education

REFERENCES

1. Aggarwal J.C. *Philosophical and Sociological Basis of Education*, 8th Edition. Vikas Publishing House Pvt. Ltd. New Delhi.
2. Allport: *Encyclopaedia of Educational Research*, Revised Edition. The Macmillan Company, New York, Page (27).
3. Grewal, Rs. "A Comparative Study of Values of Rural and Urban Senior Secondary School Students of Punjab" M.E.D. Dissertation, P.U. Chd (1996).
4. Guilford, J.P: *Fundamental Statistics in Psychology and Education*, McGraw-Hillbook Co., 1987.
5. Paul P.V.: "A Study Value Orientation of Adolescent Boys and Girls 1986" *Fourth Survey of Research in Education 1983-99*, Vol. (Page 181).

42

Sri Sathya Sai System of Education

A Model to Follow

Dr. C. Ravindranatha Reddy*

Introduction

The present day educational system which is in practice throughout the world may develops the intellect but certainly does not promote values (See Annexture-VIII). Sri Sathya Sai questioned of what value is the acquisition of all knowledge in the world if there is no character? And he declares that education without values is not only useless but certainly dangerous. One such a system of education aiming at character building would ensure a happy world. It is unfortunate that educational institutions are unable to impart value system in the students that will make them good citizens. In this connection, it is appropriate to make a mention about the tremendous services being rendered by the Sri Sathya Sai educational institutions throughout the world by adopting value oriented education which has become a model to follow.

Need of Value Oriented Education

Today everyone is being attracted to the programme of value-oriented education. The reason is the realisation that the world is in a sorry mess because of absence of values. In this critical situation the promotion of values are supremely important. Parents,

* Associate Professor, Centre for Studies on Indochina & South Pacific, S.V. University, Tirupati–517 502.

teachers, and society at large have been concerned about values and value education. There is growing realisation a fresh look at the place of values in the curriculum of educational institutions. The present situation in India demands a system of education which strengthen national unity and social solidarity through meaningful constructive value education.

Whatever be the cause of present value crisis, the fact that weakening of moral values in our social life is creating serious unrest in the society. It is this declining moral standards behind the recommendations, stressing the importance of value-oriented education. Unfortunately education has become more or less materialistic and value traditions being slowly given up. The degeneration in the present day life and the utter disregard for values, are all traceable to the fact that moral, religious and spiritual education has not been given due place in our educational system.

Students today are pursuing only worldly education. Mere secular or worldly education is not enough. It must be supplemented with spiritual education which inculcates values like truth, right conduct, peace, love etc. and bring about transformation among the students. The harmonious blend of secular and spiritual education is ideally suited to the present day world. The importance of this type of integral education is being recognised in world today. Against this background Sri Sathay Sai educational institutions are perhaps one of the few institutions in the world in the field of education while emphasis character building as much as academic excellence. It is based on Sai Sathya Sai outstanding contribution to world of learning in the form of human values as extended to education. The underlying principle of all activities of the institutes—curricular, co-curricular and extra-curricular in that education is for life and not for living.

Sri Sathya Sai Baba

Sri Sathya Sai is highly spiritual leader and the world teacher. His life and message are inspiring millions of people throughout the world to lead more purposeful spiritual and moral lives. He urges people to become better followers of their respective religions.

Sri Sathya Sai Baba born on November 23, 1926 to the parents of modest means in the obscure hamlet Puttaparthi in Ananthapur district, Andhra Pradesh. He occupies a distinct place in the galaxy of holy men of India for all he does in the cause of education and the social and moral upliftment of the people as a whole. He did not even complete his school education but could write commentaries on Vedas and Upanishads, a great task even for the very learned. At the tender age, he threw away his books, declaring he had a mission to undertake.

In our own time, he has given to the world a blue print for an ideal system of education, taught us how to go about, beginning with Balavikas (child development). Then he himself evolved a new pattern of education for school and college students, known as 'Education in Human Values' and then 'Educare' which are even acceptable and applicable to all sections of people. He has set up schools and colleges and even a university at Prasanthi Nilayam where what is teached is practiced. The university which is known as Sathya Sai Institute of Higher Learning received high praise from eminent people (See Annexure-IV).

Sathya Sai System of Education in Practice

The new system of education of Sathya Sai guides the governance of schools and colleges founded by Baba and his devotees. The new education emphasise integral education to make the 'New Man' with an integrated personality (See Annexure-VI). Spiritual education is the basis of integral education. Integral education seeks to develop all the aspects of human personality—Physically, intellectual, emotional and spiritual, inculcation of spiritual insight alone can provide the foundation for a noble, able and stable character. The cornerstone of philosophy of life is—truth, right conduct, peace, love and non-violence. But love is the underlying principle in the other three values. Love for God and fellow beings is the foundation of integrated personality.

In view of the strong emphasis laid on moral, ethical and spiritual values, courses are also given on spiritual awareness both at UG and PG levels. The integral items of education are applicable to all students, irrespective of the course they are admitted to. The institute attaches great importance to this component of education.

The items included in the integral education are: (a) Yogasanas, games and sports; (b) prayer and meditation (in the hostel); (c) college prayer; (d) social work and self-reliance programmes; (e) regular attendance at class; (f) disciplined behaviour in the classroom as well as elsewhere. Students are continuously assessed on these items. The final grade statement of the students takes into account the grades awarded under category of integral items also.

The Sai path of education does not leave anything to chance, as our system did so far. Sri Sathya Sai has laid a firm foundation to his system, beginning with the right type of education from the stage of childhood. He called it as Balavikas (child development). Then Education in Human Values (EHV) runs through Sri Sathya Sai schools and colleges under the care of a university. Here the medium of instruction is love, the first, second and third languages being discipline, devotion and duty. The maintenance of very high academic standards is ensured by highly motivated and dedicated teachers who live in the campus. Character moulding is the most important aspect of education. The emotional integration is achieved silently in community in the hostels. Physical education is given importance. Students are provided opportunities for the cultivation of their talents and participate in cultural programmes and discourses and speeches. Students are being moulded in a spirit of sacrifice and service to the community.

Sri Sathya Sai Institutions

A deemed university—Sri Sathya Sai Institute of Higher Learning comprises three campuses at Anantapur, Bangalore and Prasanthi Nilayam. (see Annexure-I). It provides free education in graduate and post-graduate courses in Arts, Science and Management including B.Ed., M.B.A. and M.Tech. in Computer Science and Ph.D. (see Annexure-II). Apart from the above there are also a music college, a couple of High Secondary Schools and several primary and middle schools. The five year integrated courses evolved by the institute given an option to the students to take degree at the end of third year at a lower level or fifth year for a master degree at a higher level. In addition to the core subjects and languages, the students have to study four awareness courses in Indian culture, unity of religions, Methods of Science and Economic, Social and Political problems of India. They have also to take an elective course in world literature and Fine Arts, the evolution of cosmos and life or evolution of man and human society. They are examined in these subjects and their marks are counted towards final grade.

The institute offers a comprehensive modern teaching programme. The semester system of study makes for the intensive and steady participation of the students in the learning process. Modern syllabi and monthly and semester end tests carefully devised in line with the latest concepts and techniques, make learning process a joy and an adventure to the students. A cumulative grading system based on all these tests brings a correct profile of the capacities and achievements of the students. The institute seeks to shape the students sensitive to and aware of the problems of the people living around in the society. Through social work and extension programmes, students realise their duties towards the poor and handicapped. Six hours of social work per month are compulsory and count towards the final grade of the students. In practical terms the students are taught love all and serve all and help ever and hurt never.

Unique Features of Sathya Sai Institute of Higher Learning

There are many unique features in Sri Sathya Sai University, they are: (i) Sai is the Chancellor of the University. As Dr. Gokak, former Vice-Chancellor of the institute put it, "the Chancellor of the university is himself the chancellor of the university", (ii) It is the only university in India that has campuses more than one state; (iii) what makes the institute unique is Sai personal contact and direct personal interest in the students; (iv) instruction is absolutely free, no fee of any kind is charged; (v) hostel residence is a must and hostel life is based on *Gurukula* pattern; (v) the institute runs like a clock. In particular there is never any student unrest. Admissions are always made at the same time of the year; exams are never postponed; the results are never delayed and the convocation is always held on 22nd November; (vi) Research programme of the institute is designed to keep up in view of their relevance to the social needs; (vii) The laboratories and work of the institute provided with most modern equipment, instruments and amenities; (viii) The student lecture ratio is very favourable for closer rapport between students and faculty; (ix) English as the medium of instruction at all levels; (x) An open admission policy from all over the country irrespective of income, class, creed, religion and region; (xi) Merit based selection through test and interview giving weightage to intelligence of the students; (xii) The NAAC has granted accreditation at the A++ level to the institute for five year from 2002-03 (see Annexure-III).

Sri Sathya Sai Value Obtained Model Schools

Inspired by the shining example and excellent results of Sri Sathya Sai educational institutions in India, similar schools are being established around the world including India. These schools have become model schools to develop young men and women of noble character. By leading exemplary lives, these young people illustrate the importance of good character simultaneously keeping pace with the advancement of intellectual knowledge. The first Sathya Sai School was launched in Zambia by Dr. Victor Kanu, former High Commissioner of Sierra Leone. Much such schools were started all over the world and more are opened every where.

With such an expansion there around a parallel need for teachers who were trained to impart spiritual education along with secular education. Anticipating the situation, in 1991 an institute of Sathya Sai Education was established in Japan. Based on the manual on human values used by Balavikas gurus in India, they evolved a curriculum of 'Education in Human Values' (EHV) in the various languages of the world for global use. The movement achieved a purpose and direction when Dr. Artong Jum Sai an ex-NASA scientist and three time parliamentarian established the Institute of Sathya Sai Education in 1998 with the clear goal of imparting teacher training in Education in Human Values (see Annexure-VII). A new chapter was added to the value Education of Sri Sathya Sai when a galaxy of over 600 delegates from 78 countries of the world congregated at Prasanthi Nilayam to participate in the "International Conference on Strengthening Value Education from 25th and 29th September, 2000. This conference was organised by the Institute of Sathya Sai Education,

Thailand. At the end of the conference 'Prasanthi Nilayam Declaration' was adopted unanimously by the delegates (see Annexure-V).

For the propagation of Human values' 'think global but act local' motto has been adopted. Tradition, religion, aspiration and culture (TRAC) of the people concerned are integrated into EHV. For example in Brazil, a Christian approach to EHV has been adopted. In Indonesia, the Islamic approach to EHV has been taken up, in Nepal, the principles of the Hindu kingdom apply, in Bangkok, the Buddhist perspective in emphasised. To ensure that high standards of spiritual and secular education is maintained at these schools, the Institute of Bangkok worked out a standardisation—Accreditation—Inspection (SAI-2000). Sri Sathya Sai schools, other than those adopted, and which are affiliated to quality control under SAI-2000 accreditation programme have been established in the following countries: Australia, Brazil, Canada, Fiji, Indonesia, Kenya, Maritius, Nepal, the Philippines, Sri Lanka, South Africa, Taiwan, Thailand the USA, Zambia.

Studies done by independent observers in various parts of the world are pointing to the fact that EHV curriculum is working. In Zambia, Dr. Manchishi, a lecturer of University of Zambia, did an indepth study on the effect of value education on the students of the Sathya Sai School at Ndola, Zambia. The Zambian media has praised the school as "the miracle school" and the Zambia Department of Education is extending EHV curriculum to other schools. In the USA, a year long study of Dr. Ronne Marantz on the implementation of EHV in fourteen public schools in New York, Chicago and San Diego from kindergarden through grade eight showed that students had improved relationships at home and school. In Britain the EHV wing of the Sri Sathya Sai service organisation has been coordinating with educational authorities in the implementation of the EHV programmes in the schools.

In India, independent research studying the impact of EHV in the eighteen schools adopted by the Institute of Sathya Sai Education at Mumbai showed that along with practice of human values taught, there was also an improvement in academic performance. The school at Vandalur run by old students of Sri Sathya Sai Women's College, Anantapur has become famous at

Chennai for year after year because the rural children have been sweeping prizes at inter school competitions beating all the high profile city schools. The confidence displayed by these under-privileged rural children of the school testified to the success of EHV programme.

Conclusion

Sri Sathya Sai has made very meaningful contribution in providing a much needed corrective to the prevailing educational system in the world at a crucial time. Its virtues lies in its universal acceptance. Most states in India appreciate the Sai path to progress through education with emphasis on human values—truth, righteousness, love, peace and non-violence.

Many Sathya Sai centres abroad have also reported its whole hearted acceptance by some of their educational institutions. The Dept. of Human Resource Development, Govt. of India, announced that value education would be introduced in schools and colleges. But the government seems to have forgotten the resolve. In India, we are quarrelling over petty issues like text errata, saffronisation of education when the rest of the world is making strides by following the lead shown by Sri Sathya Sai.

ANNEXURE—I

THE INSTITUTE AND ITS CAMPUSES

The central administrative office of the institute is located in Prasanthi Nilayam, A.P., while academic instruction is imparted in three constituent colleges located in three different campuses. To each college is attached a residential hostel.

The three campuses are:

1. Anantapur campus (for women);
2. Brindvan campus (for men);
3. Prasanthi Nilayam campus (for men).

Of the above, the Prasanthi Nilayam campus is the main one, as it does not only have specialised research and computer facilities, but also the central library, the Planetarium, and the Museum of External Heritage. The addresses of the three campus are as below:

Anantapur Campus

Sri Sathya Sai Institute of Higher Learning
Anantapur Campus
Anantapur–515 001
Andhra Pradesh
Phone: (08554) 272567, Hostel: 273122

Brindavan Campus

Sri Sathya Sai Institute of Higher Learning
Brindavan Campus
Kadugodi P.O.
Bangalore–560 067
Karnataka
Phone: (080) 845329 Hostel: 8452233

Prasanthi Nilayam Campus

Sri Sathya Sai Institute of Higher Learning
Prasanthi Nilayam Campus
Prasanthi Nilayam–515 134
Anantapur District
Andhra Pradesh
Phone: (08555) 287235 Hostel: 287234

Source: Sri Sathya Sai Institute of Higher Learning. Information Handbook, 2004-05 (Prasanthi Nilayam), pp. 4-5.

ANNEXURE—II

COURSESS OFFERED

The following courses are offered in the three campuses:

Anantapur Campus: (for women)

Undergraduate courses: Duration 3 years

(a) B.A. (with one of the following subjects being the major subject during third year: History, Economics, Philosophy, Political Science, Optional English, Optional Telegu).

(b) Bachelor of Home Science

(c) B.Com. (Hons.)

(d) B.Sc. (Hons.) Mathematics

(e) B.Sc. (Hons.) Physics

(f) B.Sc. (Hons.) Chemistry

(g) B.Sc. (Hons.) Botany

(h) B.Sc. (Hons.) Zoology

Postgraduate Courses: Duration 2 years

(a) M.A. (English Language & Literature)

(b) M.A. (Telegu Language & Literature)

(c) Master of Home Science

Professional Course: Duration 1 year

(a) B.Ed. (Bachelor of Education)

Brindavan Campus: (for men)

Undergraduate Courses: Duration 3 years

(a) B.Com. (Hons.)

(b) B.Sc. (Hons.) Mathematics

(c) B.Sc. (Hons.) Physics

(d) B.Sc. (Hons.) Chemistry

(e) B.Sc. (Hons.) Biosciences

Prasanthi Nilayam Campus: (for men)

Undergraduate courses: Duration 3 years

(a) B.A. (with one of the following subjects being the major subject during third year: Economics, History, Political Science, Optional English).

(b) B.Sc. (Hons.) Mathematics

(c) B.Sc. (Hons.) Physics

(d) B.Sc. (Hons.) Chemistry

(e) B.Sc. (Hons.) Biosciences

(f) B.Sc. (Hons.) Economics

Postgraduate courses: Duration 2 years

(a) M.A. Economics

(b) M.Sc. Mathematics

(c) M.Sc. Physics

(d) M.Sc. Chemistry

(e) M.Sc. Biosciences

Professional Courses

(a) M.B.A. — Duration: 2 years

(b) M.B.A. Finance — Duration: 2 years

(c) M.Tech. (Comp. Science) — Duration 1½ years

Postgraduate Diploma Course

(a) Postgraduate diploma in 'Indian culture and philosophy'

(PGDICAP)–Duration: 1 year

Note: The M.A. and M.Sc. courses have been designed as a part of a comprehensive five-year programme, leading from the UG level to the Master degree. Candidates admitted to the UG programme are eligible for admission to the above courses, provided they secure a minimum CGPA as prescribed by the Institute in Bachelor's degree.

Doctoral Programme

Students of high academic caliber may be enrolled for Doctoral programme, subject to their meeting various criteria. While the Prasanthi Nilayam campus offers such programmes in Science, Business Management and Arts, the Anantapur campus offers doctoral programmes in English, Telugu and Home Science.

Source: Sri Sathya Sai Institute of Higher Learning. Information Handbook, 2004-05 (Prasanthi Nilayam), pp. 5-6.

ANNEXURE—III

ACCREDITATION BY NAAC

The National Assessment and Accreditation Council (NAAC) was established by UGC in 1994 with its headquarters at Bangalore, for the assessment and accreditation of higher education institutions. For carrying out this exercise of assessment and accreditation in an objective and realistic manner it has evolved seven criteria based on international parameters contextualised in Indian conditions: (1) Curricular aspects, (2) Teaching—Learning and evaluation, (3) Research, Consultancy and Extension, (4) Infrastructure and Learning Resources, (5) Student support and progression, (6) Organisation and management, and (7) Health Practices.

The peer team from the NAAC visited the institute from 2nd to 4th December, 2002.

Some Excerpts from NAAC Report

"The peer term puts on record its appreciation for providing the members of the team the opportunity to spend time with the institute faculty and the students so as to develop a thorough insight into the higher education process of the Sri Sathya Sai Institute of Higher Learning, particularly the integral higher education interwoven in the blue print and design of higher education products. This made us utilise that there is a way to correct our already degrading university education system in India, if we decide to do so".

"In the present context, when we witness, conflicts all over globally, there is a need for the role of higher education, in shaping the character and inculcating higher principles in individuals. Education in human values is imperative for rebuilding the fabric of society and ushering harmony and peace all round. The integral education system of this institute is a tested model designed to provide a balanced combination of academic excellence and social awareness among the students, with beneficial consequences to the individual and the society".

"The peer team feels that this institute stands out as a crest-jewel among the University education system in the country and this model is worthy of emulation by the institutions of higher learning in the country and elsewhere, so that these benefits would be reaped fast and on the widest possible scale".

Accreditation Status

The National Assessment and Accreditation Council has granted accreditation at the A++ level to the Sri Sathya Sai Institute of Higher Learning for five years, from 2002-03. This places the institute in the top bracket of the Indian universities.

Source: Sri Sathya Sai Institute of Higher Learning. Information Handbook, 2004-05 (Prasanthi Nilayam), p. 4.

ANNEXURE—IV

HIGH PRAISE FOR THE INSTITUTE FROM EMINENT PERSONS

Understandably, the institute has received high praise form eminent people, as the following quotes testify:

"The purpose of real education is to initiate a learning process that transforms students into good human beings with knowledge and value systems. Is value based education possible? Sri Sathya Sai Institute of Higher Learning has given an answer in the affirmative. I am in a place where university learning takes place in a divine environment. Here students get education with a value system. I would like to congratulate Sri Sathya Sai Institute of Higher Learning for this noble education)."

Dr. A.P.J. Abdul Kalam, President of India (Convocation, Nov. 2002).

"The students of this university are not just students, but seekers of truth. The divine guidance of Bhagavan Baba has elevated even education to the level of worship of God. The education imparted here is of the liberative kind. It addresses both 'apara' and 'para' aspects of man and society. The higher learning which the pupils here receive facilitate their integral development, and enables them to become better human beings with a finer, culturally richer character.

Shri Atal Bihari Vajpayee, Prime Minister of India (convocation, Nov. 1998).

"I am deeply impressed by the infrastructure, atmosphere, equipment and human resources organised for imparting education at Vidyagiri. The campuses at Prasanthi Nilayam, Brindavan and Anantapur are an invaluable asset in the crucial task of promoting integral education. Indeed, these constitute a blessing of far-reaching significance. There is much to be learnt hereby the student, the teachers, educationists and policy-makers."

Dr. Shankar Dayal Sharma, President of India
(Convocation, Nov. 1992)

"It is indeed rare to find institutions of higher learning like the Sri Sathya Sai institute of Higher Learning, where students receive free education, where voluntary service prevails, and where the acquisition of knowledge and wisdom is combined with duty and devotion."

"What is unique at this institute is that it is founded by Bhagavan Baba, it is inspired by His teaching, and is guided by His concept of a wholesome education based on the fundamental values of Truth, Righteousness, Peace, Love and Non-violence."

Rt. Hon. Anerood Jugnauth, Prime Minister of Mauritius
(Convocation, Nov. 1993)

"This institute is a pioneering and unique seat of Learning, spiritual and ethical values permeate this university. The atmosphere here is calm, solemn and serene, and is surcharged with spiritual ethos. It is in such an environment that our ancient Rishis transmitted knowledge to their disciple. It is for this reason that I feel happy to be here. For myself, I would like to humbly study this institution, understand the process of how it grew from strength to strength, and then see what can be done to extend the influence and the halo of this institute for and wide in India."

Shri P.V. Narasimha Rao, Prime of India
(Convocation, Nov. 1991)

"To the graduates, I would like to say...you have received all round instruction through the system which your institute appropriately calls 'integral education'. But above all, you have received here a sense of human values—values which are common to all the religious faiths of the world, indeed common to human—kind."

Shri R. Venkataraman, President of India
(Convocation, Nov. 1990)

Source: Sri Sathya Sai Institute of Higher Learning, Information Handbook, 2004-05 (Prasanthi Nilayam), p. 3.

ANNEXURE—V

PRASANTHI NILAYAM DECLARATION
29TH SEPTEMBER 2000

Human Values for All Through Education

It is hereby declared:

All children have a right to equal opportunity to receive the best and free education that would bring about good character and human excellence; and

Human values must be an integral part of all subjects taught in the education systems of the world; and

All governments should be encouraged to develop and implement laws and policies which enable values in education to be an integral component of teacher education, professional development and student learning experiences; and

Education in human values, peace and international understanding should be taught across the entire teacher education curriculum; and

In order to implement the above, a voluntary network of educators sharing the education goal of human excellence will be established for educators to exchange ideas, experience and promote value education.

The Prasanthi Nilayam Declaration will be submitted to UNESCO, the United Nations and other international organisations for further consideration and action.

Source: *Sanathana Sarathi* (Monthly) October 2000, p. 320.

ANNEXURE—VI

Chart showing how the philosophy of Integral Education is put into practice in Sri Sathya Sai Institute of Higher Learning

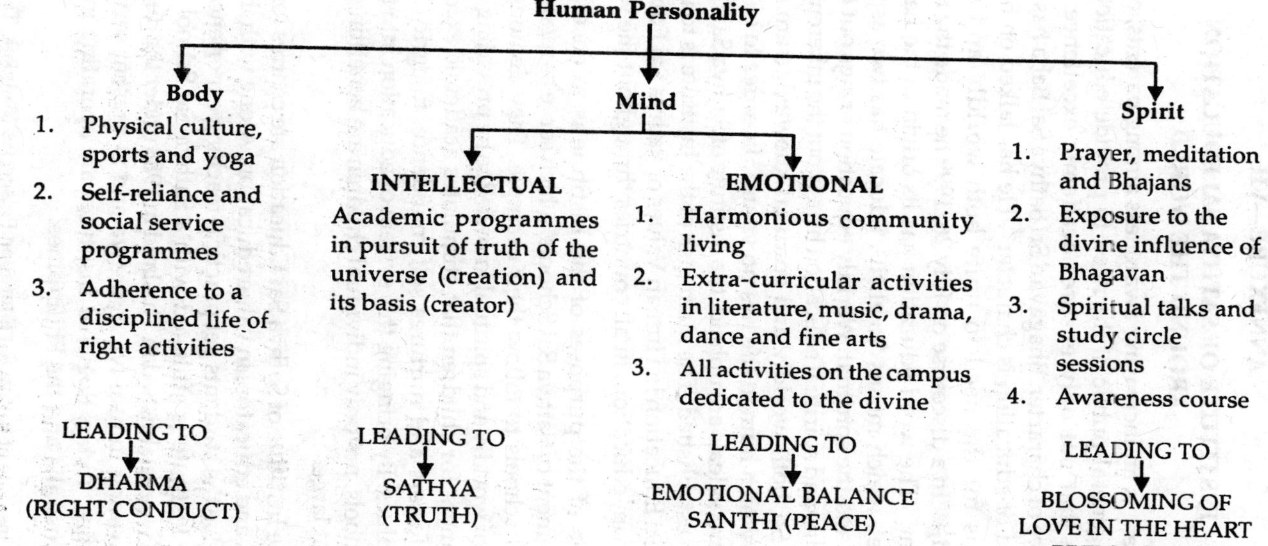

Source: B.N. Narasimha Murthy: 'New Education for a New Word' in a *Sanatha Sarathi (Monthly) (Special issue) November 1999, p. 339.*

ANNEXURE—VII

INSTITUTE OF SATHYA SAI EDUCATION AROUND THE WORLD

There is an increasing awareness among parents, educators and the general public of the need to provide education for our children that not only ensures academic excellence but also excellence of character. Bhagavan Sri Sathya Sai Baba has declared "The end of education is character". He has talked on numerous occasions for the need to unite both worldly and spiritual knowledge. In a discourse on July 26, 1999 he made the following statement: "The word education has its origin in the Latin word 'Educare', which means 'to elicit'. Educare has two aspects, the worldly and the spiritual. Worldly education brings out the latent knowledge and spiritual education brings out the inherent divinity in man. So, both worldly and spiritual knowledge are essential, without which human life has no value". In order to ensure that these sacred ideals are upheld, the institute of Sathya Sai Education has been established. The main task of the Institute is to introduce Sathya Sai Education in Human Values or Sathya Sai Educare into mainstream education, in all countries throughout the world.

One of the purposes of the Institute is to encourage the establishment of Sathya Sai Schools, which serve as model schools for other schools to follow their example. They demonstrate the balance of worldly and spiritual knowledge by providing a suitable environment for children that stimulates academic excellence as well as fosters and nurtures self-confidence, integrity, love and moral values. By bringing this system of education into more and more schools, not only individual children are benefiting, but also society at large.

The Institute of Sathya Sai Education are centres for training teachers and educators in value education. Along with theoretical knowledge the students get practical teaching experience, as each training Institute is affiliated with a Sathya Sai School. The first institute was established in Thailand in 1988 under the directorship of Dr. Art-ong Jumsai Na Ayudhya and at present serves as the main office. Today, Regional Institutes are operating in Zambia, India, Australia and the Philippines.

Source: Institute of Sathya Sai Education Prospectus (Bangkok, Thailand).

ANNEXURE—VIII

SRI SATHYA SAI QUOTATIONS ON EDUCATION AND VALUES

Education

E for Enlightenment

D for Duty and devotion

U for Understanding

C for Character

A for Action

T for Thinking

I for Integrity

O for Oneness

N for Nobility

Education is for life, not for mare living: Give up false notion that education is meant for acquiring jobs and earning money. Acquiring good qualities can be only purpose of education. What is the use of education, if one cannot give up evil qualities. Education is for elevation.

The end of education in Character. Education without character is useless.

- True education is that which develops in you love for your fellow beings and motivates you to serve the community.
- Humility, reverence, compassion, forbearance sacrifice, discipline and self control are the qualities which reveal the outcome of true education.
- Educated man must realise that he has more obligations than privileges, more duties than rights.
- Educational institutions must endeavour to produce students with integrity, character and self-confidence. Cultivation of knowledge is secondary.

- If the educational system could contribute to the turning out of students of good character, committed to human values, the country will become stronger and greater as a nation and be a model to the world.
- Among all professionals, teaching profession is the noblest, the most difficult and most important. Teachers have to mould the young today so that they will grow up into worthy citizens of tomorrow.
- Spirituality is discovering who you really are. Spirituality is not merely singing Bhajans, performing worship, visiting temples, going on pilgrimages and undertaking any other good activity. Recognising oneness of all brings in spirituality. Seeing unity in diversity is spirituality.
- Whatever job a student may take up wherever he may be working, he must continue to practice spiritual discipline. Without a spiritual basis, education would be wasted.
- Science is below the mind.
  Spirituality is the beyond the mind.
- Values for education
  Education for Life
  Life for Love
  Love for Man
  Man for Service
  Service for Spirituality
  Spirituality for Society
  Society for Nation
  Nation for World
  World for Peace
- See no evil—See what is good
  Here no evil—Hear what is good
  Talk no evil—Talk what is good
  Do no evil—Do what is good
  That is the way to God
- See Good—Do Good—Be Good

- Love + Thought = Truth
  Love + Action = Right conduct
  Love + Feeling = Peace
  Love + Understanding = Non Violence
  So love is the under current in all human values
- Sow a seed of good thought,
  Reap a harvest of good action;
  Sow a seed of good action;
  Reap a harvest of good habit;
  Sow a seed of good habit;
  Reap a harvest of good character;
  Sow a seed of good character;
  Reap a harvest of good destination.
- Money comes and goes
  Morality comes and grows
- Removal of immorality is the only way to immortality.
- Attach importance to values than money.
- You cannot always oblige.
  But you can speak always obligingly.
- Parents have primary responsibilities to mould the character of their children.
- If wealth is lost—nothing is lost
  If health is lost—something is lost
  If character is lost—everything is lost
- Duty is God—Work is worship
- Love all—Serve all
- Help ever—Hurt never
- Man is to born share and serve not to grab and grieve
- Leanr to adopt, adjust and accommodate
- Ego wants to get and forget
  Love wants to give and forgive.
- If there is righteousness in the heart;
  There will be beauty in the character;
  If there is beauty in the character;
  There will be harmony in the home;

If there is harmony in the home;
There will be order in the nation;
If there is order in the nation;
There will be peace on the earth.

REFERENCES

Books

1. Sri Sathya Sai Baba, *Vidhya Vahini* (Prasanthi Nilayam).
2. Loraine Burrows (Comp.), *Sathya Sai Education in Human Values* (Prasanthi Nilayam, 2001).
3. *The Beacon* (World Council of Sri Sathya Sai Organisation, Bombay, 1985).
4. N.B.S. Rama Rao, *Sri Sathya Sai Era, 2000 AD* (Prasanthi Nilayam, 2002).
5. *Sri Sathya Sai Educare. Route to Global Peace and Happiness* (Institute of Sathya Sai Education, Mumbai, 2001).
6. *Sri Sathya Sai Educare for Devotees* (Institute of Sri Sathya Sai Education, Mumbai, 2001).
7. *Institute of Sathya Sai Education, Prospects*, (Institute of Sathya Sai Education, Bangkok, Thailand, ND), 2001).
8. N.B.S. Rama Rao, *Sri Sathya Sai Educare,* (Prasanthi Nilayam, 2002).
9. *Sri Sathya Sai Institute of Higher Learning: Information Handbook*, 2004-05 (Prasanthi Nilayam, 2004).
10. *Human Excellence*, (Vivekananda Institute of Human Excellence, Hyderabad, 2000).

Articles

1. B.N. Narasimha Murthy, "New Education for a New World," *Sanathana Sarathi* (Monthly) (Prasanthi Nilayam), November, 1999, pp. 337-341.
2. Sri Sathya Sai Baba, "Sathya Sai Educare and its Significance" *Sanathana Sarathi*, March, 2002, pp. 65-76.
3. Sri Sathya Sai Baba, "True Education Leads to Divinity," *Sanathana Sarathi*, June 2000, pp. 169-76.
4. Sri Sathya Sai Baba, "Education for Supreme Bliss," *Sanathana Sarathi*, December, 2000, pp. 405-413.
5. Sri Sathya Sai Baba, "Humility and Character are the Hallmarks of True Education," *Sanathana Sarathi*, January, 2002, pp. 23-29.
6. Sri Sathya Sai Baba, Education Should Foster Values, *Sanathana Sarathi*, October, 2000, pp. 308-315.

7. "International Conference on Strengthening Value Education," *Sanathana Sarathi*, October, 2000, pp. 316-320.

8. Sri Sathya Sai Baba, "Excellence of Ancient Indian System of Education," *Sanathana Sarthi*, July 2002, pp. 210-221.

9. Sri Sathya Sai Baba, "What Should Education Aim At" *Sanathana Sarathi*, July 2002, pp. 209-14.

10. "Summer Course in Indian Culture and Spirituality," *Sanathana Sarathi*, December 2000, pp. 405-413.

11. Victor Kanu, "Sai System of Education," *Sanathana Sarathi*, November, 1999, pp. 316-320.

12. S.V. Giri "Satya Sai Institute of Higher Learning." An Instrument in Bhagavans Mission. *Sanathana Sarathi*, November, 1999, pp. 329-333.

13. Sri Sathya Sai Baba, "The End of Education is Character," *Sanathana Sarathi*, March 2003, pp. 65-73.

14. Sri Sathya Sai Baba, "Education for Transformation of the Study," *Sanathana Sarathi*, December 1999, pp. 369-71.

15. Seminar of Vice-Chancellors on Value Education and Ethics, *Sanathana Sarathi*, November 2003, pp. 351-52.

16. "Sri Sathya Sai Baba and Human Values," *The Hindu*, November 23, 2003.

17. N.N. Prahlada, "Strengthening Positive Sentiments," *The Hindu*, February 11, 2003.

18. J.S. Rajput, "Towards God Citizenship," *The Hindu*, January 21, 2003.

19. Hiramalini Seshadri, "Nurturing Human Values," *The Hindu*, April 15, 2003.

20. V. Mahadev Iyer, "Making a Good Teacher," *The Hindu*, August 28, 2002.

21. J.S. Rajput, "Education in Values," *The Hindu*, October 16, 2001.

22. K. Srinivasa Rao, "Value Crisis and the Need for Value Based Education," *Journal of Educational Research and Extension*, July, 1995, pp. 41-50.

23. J.S. Rajput, "Education in Values," *The Hindus*, October 16, 2001.

43

Value Education

The Saviour of Human Society

Dr. Digumarti Bhaskara Rao*

Modern science has placed a proverbial Alladin's lamp in the hands of man. The jinn is at his command now. Man can order the jinn to annihilate the structure which his predecessors have taken several millennia to create or else ask the jinn to usher in an era of prosperity in the world. The choice rests with the modern man, and in making a choice he will inevitably guided by his sense of values. So, the question of values becomes important.

With the progress of technology, there has been a continuous flow of population non-potential areas to potential urban and industrial areas. In the process of migration, group loyalties and consequently the value system of the migrants get temporarily or permanently disoriented. Resolution of conflict between the value systems, of different groups, brought together by political, economic or other compulsions is necessary, if mankind is to live in peace and happiness.

Anxiety is the order of the day. Anxiety in its higher order may lead to a nuclear catastrophe which can destroy the whole universe within minutes. Political anxiety causes national and international disputes. There is a spate of terrorist activities encouraged by groups or nations against one another. There are

* **Reader, R.V.R. College of Education, Member, Board of Studies in Education, Acharya Nagarjuna University, Guntur–522 006 (India).**

the ethnic disputes which are getting multiplied rather than resolved, and lastly there are problems of territorial adjustments, river-waters distribution and sometimes even ever non-issues. Economic anxiety also emerges from monopolisation of resources by a few, at the level of the state or that of the individual. In a close-circuited, fast-shrinking, and mutually-interacting world, economic imbalances and exploitation of the havenots by the haves is resulting in unrest and violence of varying dimensions.

Conflict is also the passion of the day. The age of science and technology has aggravated this conflict manifold. To be secular or religions, to accept or to reject the tradition, to prefer cultural isolation or to allow cultural interaction are some of the dimensions of this conflict. Conflicts also arise, when an old code loses relevance or new values emerges. This occurs due to changes in the population graph, advancement of knowledge and technological vistas, or some other similar strongly influencing factors. Exploding population may call for new values like family-planning, reproduction by genetic selection and even a legislation such as reproduction only by those who are genetically suitable.

The high rate of suicides, increase in husband-wife divorces and a large number of broken homed demonstrate that wealth alone cannot buy mental peace, happiness, or contentment. Something more is to be searched for so that life becomes more worth living.

At the global level, the anxiety and conflict have been sought to be lessened by setting up organisations like the United Nations, Non-Aligned Movement, Commonwealth of Nations and other regional and sub-regional, associations and by signing various pacts, but conflicts continue and man's anxiety remains. Possibly, this state of affairs would continue till such time we identify the basic cause of the entire malaise rather than tinkering with externalities.

India in the past, has made a substantial contribution to the evolution of mankind's culture and moral values. According to the Encyclopaedia Britannica, the Vedas are the oldest philosophical literature and philosophical ethics of mankind. Numerous foreign travellers and writers of historical records have, from time to time, written in praise of the high standards of Indian morality. This contribution is as significant as that of modern Europe in the fields of science and technology. Today, man with a power-house of knowledge at his command is in greater need of the cultural reorientation that he was at any time in the past. Value education may, therefore, be destined, once again, to lead mankind out of the present stage of multiple crisis and more so of the moral crisis or the crisis of values which is at the root of all these crises.

Value Education

Value-system is the fusion of moral and spiritual values. The Report of the Religious and Moral Education defined moral behaviour as the conduct of man towards man in various situations in which human beings come together in home, social and economic fields and in outside world generally. Anything that helps us to behave towards others is of moral value.

It may be conceded here that there is no universally accepted definition of good or bad. These terms are related to time, place and persons. Good may, by some persons, be equated with the will of God and evil as an inducement of satan. Good is also identified with pleasure and evil with suffering. There is hardly any defined frontier between licit and illicit. Such a definition is only possible on the basis of certain socially accepted norms or governmental laws. It is easier to discriminate the lawful from the unlawful.

Morality is concerned with beliefs and actions which are in conformity with the social norms shaped, modified and chiselled over a length of time. In ancient Greece, there was emphasis on beliefs whereas in ancient India, the stress was on action. However, action had to be in conformity with Dharma, thus action itself had moral and spiritual base. Manu, the great Indian Codifier, on the strength of the Vedas and the Smritis, said that doing noble actions is the highest duty (dharma) of man. To be frank, it is difficult to precisely define the philosophical and abstract concept of morality. One may attempt to understand this term in the following ways. (1) The basis of morality is right belief and right action. (2) The element of free-will of the dos is fundamental to any moral act, the dos must adhere to the moral act inspite of a temptation to deviate from it. (3) Moral acts extends both over physiological and psychological domains.

Values are classified in several ways. In terms of importance, values may be divided into these groups:

1. Trivial values, such as the type of clothes one should wear while going to a particular place.
2. More substantial beliefs, such as the ones which also effect people other than the belief-holder himself. These include punctuality, cleanliness, courtesy etc.
3. Fundamental or perennial and emperical beliefs, such as practice of truthfulness, spirit of patriotism, kindness towards all like, etc.

The great Indian sage Vatsyayana related virtues and vices to human faculties are classified them as:

1. *Virtues of body:* charity, helping the needy, social service.
2. *Virtues of speech:* truthfulness, benevolence, gentleness, recitation of scriptures.
3. *Virtues of mind:* kindness, unworldness, piety.
4. *Vices of body:* cruelty, theft, sexual indulgence.
5. *Vices of speech:* falsehood, harshness, scandal.
6. *Vices of mind:* hatred, covetousness, disbelief.

In terms of social order, values may be classified as political, economic, social, cultural, spiritual, aesthetic and individual. Thus values encompasses the entire gamut of life.

According to the Indian philosophy, individual interest may be scarified for that of the family, the interest of the family for that of the clan and all interests for that of the soul. Individual soul, according to Indian philosophers, is a part of the universal soul.

Our world is undergoing radical social changes. So the students who are the future citizens have to be trained to respond to and adjust with these social changes satisfactorily by equipping themselves with desirable skills and values. The modern world has been committed to the guiding principles of socialism, secularism, democracy, and so on. These guiding principles should be emphasised in the educational system and suitable values are to be inculcated in the pupils and public for promoting equality, social justice, national and international cohesion and democratic citizenship. With these aims in view, radical reforms in the present lopsided education are to be introduced and all attempts need to be made for developing well integrated personalities of our individuals. Hence, the need for inculcating desirable values is felt more important.

"We are behind until we see that in the human plan, nothing is worth the making if it does make the man. Why build these cities glorious if man unbuilded goes? In vain we build the world, unless the builder also grows".

Decline in Values

There is hardly any issue on which one may find complete unanimity of views in the society. The situation is no different in the case of value systems. Many people fell that there is, at present, a state of total chaos in the society so far as values are concerned. However, a number of people do not share deep concern over the so-called deterioration of values. It is difficult to say that values have totally declined. But, there is a decline in values and the reasons for that are:

1. The gap between the material and spiritual progress is an important cause of the present moral crisis. Nuclear capability is such a material achievement, but our failure to coordinate it with moral values poses serious dangers to the human race. We have, somehow, forgotten that there is a psychological man behind the physical man. Stating this idea philosophically, the ancient Indians have declared that the cosmic matter coupled with cosmic spirit alone gives meaning to life. The importance of this great thought seems to have been lost somewhere.
2. The fall in values in modern times is attributable to over-emphasis on wealth, power and consumerism.
3. The present social milieu, as some people believe, is such that it takes us to the moral downfall. While criticising the social environs, we should remember that the individual is a block as well as a builder of the social

system. The social ethos depend on the ethos of the individuals constituting the group, therefore, why not to start the process of moral regeneration of the society with ourselves?

4. Consumer-goods civilisation is dominating the society. It developed a glamour for every developing nation. This promoted the people to sacrifice the values.
5. Literature of advanced nations introduced new unhealthy trends in mankind. These trends were brimmed with sex, crime and violence. This had an adverse impact on social ethos. What is true of literature, is true of films also, which is literature on a silvery-screen.
6. There has been a great change in the political, economic and social structure of the human society during the last 150 years. Altruism has been replaced by self centredness, acquisition and consumerism. Gallopping, urbanisation has ushered in the apartment-culture and pushed off the rural life values, including socialisation. With the ever-increasing speed in life there is limited socialisation even at home. All this has brought about changes in our outlook to the existing value-system.
7. Democracy has made a great contribution in alleviating the common man, particularly the down-trodden. However, one cannot be obvious to its negative role in regard to nurturing of higher moral values. Winston Churchill once described democracy as the worst form of government till a better alternative was available.

All this highlights the need for an enlightened and a fresh approach to the important question of value education.

Syllabus for Value Education

To make the value aspect of our educational programmes more prominent, the following ideas may be incorporated in the educational programmes.

1. Developing self-respect, awareness of self-growth, of one's uniqueness, self-confidence.

2. Promoting selflessness, cooperative spirit, spirit of sharing.
3. Cultivating respect for property, one's own and that of others.
4. Understanding the contribution of home towards the physical, emotional, cultural and spiritual development of young people.
5. Imparting clear directions on cleanliness, punctuality, use of refined language, courtesy, proper manners, respect for elders.
6. Knowing the surroundings—visiting slums, villages, hospitals orphanages, old people's homes.
7. Becoming aware of the needs of the others.
8. Promoting civic sense, awareness of oneself as a member of a community, civic duties.
9. Awareness of one's strengths and weakness, of those others.
10. Love of friends, classmates, the not-so-fortunates.
11. Seeking to realise one's potentialities and talents, disciplined learning in academics, sports, cultivating the scientific temper.
12. Independent thinking, not blindly following others.
13. Exposure to the great personalities.
14. Knowledge of the Constitution, the rights, the duties.
15. Knowing the provisions to promote human dignity and justice.
16. Patriotism, national integration, international understanding, builders of modern world.
17. Protection of environment.
18. Dissemination of cultural heritage.
19. Modifying human behaviour through values.
20. Knowing the own village/city, state, country.

21. Promotion of equality and justice for all the citizens.
22. Prayers of various religions.
23. Awareness of the good points in other religions.
24. Appreciating the useful views of others and their cultural traditions.
25. Propagation of value philosophy.

Programmes for Value Education

The Education Commission (1964-66) suggested that social, moral and spiritual values should be imparted both through indirect and direct methods. The Commission remarked "We attach great importance to the role of indirect influence in building up good character. The school atmosphere, the personality and behaviour of the teachers, the facilities provided in the campus will have a large say in developing a sense of values. We would like to emphasise that the consciousness of values must permeate the whole curriculum and programme of activities in the campus. It is not only the teachers incharge of normal instruction who are responsible for building character, every teacher, whatever be the subject, the teachers must necessarily accept this responsibility. The school assembly, the curricular and co-curricular activities, the celebration of festivals of all religions, work experience, team games, subject clubs, social service programmes—all these can help in inculcating the values of cooperation and mutual regard, honesty and integrity, discipline and social responsibility. These values have a special significance in society today, when young men and women are passing through a crisis of character".

Ethics should be taught only through parable, stories, religion, and sayings of great people and their lives. Right from the start, children should be taught about the founders of great religions of the world. Films should be shown to them depicting temples, mosques, churches, etc.

Based on past experiences and looking into the present social context, the following programmes have to be incorporated in educational programmes to promote value education in the campus and neighbourhood.

1. Community prayer everyday in the campus and at occasions in social functions.
2. Health and cleanliness programmes.
3. Socially useful productive work.
4. Training in citizenship.
5. Various cultural programmes.
6. Dramas, folks dances, recitations related to the unity of our heritage.
7. Art exhibitions, musical performances, literary displays which promote integration.
8. Running literacy centres in villages.
9. Promoting subject clubs.
10. Organisation of cooperative societies.
11. Mock parliaments and debates.
12. Excursions to historic monuments and religious places.
13. Celebration of national and international festivals.
14. Participation in traffic control, elections, etc. voluntarily.
15. Programmes for the protection of environment.
16 Actions to bring social justice.
17. Arrangement of seminars to propagate value-oriented ideas.
18. Programmes to curtail the anti-social behaviours such as bribing, drinking, smoking, participating in wrong actions, sex indulgence etc.
19. Forming voluntary forces to propagate values through various means and modes.
20. Arrangement of guest lectures by reputed personalities.
21. Participation in religious prayers by the students in the campus as well as in the socio-religious programmes.
22. Promotion of civic sense by making them participate in the social organisations and social activities.

23. Family welfare programmes.
24. Explaining the problems associated with population explosion.
25. "Save the Environment" programmes can be launched.

Value education is the only answer to promote peace throughout the world to save the human society. Let us dedicate ourselves to impart value education directly or indirectly in our educational campuses.

44

Memories of UGC National Seminar on Value-Oriented Education

Inauguration of the Seminar by Prayer

Welcome Address by the Organising Secretary of the Seminar, Dr. V. Dayakara Reddy

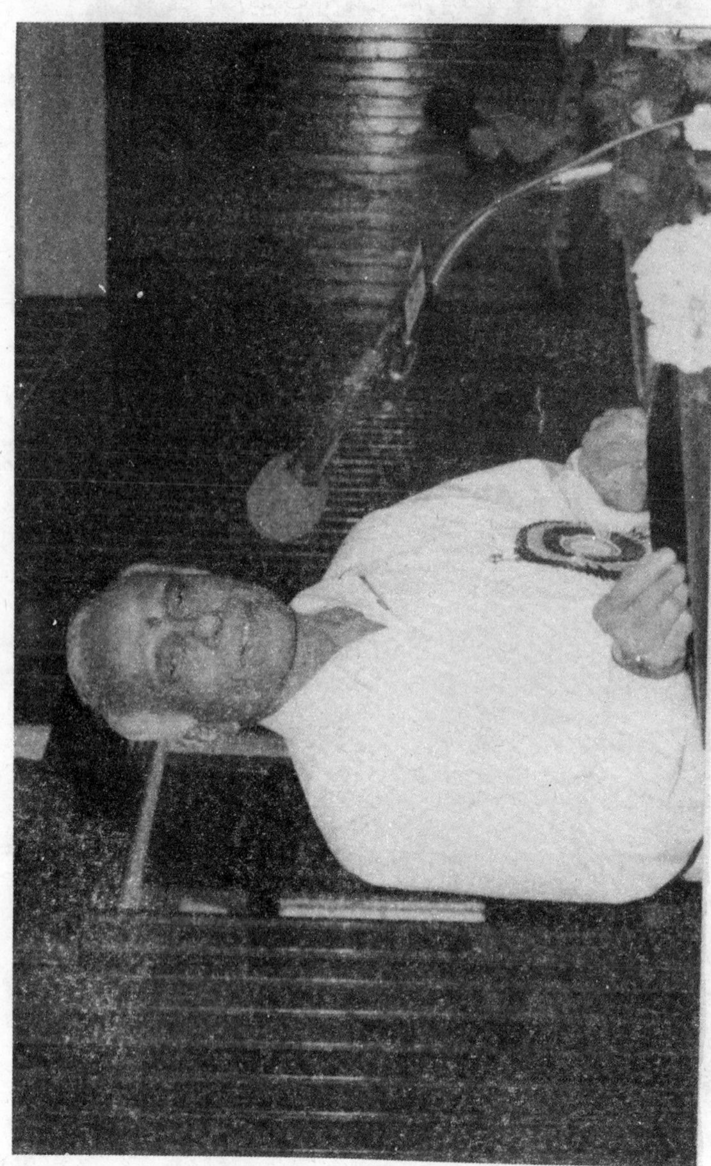

Plenary Speech by Prof. R. Srinivasa Rao

Discussions during Seminar Breaks

Special Talk by Prof. Ashok V. Jain

Seminar Participants Discussing about the Deliberations with the Organising Secretary

Expressing the Views of Participants

Felicitation to the Organising Secretary, Dr. Reddy, for Successfully Organising the UGC National Seminar

Additional Reading

Bhaskara Rao, Digumarti (1994). *Scientific Aptitude*. New Delhi: Ashish Publishing House. ISBN 81-7024-658-X.

Bhaskara Rao, Digumarti (1995). *Animal Kingdom*. New Delhi: Discovery Publishing House. ISBN 81-7141-274-2.

Bhaskara Rao, Digumarti (1995). *Batracology*. New Delhi: Discovery Publishing House. ISBN 81-7141-279-3.

Bhaskara Rao, Digumarti (1997). *Scientific Attitude*. New Delhi: Discovery Publishing House. ISBN 81-7141-381-1.

Bhaskara Rao, Digumarti (1996). *Scientific Attitude vis-à-vis Scientific Aptitude*. New Delhi: Discovery Publishing House. ISBN 81-7141-308-0.

Bhaskara Rao, Digumarti (2004). *Scientific Attitude, Scientific Aptitude and Achievement*. New Delhi: Discovery Publishing House. ISBN 81-7141-781-7.

Bhaskara Rao, Digumarti (2004). *Educational Administration*. New Delhi: Discovery Publishing House. ISBN 81-7141-842-2.

Bhaskara Rao, Digumarti, editor (1996). *Encyclopaedia of Education For All*, 5 volumes. New Delhi: APH Publishing Corporation. ISBN 81-7024-759-4 (set).

Vol. I *Education For All: The World Conference*. ISBN 81-7024-760-8.

Vol. II *Education For All: The EPA-9 Summit*. ISBN 81-7024-761-6.

Vol. III *Education For All: Quality Education For All*. ISBN 81-7024-762-6.

Vol. IV *Education For All: Planning and Monitoring*. ISBN 81-7024-763-4.

Vol. V *Education For All: The Indian Scenario*. ISBN 81-7024-764-0.

Bhaskara Rao, Digumarti, editor (1996). *Global Perceptions on Peace Education*, 3 volumes. New Delhi: Discovery Publishing House. ISBN 81-7141-319-6.

Bhaskara Rao, Digumarti, editor (1996). *National Policy on Education*, 2 volumes. New Delhi: Anmol Publications Pvt. Ltd. ISBN 81-7488-323-1.

Bhaskara Rao, Digumarti, editor (1997). *Care the Child*, 2 volumes. New Delhi: Discovery Publishing House. ISBN 81-7141-394-3.

Bhaskara Rao, Digumarti, editor (1997). *Education for the 21st Century*. New Delhi: Discovery Publishing House. ISBN 81-7141-389-7.

Bhaskara Rao, Digumarti, editor (1997). *Reflections on Scientific Attitude*. New Delhi: Discovery Publishing House. ISBN 81-7141-319-6.

Bhaskara Rao, Digumarti, editor (1997). *Success Story of a Primary Education Project*. New Delhi: APH Publishing Corporation. ISBN 81-7024-850-7.

Bhaskara Rao, Digumarti, editor (1997). *World Food Summit*. New Delhi: Discovery Publishing House. ISBN 81-7141-386-2.

Bhaskara Rao, Digumarti, editor (1998). *Adolescence Education*. New Delhi: Discovery Publishing House. ISBN 81-7141-432-X.

Bhaskara Rao, Digumarti, editor (1998). *Community and School Nutrition Education*. New Delhi: Discovery Publishing House. ISBN 81-7141-435-4.

Bhaskara Rao, Digumarti, editor (1998). *District Primary Education Programme*. New Delhi: Discovery Publishing House. ISBN 81-7141-396-X.

Bhaskara Rao, Digumarti, editor (1998). *Earth Summit*, 2 volumes. New Delhi: Discovery Publishing House. ISBN 81-7141-435-4.

Bhaskara Rao, Digumarti, editor (1998). *National Policy on Education: Towards an Enlightened and Humane Society*. New Delhi: Discovery Publishing House. ISBN 81-7141-426-5.

Bhaskara Rao, Digumarti, editor (1998). *Reforming School Education*. New Delhi: Discovery Publishing House. ISBN 81-7141-403-6.

Bhaskara Rao, Digumarti, editor (1998). *Teacher Education in India*. New Delhi: Discovery Publishing House. ISBN 81-7141-406-0.

Bhaskara Rao, Digumarti, editor (1998). *World Summit for Social Development*. New Delhi: Discovery Publishing House. ISBN 81-7141-420-6.

Bhaskara Rao, Digumarti, editor (2000). *Education For All: Achieving the Goal*, 3 volumes. New Delhi: APH Publishing Corporation. ISBN 81-7648-152-1 (set).

Vol. I *The Global Consensus*. ISBN 81-7648-155-6.

Vol. II *Mid-Decade Review Reports of Regional Seminars*. ISBN 81-7648-154-8.

Vol. III *Issues and Trends*. ISBN 81-7648-155-6.

Bhaskara Rao, Digumarti, editor (1999). *International Encyclopaedia of AIDS*, 11 volumes. New Delhi: Discovery Publishing House. ISBN 81-7141-522-6 (set).

Vol. 1 *Introduction to HIV/AIDS*. ISBN 81-7141-523-7.

Vol. 2 *HIV/AIDS-Issues and Challenges*, 2 parts. ISBN 81-7141-524-5.

Vol. 3 *HIV/AIDS-Socio Economic Realities*. ISBN 81-7141-524-3.

Vol. 4 *HIV/AIDS-Law Ethics and Human Rights*, 2 parts. ISBN 81-7141-526-1.

Vol. 5 *AIDS and NGOs*. ISBN 81-7141-527-X.

Vol. 6 *AIDS and Home Care*. ISBN 81-7141-528-8.

Vol. 7 *STD Case Management*. ISBN 81-7141-529-6.

Vol. 8 *HIV/AIDS Prevention and Care-Teaching Modules for Nurses and Midwives*. ISBN 81-7141-530-X.

Vol. 9 *HIV Prevention Education for Educational Institutions*. ISBN 81-7141-531-8.

Vol.10 *Instructional Modules for AIDS Education*. ISBN 81-7141-532-6.

Vol.11 *School Health Education to prevent AIDS and STD-A Package for Curriculum Planners*. ISBN 81-7141-533-4.

Bhaskara Rao, Digumarti, editor (2000). *International Encyclopaedia of Science and Technology Education*, 11 volumes. New Delhi: Discovery Publishing House. ISBN 81-7141-548-2 (set).

Vol. 1 *Science and Technology Education*. ISBN 81-7141-568-7.

Vol. 2 *Science Education in Developing Countries*. ISBN 81-7141-569-9.

Vol. 3 *Organizational Structure of Science*. ISBN 81-7141-570-9.

Vol. 4 *Science Education in Asia and the Pacific*. ISBN 81-7141-571-7

Vol. 5 *Science and Technology Education For All*. ISBN 81-7141-572-5.

Vol. 6 *Values, Ethics, Talent and Girls in Science and Technology Education*. ISBN 81-7141-573-3.

Vol. 7 *Popularization of Science and Technology Education*. ISBN 81-7141-574-1.

Vol. 8 *Science, Power and Society*. ISBN 81-7141-575-X.

Vol. 9 *Information Technology*. ISBN 81-7141-576-8.

Vol. 10 *Teacher Training in Science and Technology Education*. ISBN 81-7142-577-6.

Vol. 11 *Teacher Training in Science and Technology: A Curriculum Framework*. ISBN 81-7141-578-4.

Bhaskara Rao, Digumarti, editor (2001). *Distance Education in Different Countries*. New Delhi: APH Publishing Corporation. ISBN 81-7648-229-3.

Bhaskara Rao, Digumarti, editor (2001). *Decentralised Management of Education: Management of Education in Panchayati Raj and Municipal Bodies*. New Delhi: Discovery Publishing House. ISBN 81-7141-617-9.

Bhaskara Rao, Digumarti, editor (2001). *Electrochemistry for Environmental Protection*. New Delhi: Discovery Publishing House. ISBN 81-7141-619-5.

Bhaskara Rao, Digumarti, editor (2001). *Global Educational Studies*. New Delhi: Discovery Publishing House. ISBN 81-7141-616-0.

Bhaskara Rao, Digumarti, editor (2001). *Global Synthesis of Educational Assessment*. New Delhi: Discovery Publishing House. ISBN 81-7141-613-6.

Bhaskara Rao, Digumarti, editor (2000). *International Encyclopaedia of Human Rights*, 7 volumes in 13 parts. New Delhi: Discovery Publishing House. ISBN 81-7141-567-9 (set).

Vol. 1 *International Instruments of Human Rights*, 2 parts. ISBN 81-7141-569-4.

Vol. 2 *Regional Instruments of Human Rights*. ISBN 81-7141-604-7.

Vol. 3 *Human Rights and the United Nations*, 2 parts. ISBN 81-7141-605-5.

Vol. 4 *Fact Files of Human Rights*, 3 parts. ISBN 81-7141-606-3.

Vol. 5 *Study Stories of Human Rights*, 3 parts. ISBN 81-7141-607-3.

Vol. 6 *International Meetings on Human Rights*, 2 parts. ISBN 81-714-608-X.

Vol. 7 *Professional Training in Human Rights*. ISBN 81-7141-609-8.

Bhaskara Rao, Digumarti, editor (2001). *Jomtein Decade of Education*. New Delhi: Discovery Publishing House. ISBN 81-7141-618-7.

Bhaskara Rao, Digumarti, editor (2001). *Nuclear Materials: Issues and Concerns*, 2 volumes. New Delhi: Discovery Publishing House. ISBN 81-7141-611-X.

Bhaskara Rao, Digumarti, editor (2001). *World Conference on Education for All*. New Delhi: APH Publishing Corporation. ISBN 81-7141-274-9.

Bhaskara Rao, Digumarti, editor (2001). *World Conference on Higher Education*. New Delhi: Discovery Publishing House. ISBN 81-7141-610-1.

Bhaskara Rao, Digumarti, editor (2001). *World Conference on Science*. New Delhi: Discovery Publishing House. ISBN 81-7141-612-8.

Bhaskara Rao, Digumarti, editor (2003). *Inspiring Experiences in Teacher Education*. New Delhi: Discovery Publishing House. ISBN 81-7141-656-X.

Bhaskara Rao, Digumarti, editor (2003). *International Studies in Education*, 3 volumes. New Delhi: Discovery Publishing House. ISBN 81-7141-647-0.

Bhaskara Rao, Digumarti, editor (2003). *Military Conversion: Impact on Science and Technology*. New Delhi: Discovery Publishing House. ISBN 81-7141-578-4.

Bhaskara Rao, Digumarti, editor (2003). *United Nations Millennium Summit*. New Delhi: Discovery Publishing House. ISBN 81-7141-632-2.

Bhaskara Rao, Digumarti, editor (2003). *World Assembly on Aging*. New Delhi: Discovery Publishing House. ISBN 81-7141-637-3.

Bhaskara Rao, Digumarti, editor (2003). *World Conference on Human Rights*. New Delhi: Discovery Publishing House. ISBN 81-7141-661-6.

Bhaskara Rao, Digumarti, editor (2003). *World Education Forum*. New Delhi: Discovery Publishing House. ISBN 81-7141-639-X.

Bhaskara Rao, Digumarti, editor (2003). *Education, Employment and Human Resource Development*. New Delhi: Discovery Publishing House. ISBN 81-7141-681-0.

Bhaskara Rao, Digumarti, editor (2003). *Successful Schooling*. New Delhi: Discovery Publishing House. ISBN 81-7141-677-2.

Bhaskara Rao, Digumarti, editor (2003). *European Education and Teachers*. New Delhi: Discovery Publishing House. ISBN 81-7141-702-7.

Bhaskara Rao, Digumarti, editor (2003). *Teachers in a Changing World*. New Delhi: Discovery Publishing House. ISBN 81-7141-694-2.

Bhaskara Rao, Digumarti, editor (2004). *International Encyclopaedia of Learning to Live Together*, 4 volumes. New Delhi: Discovery Publishing House. ISBN 81-7141-848-1.

Vol. 1 *International Conference on Learning to Live Together.*

Vol. 2 *Globalization and Living Together.*

Vol. 3 *Curriculum for Learning to Live Together.*

Vol. 4 *Science Education for the Contemporary Society.*

Bhaskara Rao, Digumarti, editor (2004). *International Guidelines on Open and Distance Teacher Education*. New Delhi: Discovery Publishing House. ISBN 81-7141-777-9.

Bhaskara Rao, Digumarti, editor (2004). *Adult Learning in the 21st Century*. New Delhi: Discovery Publishing House. ISBN 81-7141-797-3.

Bhaskara Rao, Digumarti, editor (2004). *Educational Practices: Research and Recommendations*. New Delhi: Discovery Publishing House. ISBN 81-7141-835-X.

Bhaskara Rao, Digumarti, editor (2004). *General Secondary Education in the 21st Century*. New Delhi: Discovery Publishing House. ISBN 81-7141-885-6.

Bhaskara Rao, Digumarti, editor (2004). *Reforming Secondary Education*. New Delhi: Discovery Publishing House. ISBN 81-7141-843-0.

Bhaskara Rao, Digumarti, editor (2004). *Human Rights Education*. New Delhi: Discovery Publishing House. ISBN 81-7141-882-1.

Bhaskara Rao, Digumarti, editor (2004). *United Nations Decade for Human Rights Education*. New Delhi: Discovery Publishing House. ISBN 81-7141-887-2.

Bhaskara Rao, Digumarti and B.S.V. Dutt, editors (2003). *Education: Programmes and Policies*. New Delhi: APH Publishing Corporation. ISBN 81-7648-470-9.

Bhaskara Rao, Digumarti, C.A.P. Swamy and B.S.V. Dutt (1997). *Self-Evaluation in Student Teaching*. New Delhi: Discovery Publishing House. ISBN 81-7141-374-9.

Bhaskara Rao, Digumarti and D. Naresh Kumar (2004). *School Teacher Effectiveness*. New Delhi: Discovery Publishing House. ISBN 81-7141-782-5.

Bhaskara Rao, Digumarti and D. Sridhar (2002). *Job Satisfaction of School Teachers*. New Delhi: Discovery Publishing House. ISBN 81-7141-652-7.

Bhaskara Rao, Digumarti, C. Sridevi and K. Vijaya (1995). *Achievement in Social Studies*. New Delhi: Discovery Publishing House. ISBN 81-7141-281-5.

Bhaskara Rao, Digumarti and Digumarti Pushpa Latha (1994). *Achievement in Biology*. New Delhi: Discovery Publishing House. ISBN 81-7141-264-5.

Bhaskara Rao, Digumarti and Digumarti Pushpa Latha (1995). *Achievement in English*. New Delhi: Discovery Publishing House. ISBN 81-7141-283-1.

Bhaskara Rao, Digumarti and Digumarti Pushpa Latha (1994). *Achievement in Science*. New Delhi: Discovery Publishing House. ISBN 81-7141-280-70.

Bhaskara Rao, Digumarti and Digumarti Pushpa Latha (1995). *Achievement in Mathematics*. New Delhi: Discovery Publishing House. ISBN 81-7141-278-5.

Bhaskara Rao, Digumarti and Digumarti Pushpa Latha (2004). *Education for Women*. New Delhi: Discovery Publishing House. ISBN 81-7141-873-2.

Bhaskara Rao, Digumarti and Digumarti Pushpa Latha, editors (1998). *International Encyclopaedia of Women*, 5 volumes. New Delhi: Discovery Publishing House. ISBN 81-7141-410-9 (set).

Vol. 1 *Status of World's Women*. ISBN 81-7141-494-X.

Vol. 2 *Women, Education and Empowerment*. ISBN 81-7141-498-1.

Vol. 3 *Women Challenges and Advancement*. ISBN 81-7141-497-4.

Vol. 4 *Women and Family Health*. ISBN 81-7141-497-4.

Vol. 5 *Women and International Action*. ISBN 81-7141-498-2.

Bhaskara Rao, Digumarti, Digumarti Pushpa Latha and Digumarthi Harshitha, editors (2001). *Biological Warfare*. New Delhi: Discovery Publishing House. ISBN 81-7141-597-0.

Bhaskara Rao, Digumarti, Digumarti Pushpa Latha and Digumarthi Harshitha, editors (2001). *Women as Educators*. New Delhi: Discovery Publishing House. ISBN 81-7141-602-0.

Bhaskara Rao, Digumarti and Digumarthi Harshitha (2004). *Adjustment of Adolescents*. New Delhi: APH Publishing House. ISBN 81-7648-836-8.

Bhaskara Rao, Digumarti and Digumarthi Harshitha, editors (2001). *Education in India*. New Delhi: APH Publishing House. ISBN 81-7648-207-2.

Bhaskara Rao, Digumarti, Digumarti Pushpa Latha and Digumarthi Harshitha, editors (2001). *Assessing Learning Achievement*. New Delhi: Discovery Publishing House. ISBN 81-7141-601-2.

Bhaskara Rao, Digumarti, Digumarti Pushpa Latha and Digumarthi Harshitha, editors (2001). *Energy Security*. New Delhi: Discovery Publishing House. ISBN 81-7141-598-9.

Bhaskara Rao, Digumarti, Digumarthi Harshitha and K.R.S. Sambasiva Rao, editors (1999). *Advanced Biotechnology*. New Delhi: Discovery Publishing House. ISBN 81-7141-516-4.

Bhaskara Rao, Digumarti and K.R.S. Sambasiva Rao, editors (1996). *Current Trends in Indian Education*. New Delhi: Discovery Publishing House. ISBN 81-7141-311-0.

Bhaskara Rao, Digumarti and D. Naresh Kumar (2004). *School Teacher Effectiveness*. New Delhi: Discovery Publishing House. ISBN 81-7141-782-5.

Bhaskara Rao, Digumarti and E. Sreekanth Babu (2004). *Educational Interests of School Students*. New Delhi: Discovery Publishing House. ISBN 81-7141-837-6.

Bhaskara Rao, Digumarti and K. Vijaya (1995). *A Text Book Evaluation*. Ambala Cantt: The Associated Publishers.

Bhaskara Rao, Digumarti and M.A. Fayaz (2004). *Problems of Primary School Drop-outs*. New Delhi: Discovery Publishing House. ISBN 81-7141-834-1.

Bhaskara Rao, Digumarti and N.V.M. Mohana Rao (2002). *Problems of Mentally Handicapped Children*. New Delhi: Discovery Publishing House. ISBN 81-7141-645-4.

Bhaskara Rao, Digumarti and S. Chandra Mohan (2002). *Sports Management*. New Delhi: APH Publishing House. ISBN 81-7648-467-9.

Bhaskara Rao, Digumarti and S.A. Khader (2004). *Problems of Private School Teachers*. New Delhi: Discovery Publishing Corporation. ISBN 81-7141-838-4.

Bhaskara Rao, Digumarti and S.A. Khader (2004). *School Education in India*. New Delhi: Discovery Publishing Corporation. ISBN 81-7141-849-X.

Bhaskara Rao, Digumarti and Sk. Johni Basha (2004). *Teachers' Population Education Awareness*. New Delhi: Discovery Publishing House. ISBN 81-7141-832-5.

Bhaskara Rao, Digumarti, V.V. Rao, V.V. Lakshmi and V.V. Krishna, editors (1999). *Status and Advancement of Women*. New Delhi: APH Publishing Corporation. ISBN 81-7648-169-6.

Babu, P.C., author and Digumarti Bhaskara Rao, editor (2004). *Flowers of Wisdom*. New Delhi: Discovery Publishing House. ISBN 81-7141-695-0.

Amala, P.A. and Anupam, P., authors and Digumarti Bhaskara Rao, editor (2004). *History of Education*. New Delhi: Discovery Publishing House. ISBN 81-7141-860-0.

Bhagya Lakshmi, L., author and Digumarti Bhaskara Rao, editor (2000). *Reading and Comprehension*. New Delhi: Discovery Publishing House. ISBN 81-7141-543-1.

Bhasha, S.A., author and Digumarti Bhaskara Rao, editor (2004). *Methods of Teaching Geography*. New Delhi: Discovery Publishing House. ISBN 81-7141-807-4.

Bhuvaneswara Lakshmi, Gadde, author and Digumarti Bhaskara Rao, editor (2000). *Attitude Towards Science*. New Delhi: Discovery Publishing House. ISBN 81-7141-541-6.

Bhuvaneswari Lakshmi, G., author and Digumarti Bhaskara Rao, editor (2004). *Methods of Teaching Life Science*. New Delhi: Discovery Publishing House. ISBN 81-7141-804-X.

Bhuvaneswari Lakshmi, G. and K. Subba Rao, authors and Digumarti Bhaskara Rao, editor (2004). *Methods of Teaching Biology*. New Delhi: Discovery Publishing House. ISBN 81-7141-914-3.

Chowdary, S.B.J.R. and Naga Raju authors and Digumarti Bhaskara Rao, editor (2004). *Mastery of Teaching Skills*. New Delhi: Discovery Publishing House. ISBN 81-7141-861-9.

Devraj, T.A.S., author and Digumarti Bhaskara Rao, editor (1997). *Trace Analysis of Uranium and Thorium*. New Delhi: Discovery Publishing House. ISBN 81-7141-375-7.

Durga Rani, K., author and Digumarti Bhaskara Rao, editor (2000). *Educational Aspirations and Scientific Attitudes*. New Delhi: Discovery Publishing House. ISBN 81-7141-555-5.

Dutt, B.S.V. and Digumarti Bhaskara Rao (2001). *Empowering Primary Teachers*. New Delhi: Discovery Publishing House. ISBN 81-7141-615-2.

Dutt, B.S.V., author and Digumarti Bhaskara Rao, editor (2004). *Comparative Education*. New Delhi: Discovery Publishing House. ISBN 81-7141-912-7.

Ediger, Marlow and Digumarti Bhaskara Rao (1996). *Science Curriculum*. New Delhi: Discovery Publishing House. ISBN 81-7141-321-8.

Ediger, Marlow and Digumarti Bhaskara Rao (2000). *Teaching Mathematics Successfully*. New Delhi: Discovery Publishing House. ISBN 81-7141-552-0.

Ediger, Marlow and Digumarti Bhaskara Rao (2001). *Teaching Science Successfully*. New Delhi: Discovery Publishing House. ISBN 81-7141-600-4.

Ediger, Marlow and Digumarti Bhaskara Rao (2001). *Teaching Social Studies Successfully*. New Delhi: Discovery Publishing House. ISBN 81-7141-596-2.

Ediger, Marlow and Digumarti Bhaskara Rao (2002). *Philosophy and Curriculum*. New Delhi: Discovery Publishing House. ISBN 81-7141-631-4.

Ediger, Marlow and Digumarti Bhaskara Rao (2002). *Improving School Administration*. New Delhi: Discovery Publishing House. ISBN 81-7141-633-0.

Ediger, Marlow and Digumarti Bhaskara Rao (2002). *Elementary Curriculum*. New Delhi: Discovery Publishing House. ISBN 81-7141-658-6.

Ediger, Marlow and Digumarti Bhaskara Rao (2003). *Language Arts Curriculum*. New Delhi: Discovery Publishing House. ISBN 81-7141-657-8.

Ediger, Marlow and Digumarti Bhaskara Rao (2003). *Psychology and Curriculum*. New Delhi: Discovery Publishing House. ISBN 81-7141-691-8.

Ediger, Marlow and Digumarti Bhaskara Rao (2003). *Teaching Language Arts Successfully*. New Delhi: Discovery Publishing House. ISBN 81-7141-678-0.

Ediger, Marlow and Digumarti Bhaskara Rao (2003). *School Curriculum and Administration*. New Delhi: Discovery Publishing House. ISBN 81-7141-709-4.

Ediger, Marlow and Digumarti Bhaskara Rao (2003). *Teaching Mathematics in Elementary Schools*. New Delhi: Discovery Publishing House. ISBN 81-7141-687-X.

Ediger, Marlow and Digumarti Bhaskara Rao (2003). *Teaching Science in Elementary Schools*. New Delhi: Discovery Publishing House. ISBN 81-7141-698-5.

Ediger, Marlow and Digumarti Bhaskara Rao (2003). *School Curriculum and Administration*. New Delhi: Discovery Publishing House. ISBN 81-7141-709-4.

Ediger, Marlow and Digumarti Bhaskara Rao (2003). *Elementary Curriculum Improvement*. New Delhi: Discovery Publishing House. ISBN 81-7141-740-X.

Ediger, Marlow and Digumarti Bhaskara Rao (2004). *School Organisation*. New Delhi: Discovery Publishing House. ISBN 81-7141-843-0.

Ediger, Marlow and Digumarti Bhaskara Rao (2004). *Relevancy in Elementary Curriculum*. New Delhi: Discovery Publishing House. ISBN 81-7141-845-9.

Ediger, Marlow, B.S.V. Dutt and Digumarti Bhaskara Rao (2003). *Teaching English Successfully*. New Delhi: Discovery Publishing House. ISBN 81-7141-707-8.

Elizabeth, M.E.S., author and Digumarti Bhaskara Rao, editor (2004). *Methods of Teaching English*. New Delhi: Discovery Publishing House. ISBN 81-7141-809-0.

Harshitha, D. author and Digumarti Bhaskara Rao, editor (2004). *Methods of Teaching Information Technology*. New Delhi: Discovery Publishing House. ISBN 81-7141-805-8.

Indira Devi, author and J. Prasanth Kumar and Digumarti Bhaskara Rao, editors (2004). *Values in Language Text Books*. New Delhi: APH Publishing Corporation. ISBN 81-7141-833-3.

Jalaja Kumari, C., author and Digumarti Bhaskara Rao, editor (2004). *Methods of Teaching Educational Technology*. New Delhi: Discovery Publishing House. ISBN 81-7141-810-4.

Jayasree, Kandi, author and Digumarti Bhaskara Rao, editor (1999). *Correlates of Socialisation*. New Delhi: Discovery Publishing House. ISBN 81-7141-517-2.

Jayasree, Kandi, author and Digumarti Bhaskara Rao, editor (2004). *Methods of Teaching Science*. New Delhi: Discovery Publishing House. ISBN 81-7141-801-5.

John Babu, Chikati, author and T.J.R. Prasad, G.M. Madhukar and Digumarti Bhaskara Rao, editors (1996). *Problem Solving in Mathematics*. New Delhi: APH Publishing Corporation. ISBN 81-7648-273-0.

Joseph Raju, B and G.A. Anitha, authors and Digumarti Bhaskara Rao, editor (2004). *Population Education*. New Delhi: Sonali Publications. ISBN 81-88836-31-3.

Lalitha, T., author and K.S. Prabhakaram, D.S.N. Sastry and Digumarti Bhaskara Rao, editors (2004). *Educational Philosophic Beliefs*. New Delhi: Discovery Publishing House. ISBN 81-7141-765-5.

Madhu Bala, Jampala, author and Digumarti Bhaskara Rao, editor (2004). *Adjustment Problems of Hearing Impaired*. New Delhi: Discovery Publishing House. ISBN 81-7141-831-7.

Madhu Bala, Jampala, author and Digumarti Bhaskara Rao, editor (2004). *Methods of Teaching Exceptional Children*. New Delhi: Discovery Publishing House. ISBN 81-7141-802-3.

Marja, Talvi and Digumarti Bhaskara Rao, editors (1996). *Educational Leadership and Social Changes*. New Delhi: Discovery Publishing House. ISBN 81-7141-320-X.

Nageswara Rao, S. and M. Srihari, authors and Digumarti Bhaskara Rao, editor (2004). *Guidance and Counselling*. New Delhi: Discovery Publishing House. ISBN 81-7141-840-6.

Nageswara Rao, S. and P. Sridhar, authors and Digumarti Bhaskara Rao, editor (2004). *Methods and Techniques of Teaching*. New Delhi: Sonali Publications. ISBN 81-88836-33-8.

Nirmala Jyothi, M., author and Digumarti Bhaskara Rao, editor (2003). *Non-detention System in School Education*. New Delhi: Discovery Publishing House. ISBN 81-7141-654-3.

Padma Tulasi, G., author and Digumarti Bhaskara Rao, editor (2004). *Methods of Teaching Elementary Science*. New Delhi: Discovery Publishing House. ISBN 81-7141-871-6.

Pala Prasada Rao, V., author and K. Nirupa Rani and Digumarti Bhaskara Rao, editors (2004). *Methods of Teaching Elementary Science*. New Delhi: Discovery Publishing House. ISBN 81-7141-871-6.

Prabhakaram, K.S., author and Digumarti Bhaskara Rao, editors (1998). *Concept Attainment Model in Mathematics Teaching*. New Delhi: Discovery Publishing House. ISBN 81-7141-424-9.

Prasanth Kumar, J., author and Digumarti Bhaskara Rao, editor (1998). *Effectiveness of Distance Education System*. New Delhi: Discovery Publishing House. ISBN 81-7141-437-0.

Prasanth Kumar, J., author and Digumarti Bhaskara Rao, editor (2004). *Methods of Teaching Civics*. New Delhi: Discovery Publishing House. ISBN 81-7141-806-6.

Prasanth Kumar, J., author and G. Sundara Rao and Digumarti Bhaskara Rao, editors (2000). *Open University Student Support Services*. New Delhi: Discovery Publishing House. ISBN 81-7141-550-4.

Raja Kumari, M.A. and D.R.S. Sundari, authors and Digumarti Bhaskara Rao, editor (2004). *Special Education*. New Delhi: Discovery Publishing House. ISBN 81-7141-846-5.

Raja Kumari, M.A. and D.R.S. Sundari, authors and Digumarti Bhaskara Rao, editor (2004). *Methods of Teaching Educational Psychology*. New Delhi: Discovery Publishing House. ISBN 81-7141-820-1.

Ramatulasamma, K., author and Digumarti Bhaskara Rao, editor (2002). *Job Satisfaction of Teacher Educators*. New Delhi: Discovery Publishing House. ISBN 81-7141-655-1.

Rama Krishnaiah, D., author and Digumarti Bhaskara Rao, editor (1998). *Job Satisfaction of College Teachers*. New Delhi: Discovery Publishing House. ISBN 81-7141-438-9.

Rama Kumar Ratnam, M.V., author and Digumarti Bhaskara Rao, editor (1998). *Dukkha: Suffering in Early Buddhism*. New Delhi: Discovery Publishing House. ISBN 81-7141-653-5.

Rama Krishna Prasad and P. Vide Sagar, authors and Digumarti Bhaskara Rao, editor (2004). *Methods of Teaching Physical Education*. New Delhi: Discovery Publishing House. ISBN 81-7141-868-6.

Rama Seshaiah, P. author and Digumarti Bhaskara Rao, editor (2004). *Methods of Teaching Home Science*. New Delhi: Discovery Publishing House. ISBN 81-7141-916-X.

Ramesh, Ganta and Digumarti Bhaskara Rao, editors (1998). *Environmental Education: Problems and Prospects*. New Delhi: Discovery Publishing House. ISBN 81-7141-423-0.

Ranga Rao, R., author and Digumarti Bhaskara Rao, editor (2004). *Methods of Teacher Teaching*. New Delhi: Discovery Publishing House. ISBN 81-7141-812-0.

Rathaiah, Lavu and Digumarti Bhaskara Rao, editors (1996), *International Innovations in Education*. New Delhi: Discovery Publishing House. ISBN 81-7141-359-5.

Rathaiah, Lavu and Digumarti Bhaskara Rao (1997). *Achievement Correlates*. New Delhi: Discovery Publishing House. ISBN 81-7141-385-4.

Ravi Krishna, M., author and Digumarti Bhaskara Rao, editor (2004). *Examination System*. New Delhi: Discovery Publishing House. ISBN 81-7141-824-4.

Ravi Kumar, M., author and Digumarti Bhaskara Rao, editor (2004). *Methods of Teaching Computer Science*. New Delhi: Discovery Publishing House. ISBN 81-7141-823-6.

Reddy, Sudhakar Y., author and Digumarti Bhaskara Rao, editor (2003). *Creativity in Adolescents*. New Delhi: Discovery Publishing House. ISBN 81-7141-659-4.

Reddy, M. S., author and Digumarti Bhaskara Rao, editor (2004). *Creativity in College Students*. New Delhi: Discovery Publishing House. ISBN 81-7141-697-7.

Rudramamba, B., author and Digumarti Bhaskara Rao, editor (2003). *Problems of Teaching*. New Delhi: APH Publishing Corporation. ISBN 81-7648-462-8.

Rudramamba, B. and V. Lakshmi Kumari, authors and Digumarti Bhaskara Rao, editor (2004). *Methods of Teaching Economics*. New Delhi: Discovery Publishing House. ISBN 81-7141-900-3.

Sanjeeva Rao, P.C., author and Digumarti Bhaskara Rao, editor (1996). *A Text Book of Geology*. New Delhi: Discovery Publishing House. ISBN 81-7141-313-7.

Satya Narayana, V., author and Digumarti Bhaskara Rao, editor (2001). *Physical Education, Social Attitudes and Leadership Qualities*. New Delhi: Discovery Publishing House. ISBN 81-7141-593-8.

Satya Narayana, P.V.V. and G. Krishna, authors and Digumarti Bhaskara Rao, editor (2004). *Curriculum Development and Management*. New Delhi: Discovery Publishing House. ISBN 81-7141-813-9.

Siva Lakshmi, G.V. and G.L. Subbaiah, authors and Digumarti Bhaskara Rao, editor (2004). *Methods of Teaching Environmental Science*. New Delhi: Discovery Publishing House. ISBN 81-7141-839-2.

Srinivas, M. and I. Prasada Rao, authors and Digumarti Bhaskara Rao, editor (2004). *Methods of Teaching History*. New Delhi: Discovery Publishing House. ISBN 81-7141-803-1.

Srinivasulu Reddy, M. and K.R.S. Sambasiva Rao, authors and Digumarti Bhaskara Rao, editor (1999). *A Text Book of Aquaculture*. New Delhi: Discovery Publishing House. ISBN 81-7141-482-6.

Srinivasa Rao, Mandalapu, author and Digumarti Bhaskara Rao, editor (2003). *Achievement Motivation and Achievement in Mathematics*. New Delhi: Discovery Publishing House. ISBN 81-7141-674-8.

Sunil Kumar, K. and K. Rama Krishana, authors and Digumarti Bhaskara Rao, editor (2004). *Methods of Teaching Chemistry*. New Delhi: Discovery Publishing House. ISBN 81-7141-913-5.

Sunita, E. and R. Sambasiva Rao, authors and Digumarti Bhaskara Rao, editor (2004). *Methods of Teaching Mathematics*. New Delhi: Discovery Publishing House. ISBN 81-7141-915-1.

Swarupa Rani, T. and J.R. Priyadarshini, authors and Digumarti Bhaskara Rao, editor (2004). *Educational Measurement and Evaluation*. New Delhi: Discovery Publishing House. ISBN 81-7141-859-7.

Vanaja, M., author and Digumarti Bhaskara Rao, editor (1999). *Inquiry Training Model*. New Delhi: Discovery Publishing House. ISBN 81-7141-515-6.

Vanaja,M., author and Digumarti Bhaskara Rao, editor (2004). *Methods of Teaching Physics*. New Delhi: Discovery Publishing House. ISBN 81-7141-867-8

Valeri V. Koustiouk, author and Digumarti Bhaskara Rao, editor (2002). *A Text Book of Cryogenics*. New Delhi: Discovery Publishing House. ISBN 81-7141-642-X.

Vamsi Krishana, V., author and Digumarti Bhaskara Rao, editor (2004). *School Psychology*. New Delhi: Discovery Publishing House. ISBN 81-7141-880-5.

Veena Kumari, Balusu and Digumarti Bhaskara Rao (1996). *Operation Black Board*. New Delhi: APH Publishing Corporation. ISBN 81-7024-711-X.

Veena Kumari, B. author and Digumarti Bhaskara Rao, editor (2004). *Methods of Teaching Social Studies*. New Delhi: Discovery Publishing House. ISBN 81-7141-899-6.

Veena Kumari, Balusu, author and Digumarti Bhaskara Rao, editor (2000). *Psycho-Social Correlates of Achievement*. New Delhi: Discovery Publishing House. ISBN 81-7141-547-4.

Venkata Rao, P. and Digumarti Bhaskara Rao (1989). *A Text Book of Zoology-Junior Intermediate*. Guntur: Vignan Publishers.

Venkata Rao, P. and Digumarti Bhaskara Rao (1989). *A Text Book of Zoology-Senior Intermediate*. Guntur: Vignan Publishers.

Venkateswara Reddy, L. and Lakshmi Narayana, M., authors and Digumarti Bhaskara Rao, editor (2004). *Methods of Teaching Rural Sociology*. New Delhi: Discovery Publishing House. ISBN 81-7141-811-2.

Venkateswara Rao, V., author and Digumarti Bhaskara Rao, editor (2004). *Problems of Education*. New Delhi: Discovery Publishing House. ISBN 81-7141-841-4.

Venkateswara Rao, V., V. Vijaya Lakshmi and V. Vamsi Krishna, authors and Digumarti Bhaskara Rao, editor (2004). *Education For All*. New Delhi: Sonali Publications. ISBN 81-88836-30-3.

Venkateswara Rao, V., V. Vijaya Lakshmi and V. Vamsi Krishna, authors and Digumarti Bhaskara Rao, editor (2004). *Education in India*. New Delhi: Sonali Publications. ISBN 81-88836-858-9.

Venkateswara Reddy, L. and Lakshmi Narayana, M., authors and Digumarti Bhaskara Rao, editor (2004). *Education for Dalits*. New Delhi: Discovery Publishing House. ISBN 81-7141-872-4.

Venkateswarlu, K. and S.J. Basha, authors and Digumarti Bhaskara Rao, editor (2004). *Methods of Teaching Commerce*. New Delhi: Discovery Publishing House. ISBN 81-7141-808-2.

Venugopala Rao, K., author and Digumarti Bhaskara Rao, editor (2000). *Teacher Morale in Secondary Schools*. New Delhi: Discovery Publishing House. ISBN 81-7141-551-2.

Vidya, C., author and Digumarti Bhaskara Rao, editor (1996). *A Text Book of Nutrition*. New Delhi: Discovery Publishing House. ISBN 81-7141-309-9.

Vijaya Bharathi, D., author and Digumarti Bhaskara Rao, editor (2000). *Educational Philosophies of Swami Vivekananda and John Dewey*. New Delhi: APH Publishing House. ISBN 81-7648-309-9.

Vijaya Lakshmi, D., author and Digumarti Bhaskara Rao, editor (2004) *Basic Education*. New Delhi: Discovery Publishing House. ISBN 81-7141-881-3.

Books in Telugu Language

Bhaskara Rao, Digumarti (1986). *Dhrushya Sravana Bodhanapakaranalu (Audio Visual Teaching Aids)*. Guntur: Nagarjuna Publishers.

Bhaskara Rao, Digumarti (1993). *Jeevasashtra Bodhana (Teaching of Biology)*. Guntur: Nagarjuna Publishers.

Bhaskara Rao, Digumarti (1995). *Vignanasasthra Bodhana (Teaching of science)* Guntur: Nagarjuna Publishers.

Bhaskara Rao, Digumarti (1997). *Vidya Manovignana Seshtram (Educational Psychology)*. Guntur: Creative Press.

Bhaskara Rao, Digumarti (1998). *DSC Study Material*. Guntur: Nagarjuna Publishers.

Bhaskara Rao, Digumarti (1998). *Upadhyayudu Vidya. (Teacher and Education)* Guntur: Nagarjuna Publishers.

Bhaskara Rao, Digumarti (1998). *Vidya Drukpadalu (Perspectives of Education)*. Guntur: Nagarjuna Publishers.

Bhaskara Rao, Digumarti (1999). *EdCET Teaching Aptitude*. Guntur: Nagarjuna Publishers.

Bhaskara Rao, Digumarti (2001). *Bharata Samajamulo Upadyayudu Vidya (Teacher and Education in Emerging Indian Society)*. Guntur: Sri Nagarjuna Publishers.

Bhaskara Rao, Digumarti (2001). *Bhoutika Sastra Bodhana Paddathulu (Methods of Teaching Physical Science)*. Guntur: Sri Nagarjuna Publishers.

Bhaskara Rao, Digumarti (2001). *Jeeva Sastra Bodhana Padhathulu (Methods of Teaching Biology)*. Guntur: Sri Nagarjuna Publishers.

Bhaskara Rao, Digumarti (2001). *Vidya Manovignana Sastram (Educational Psychology)*. Guntur: Sri Nagarjuna Publishers.

Bhaskara Rao, Digumarti (2003). *Paiasala Yajamanyam/Paripalana (School Management and Administration)*. Guntur: Sri Nagarjuna Publishers.

Gopala Krishna, G., A. Ramkrishna, K. Subba Rao and Bhaskara Rao, Digumarti (2004). *Jeevasashtra Bodhana Padhatulu (Methods of Teaching of Biological Science)*. Guntur: Sri Nagarjuna Publishers.

Krishna Murthy, V., K.S. Sudheer Reddy and Digumarti Bhaskara Rao (2004). *Vidya Manovignana Sastra Adharalu (Foundations of Educational Psychology)*. Guntur: Sri Nagarjuna Publishers.

Lalini, V., V. Dayakara Reddy, M. Srihari and Digumarti Bhaskara Rao (2004). *Vidya Adharalu (Foundations of Education)*. Guntur: Sri Nagarjuna Publishers.

Subba Rao, K.P., P. Ayodhya and Digumarti Bhaskara Rao (2004). *Patasala Yajamanyam-Vidhya Vyavasthalu (School Management and Systems of Education)*. Guntur: Sri Nagarjuna Publishers.

Sudhakar, V., B. Ravindra Babu, D.S. Kumar and Digumarti Bhaskara Rao (2004). *Vidya Sanketika Sastram-Computer Vidya (Educational Technology and Computer Education)*. Guntur: Sri Nagarjuna Publishers.